# THE CHAMBER CANTATAS OF
# ANTONIO VIVALDI

for Lowell Lindgren

# THE CHAMBER CANTATAS OF ANTONIO VIVALDI

Michael Talbot

ISTITUTO ITALIANO
ANTONIO VIVALDI
*fondazione*
GIORGIO CINI

THE BOYDELL PRESS

First published 2006
The Boydell Press, Woodbridge
with the support of
Fondazione Giorgio Cini
Istituto Italiano Antonio Vivaldi
Venezia


ISBN  1 84383 201 1


The Boydell Press is an imprint of Boydell & Brewer Ltd
PO Box 9  Woodbridge  Suffolk IP12 3DF  UK
and of Boydell & Brewer Inc.
668 Mt Hope Avenue  Rochester  NY 14620  USA
website: www.boydellandbrewer.com


A CIP catalogue record for this book is available
from the British Library


Typeset by Pru Harrison, Hacheston, Suffolk
Printed in Great Britain by
Antony Rowe Ltd, Chippenham, Wiltshire

# Contents

# List of Music Examples

# List of Tables

# Preface

Without any doubt, Vivaldi's cantatas for solo voice remain the least explored corner of his music. Least researched, least discussed, least performed, least familiar. Many obvious reasons for this comparative neglect spring to mind. The genre itself is not especially favoured by musicologists concerned with the repertory of the Baroque period, who are more likely to win their laurels with studies of sonatas, concertos, sacred vocal music or – increasingly – opera. Except for specialists, singers tend to avoid them: they are hard to 'sell' to a modern audience, presupposing, as they do, not merely a knowledge of Italian but also a connoisseurship of Italian poetry in all its aspects. The music can be difficult to find and decipher, and technically very challenging. In any case, this is a repertory from which the male singer, except for the fortunate counter-tenor, is virtually excluded.

But perhaps the most potent reason for the marginalization of the chamber cantata – and this is as true for composers specializing in the genre, such as Alessandro Scarlatti and Benedetto Marcello, as it is for Vivaldi – is that, historically speaking, the Baroque cantata is a dead end. Unlike most other genres, which navigated the passage from Baroque to Classical (and beyond) smoothly, despite undergoing much change on the way, the single-voice cantata (we are not speaking here of the dramatic cantata, or serenata, which proved longer-lived) simply petered out in the course of the second half of the eighteenth century: it was replaced by arias and songs of various descriptions that rejected, rather than transplanted, its musical substance.

Its lack of historical progeny should not, of course, push the cantata into insignificance. The beauty of a composition as experienced by the listener is diminished not a whit by the knowledge that it 'leads' nowhere in particular. However, we are nowadays so strongly conditioned to view music through the prism of music history, so influenced by the 'babble' around music as opposed to the music itself, that, knowingly or unknowingly, we have allowed the Baroque cantata to recede somewhat from our consciousness. It is hard to conceive that during what the first historian of the cantata, Eugen Schmitz, called its 'springtime' (*Blütezeit*), in the second half of the seventeenth century, probably more works of this kind than of any other were written in Italy. Far from being a genre 'on the way out', this was for its contemporaries the last word in novelty, topicality, intellectual sophistication and artistic finesse.

Vivaldi is rightly seen by experts and the lay public alike as a pioneer – indeed, the first great pioneer – in the history of the concerto. It is possible to make him out to be a significant innovator in the worlds of opera and sacred vocal music, and even (in a few respects) the sonata. For his cantatas, no such grand claims can be made. Vivaldi was too much of an individualist in musical style for these compositions not to be distinctive, and too skilled a workman for them not to be effective. On occasion, they reach high levels of inspiration. But they remain highly conventional in concept and structure. For once, our composer does not set parameters: he conforms to them. Accordingly, a discussion of the general background to the cantata is not a preliminary to be despatched dutifully at the start of the book and subsequently ignored. It has to be woven into the narrative all the way through. To state things simply: the study of Vivaldi's cantatas has no option but to go hand in hand with that of the late Baroque cantata *tout court*.

My interest in the Baroque cantata dates back almost forty years to the time when, in the course of my doctoral research into the instrumental music of Vivaldi's Venetian contemporary Tomaso Albinoni (1671–1751), I stumbled on a lost published collection of cantatas (Op. 4) by this composer. I subsequently gave considerable coverage to the cantata, including its historical and literary background, in life-and-works studies of Albinoni and of a slightly older composer, Benedetto Vinaccesi (1666–1719). In addition, I have written various articles and papers on selected aspects of the cantatas of Albinoni and, latterly, Vivaldi. However, what one is able to say in a chapter or an article is far less than the subject merits – whether that subject is the Baroque cantata in general or Vivaldi's cantatas in particular. Writing a book-length study of Vivaldi's cantatas has now given me a chance to kill two birds with one stone: to fill a void (indeed, the last great void) in the literature on that composer's music, and to present a well-rounded picture of the Baroque cantata in its last phase (a phase identified rather unkindly by Schmitz as a 'time of decay', *Zeit des Verfalls*).

Prefaces customarily end with acknowledgements and expressions of thanks. The difficulty in the present case is that this book has matured for so long that I hardly know where to start. I owe a special debt of gratitude to Colin Timms, not only for his friendship over several decades but also for having been the first British scholar to have applied a general expertise in the Baroque cantata (itself an uncommon thing) to the Vivaldian canon. I am grateful to him for his willingness to read through, and comment on, the text of this book. Of his insights and findings much will be written in subsequent pages. Other friends and colleagues who have helped me in various ways and at various times to prepare this book include Marco Bizzarini, the late Malcolm Boyd, Clemens Brenneis, Enrico Careri, Luigi Cataldi, Karl Geck, Elizabeth Gibson, Karl Heller, Lowell Lindgren, Berthold Over, Rashid-Sascha Pegah, Brian Pritchard, Paul Raspé, Peter Ryom, Federico Maria Sardelli, Reinhard Strohm, Carole Taylor, Roger-Claude Travers, Carlo Vitali, and John Whenham.

I am indebted in quite a special way to the Istituto Italiano Antonio Vivaldi, which since 1978 has been one of the institutes supported by, and housed at, the Fondazione Giorgio Cini in Venice. Its directors, Antonio Fanna and (latterly) Francesco Fanna, have been generous in supporting my research and publication both morally and materially – and the fact that I have assisted, as translator and checker, in the publication of all thirty-seven Vivaldi cantatas issued individually by the IIAV in collaboration with Ricordi has only increased my appetite for the subject. I am likewise grateful to Francesco Degrada, the principal editor of the cantata volumes, for the repeated opportunities to trade information and ideas. Finally, this book would have been impossible in its present shape without the advice, over many years, of Paul Everett, many of whose findings regarding the physical characteristics of Vivaldi's manuscripts, often with profound consequences for dating, remain unpublished.

And how can I end without thanking my wife Shirley yet again for her love, encouragement, and (when required) tolerant forbearance?

# Conventions and Abbreviations

Notes of specified pitch are identified by the old German system (often called the 'Helmholz' system), where Middle C is *c'*, italicized. Notes of unspecified pitch (as in the description of keys) use capital letters in roman font.

In the music examples, the notation, including the choice of clefs, has been modernized, and the underlaid text normalized according to modern conventions. It can be assumed that the original clef for the vocal part of a soprano cantata is the C clef on the lowest stave line; that for an alto cantata is the C clef on the middle line. The original bass parts for the continuo instruments use the bass clef as the 'default' option but move freely to the tenor clef for passages in a high register.

The abbreviation 'B.c.' in the music examples stands for 'Basso continuo'.

# CHAPTER ONE

# The Rediscovery of Vivaldi's Cantatas

## *How Contemporaries saw them*

In his own day Vivaldi's cantatas went almost unnoticed. The thirty-seven that survive today, which probably represent a high proportion of the original total, may seem a respectable enough number, but viewed as a segment of his oeuvre, or in comparison with the cantata output of the 'big producers' of his time, they make little impression. This rather negative statistical assessment is based on a general impression, but the thrust of the argument receives support from Table 1.1, in which the output of six major composers of Vivaldi's time in four genres (opera, cantata, concerto, sonata) is compared.[1] Vivaldi's cantatas represent only about 6 per cent (the bracketed figure) of his works in the four categories, and this percentage would reduce further if his sacred works of all kinds and his serenatas were thrown into the balance. The composer among the five others whose profile resembles his most closely is Albinoni, who, as a fellow Venetian, enjoyed similar opportunities as a composer. But even here, the difference between 19 and 6 per cent is not negligible. Scarlatti, Marcello, and Bononcini emerge from the table as the specialists in the genre, and one is not surprised to find their names singled out frequently in this connection in the literature contemporary with Vivaldi.

Table 1.1  Statistics for works in four genres by Vivaldi and five contemporaries

| Composer | Operas | Cantatas | Concertos | Sonatas | Total |
|---|---|---|---|---|---|
| T. Albinoni (1671–1751) | 53 (20) | 48 (19) | 59 (23) | 99 (38) | 259 (100) |
| G. Bononcini (1670–1747) | 31 (7) | 295 (70) | 0 (0) | 95 (23) | 421 (100) |
| F. Gasparini (1668–1727) | 63 (44) | 71 (50) | 0 (0) | 9 (6) | 143 (100) |
| B. Marcello (1686–1739) | 0 (0) | 378 (81) | 18 (4) | 68 (15) | 464 (100) |
| A. Scarlatti (1660–1725) | 65 (9) | 620 (87) | 12 (2) | 18 (2) | 715 (100) |
| A. Vivaldi (1678–1741) | 48 (7) | 37 (6) | 475 (74) | 82 (13) | 642 (100) |

*Note: figures in parentheses are rounded percentages.*

[1]  The quoted figures, which apply only to compositions whose existence is confirmed, should be taken merely as working approximations based on the best available evidence. The table makes no attempt to show the general profile of the music by the six composers, since it includes no sacred vocal genres (e.g., oratorio, motet) and omits some important secular vocal genres (e.g., serenata, chamber duet).

Of course, gross numbers are not everything. Pergolesi achieved stardom in the domain of sacred vocal music with a single work, his *Stabat Mater* (1736), which circulated everywhere in Europe, not excluding Protestant regions. By the time Vivaldi started to compose chamber cantatas, which may have been as late as the second half of the 1710s, virtually the only way in which cantatas could circulate was via manuscript transmission. In Italy the copyists were predominantly professional scribes working in copying shops (*copisterie*). On the one hand, they fulfilled commissions from composers or the latter's patrons, making copies as instructed. On the other hand, they operated as independent retailers, supplying music to an open market that in Italy included many foreign visitors. In northern Europe music copying was carried out most often by members of the musical profession itself, since there were few persons fully dedicated to it (the famous house of J. G. I. Breitkopf in Leipzig furnishes the sole notable exception to this picture).

The dominance of manuscript transmission had not always been unchallenged. In the heyday of the cantata (its *Blütezeit*, as Eugen Schmitz described it) in the second half of the seventeenth century, Italian cantatas were frequently published, usually in sets of twelve. Indeed, composers often made a set of cantatas their first essay in the medium of published music. The centres that dominated the publication of cantatas were, not surprisingly, those that were most active in music publication generally. Before 1700 Bologna (Monti, Silvani, Micheletti) led the field, although Venice (Sala, Bortoli) ran it close after 1690. At various times Lucca (Gregori), Rome (Mascardi), Modena (Rosati), and Florence briefly participated. Outside Italy, the Amsterdam firm of Estienne Roger flirted, in the years immediately surrounding 1700, with the publication of cantatas (from movable type rather than via the process of engraving, from which Roger was later to draw his fame), and in the 1720s and 1730s the publication of cantatas (this time employing engraving) enjoyed an Indian summer in London, fuelled by the ambition of Italian émigrés. The general picture is shown in Table 1.2, which lists in chronological order all the identified publications containing Italian cantatas (sometimes appearing alongside other genres) from 1659 to 1735, and Table 1.3, which orders the same items according to the place of publication.

The two questions to which an answer is particularly urgent are these: why did the publication of cantatas collapse so spectacularly in Italy after 1708, and why did it not take root in Amsterdam subsequently?

One's reply to the first question, which applies in equal measure to instrumental music (sonatas, concertos, etc.), has to be that towards 1710 adverse economic conditions evidently reduced the competitiveness of printed music vis-à-vis manuscript music to a point where it was no longer sustainable. Even under the pressure from their competitors in Amsterdam, and before long also in London and Paris, Italian publishers failed to establish effective retail outlets north of the Alps, where, even for vocal genres, a large part of the international market for Italian music lay. So the remedy for local uncompetitiveness could not be sought via export.[2]

---

[2]   It has to be said that Roger seems to have made little effort to penetrate the Italian market. One factor in the decline of Italian instrumental music in the course of the eighteenth century must have been its failure (relatively speaking) to re-enter its homeland after publication abroad.

Table 1.2  Published cantatas, 1659–1735: listed by year of publication (col. 1)

| Year | Composer | Short description | Publisher | City |
|------|----------|------------------|-----------|------|
| 1659 | Cazzati, M. | Cantate morali e spirituali, Op. 20 | Monti | Bologna |
| 1666 | Cazzati, M. | Arie e cantate a voce sola, Op. 41 | — | Bologna |
| 1668 | Mazzaferrata, G. B. | Cantate e canzonette a 2 voci, Op. 3 | Monti | Bologna |
| 1673 | Grossi, C. | *La cetra d'Apollo*, Op. 6 | Gardano | Venice |
| 1673 | Mazzaferrata, G. B. | Cantate a voce sola, Op. 4 | Monti | Bologna |
| 1673 | Petrobelli, F. | Cantate a 2, 3, e 4 voci, Op. 9 | Monti | Bologna |
| 1675 | Grossi, C. | *L'Anfione*, Op. 7 | Gardano | Venice |
| 1676 | Legrenzi, G. | Cantate e canzonette a voce sola, Op. 12 | Monti | Bologna |
| 1677 | Bononcini, G. M. | Cantate a voce sola, Op. 10 | Monti | Bologna |
| 1678 | Bononcini, G. M. | Cantate a voce sola, Op. 13 | Monti | Bologna |
| 1678 | Legrenzi, G. | Cantate e canzoni a voce sola, Op. 14 | Monti | Bologna |
| 1679* | Coya, S. | *L'amante impazzito*, Op. 1 | Camagni | Milan |
| 1680 | Bassani, G. B. | Cantate a voce sola, Op. 2 | Monti | Bologna |
| 1680 | Mazzaferrata, G. B. | Cantate morali e spirituali, Op. 7 | Monti | Bologna |
| 1681 | Grossi, C. | *Il divertimento de grandi*, Op. 19 | Sala | Venice |
| 1682 | Bassani, G. B. | Cantate a voce sola, Op. 3 | Monti | Bologna |
| 1683 | Bassani, G. B. | Madrigali e cantate spirituali a 2 e 3 voci, Op.4 | Monti | Bologna |
| 1684 | Bassani, G. B. | Cantate a voce sola, Op. 6 | Monti | Bologna |
| 1685 | Albergati, P. | Cantate morali a voce sola, Op. 3 | Monti | Bologna |
| 1685 | Amodei, C. | Cantate a voce sola | De Bonis | Naples |
| 1685 | various | *Melpomene*, cantate a voce sola | Monti | Bologna |
| 1686 | Del Ricco, A. | Cantate a voce sola | — | Florence |
| 1687 | Albergati, P. | Cantate a voce sola, Op. 6 | Monti | Bologna |
| 1687 | Alveri, G. B. | Cantate a voce sola, Op. 1 | Micheletti | Bologna |
| 1688 | Bassani, G. B. | Cantate a voce sola, Op. 7 | Monti | Bologna |
| 1688 | Perti, G. A. | Cantate morali a 1 e 2 voci, Op. 1 | Monti | Bologna |
| 1688 | Tosi, G. F. | Cantate a voce sola, Op. 2 | Micheletti | Bologna |
| 1688 | Vinaccesi, B. | *Il consiglio degli amanti*, Op. 3 | Sala? | Venice |
| 1689 | Paulato, A. | Cantate a voce sola, Op. 1 | Sala | Venice |
| 1689 | Viviani, G. B. | Cantate a voce sola, Op. 1 | Monti | Bologna |
| 1690 | Degli Antonii, P. | Cantate a voce sola, Op. 6 | Monti | Bologna |
| 1690 | Viviani, G. B. | *Veglie armoniche*, Op. 7 | — | Florence |
| 1691 | Brevi, G. B. | Cantate a voce sola, Op. 1 | Monti | Bologna |
| 1691 | Gabrielli, D. | Cantate a voce sola, Op. 2 | Monti | Bologna |
| 1692 | Porfirii, P. | Cantate a voce sola, Op. 1 | Monti | Bologna |
| 1693 | Bassani, G. B. | Cantate a voce sola, Op. 14 | Sala | Venice |
| 1694* | Alghisi, P. | Cantate | Monti? | Bologna |
| 1694 | Bassani, G. B. | Cantate a voce sola, Op. 15 | Sala | Venice |
| 1695 | Bassani, G. B. | Cantate a voce sola, Op. 16 | Monti | Bologna |
| 1695 | Brevi, G. B. | *I deliri d'amor divino*, Op. 5 | Rosati | Modena |
| 1695 | Gasparini, F. | Cantate a voce sola, Op. 1 | Mascardi | Rome |
| 1695 | Marino, C. A. | Cantate a voce sola, Op. 4 | Sala | Venice |
| 1695 | Zanata, D. | Cantate a voce sola, Op. 2 | Sala | Venice |
| 1696 | Brevi, G. B. | Cantate a voce sola, Op. 7 | Rosati | Modena |
| 1696 | Predieri, G. C. | Cantate morali a 2 e 3 voci, Op. 1 | Silvani | Bologna |

| Year | Composer | Short description | Publisher | City |
|------|----------|------------------|-----------|------|
| 1696 | Zanata, D. | Cantate a voce sola, Op. 4 | Sala | Venice |
| 1697 | Bassani, P. A. | Cantate a voce sola, Op. 1 | Silvani | Bologna |
| 1698 | Bassani, G. B. | Cantate a voce sola, Op. 19 | Silvani | Bologna |
| 1698 | Cherici, S. | Ariete o cantate, Op. 5 | Silvani | Bologna |
| 1698 | Le Grand, N. F. | Cantate e ariette a voce sola, lib. 1 | Roger | Amsterdam |
| 1698 | Le Grand, N. F. | Cantate e ariette a voce sola, lib. 2 | Roger | Amsterdam |
| 1698 | Pistocchi, F. A. | Cantate, Op. 1 | Silvani | Bologna |
| 1698 | Pistocchi, F. A. | Scherzi musicali . . . cantate, Op. [2] | Roger | Amsterdam |
| 1698 | Zanata, D. | Cantate a voce sola, Op. 6 | Sala | Venice |
| 1699* | Badia, C. A. | *Tributi armonici* | — | Nuremberg |
| 1699 | Bassani, G. B. | Cantate a voce sola, Op. 17 | Sala | Venice |
| 1699 | Caldara, A. | Cantate a voce sola, Op. 3 | Sala | Venice |
| 1699 | Coletti, A. B. | Cantate a voce sola | Gregori | Lucca |
| 1699 | Gregori, G. L. | Cantate a voce sola, Op. 3 | Gregori | Lucca |
| 1700 | Gaffi, B. | Cantate da camera a voce sola | Mascardi | Rome |
| 1701 | Aldrovandini, G. | Cantate a voce sola, Op. 2 | Silvani | Bologna |
| 1701 | Bassani, G. B. | Cantate a voce sola, Op. 28 | Sala | Venice |
| 1701 | Della Ciaia, A. B. | Cantate da camera a voce sola | Gregori | Lucca |
| 1701 | Scarlatti, A. | Cantate a 1 e 2 voci, Op. 1 | Roger | Amsterdam |
| 1702 | various | Cantate a 1 e 2 voci con tromba e flauto | Roger | Amsterdam |
| 1702 | various | Cantate e ariette a voce sola sensa violini | Roger | Amsterdam |
| 1702 | various | Cantate e ariette a voce sola con violini | Roger | Amsterdam |
| 1702 | Albergati, P. | Cantate spirituali, Op. 9 | Rosati? | Modena |
| 1702 | Albinoni, T. | Cantate a voce sola, Op. 4 | Sala | Venice |
| 1703 | Bassani, G. B. | Cantate a voce sola con violini unisoni, Op. 31 | Silvani | Bologna |
| 1703 | Braibanzi, F. | Cantate a voce sola, Op. 2 | Silvani | Bologna |
| 1704 | Canuti, G. A. | Cantate da camera a voce sola | Gregori | Lucca |
| 1704 | Motta, A. | Cantate a voce sola, Op. 2 | Silvani | Bologna |
| 1705* | Altogiri, Abate | Cantate a voce sola | Sala | Venice |
| 1706 | Ruggieri, G. M. | Cantate a voce sola, Op. 5 | Sala | Venice |
| 1707 | Silvani, G. A. | Cantate morali a 1, 2, e 3 voci, Op. 5 | Silvani | Bologna |
| 1708 | Marcello, A. | Cantate da camera a voce sola | Bortoli | Venice |
| 1713 | Keiser, R. | Divertimenti serenissimi | Greflinger | Hamburg |
| 1714 | Albergati, P. | Cantate e oratorii a 1, 2, e 3 voci, Op. 10 | Silvani | Bologna |
| 1715 | Stricker, A. R. | Cantate a voce sola, Op. 1 | — | Köthen |
| 1717 | Albergati, P. | *Corona de preggi di M.V.*, Op. 13 | Silvani | Bologna |
| 1720 | Montuoli, C. etc. | Cantate a voce sola e basso continuo | Montuoli | Bologna |
| 1721 | Bononcini, G. | Cantate e duetti | — | London |
| 1726 | D'Astorga, E. | Cantate a voce sola | — | Lisbon |
| 1727 | Kelleri, F. | Cantate e arie con stromenti | Smith | London |
| 1727* | Sandoni, P. G. | Cantate da camera . . . | — | London |
| 1728 | Ariosti, A. | [Six cantatas and six lessons] | — | London |
| 1728 | D'Alay, M. | Cantate e suonate | — | London |
| 1732 | Arrigoni, C. | Cantate da camera | Atkins | London |

| Year | Composer | Short description | Publisher | City |
|------|----------|------------------|-----------|------|
| 1735* | Duni, A. | Cantate da camera | Smith | London |
| 1735 | Porpora, N. | Cantate, Op. 1 | — | London |
| 1735* | Roseingrave T. | VI Italian cantatas | Cooke | London |

*Note: starred years are approximate.*

Table 1.3  Published cantatas, 1659–1735: listed by place of publication (col. 5)

| Year | Composer | Short description | Publisher | City |
|------|----------|------------------|-----------|------|
| 1698 | Le Grand, N. F. | Cantate e ariette a voce sola, lib. 1 | Roger | Amsterdam |
| 1698 | Le Grand, N. F. | Cantate e ariette a voce sola, lib. 2 | Roger | Amsterdam |
| 1698 | Pistocchi, F. A. | Scherzi musicali . . . cantate, Op. [2] | Roger | Amsterdam |
| 1701 | Scarlatti, A. | Cantate a 1 e 2 voci, Op. 1 | Roger | Amsterdam |
| 1702 | various | Cantate a 1 e 2 voci con tromba e flauto | Roger | Amsterdam |
| 1702 | various | Cantate e ariette a voce sola sensa violini | Roger | Amsterdam |
| 1702 | various | Cantate e ariette a voce sola con violini | Roger | Amsterdam |
| 1659 | Cazzati, M. | Cantate morali e spirituali, Op. 20 | Monti | Bologna |
| 1666 | Cazzati, M. | Arie e cantate a voce sola, Op. 41 | — | Bologna |
| 1668 | Mazzaferrata, G. B. | Cantate e canzonette a 2 voci, Op. 3 | Monti | Bologna |
| 1673 | Mazzaferrata, G. B. | Cantate a voce sola, Op. 4 | Monti | Bologna |
| 1673 | Petrobelli, F. | Cantate a 2, 3, e 4 voci, Op. 9 | Monti | Bologna |
| 1676 | Legrenzi, G. | Cantate e canzonette a voce sola, Op. 12 | Monti | Bologna |
| 1677 | Bononcini, G. M. | Cantate a voce sola, Op. 10 | Monti | Bologna |
| 1678 | Bononcini, G. M. | Cantate a voce sola, Op. 13 | Monti | Bologna |
| 1678 | Legrenzi, G. | Cantate e canzoni a voce sola, Op. 14 | Monti | Bologna |
| 1680 | Bassani, G. B. | Cantate a voce sola, Op. 2 | Monti | Bologna |
| 1680 | Mazzaferrata, G. B. | Cantate morali e spirituali, Op. 7 | Monti | Bologna |
| 1682 | Bassani, G. B. | Cantate a voce sola, Op. 3 | Monti | Bologna |
| 1683 | Bassani, G. B. | Madrigali e cantate spirituali a 2 e 3 voci, Op.4 | Monti | Bologna |
| 1684 | Bassani, G. B. | Cantate a voce sola, Op. 6 | Monti | Bologna |
| 1685 | Albergati, P. | Cantate morali a voce sola, Op. 3 | Monti | Bologna |
| 1685 | various | *Melpomene*, cantate a voce sola | Monti | Bologna |
| 1687 | Albergati, P. | Cantate a voce sola, Op. 6 | Monti | Bologna |
| 1687 | Alveri, G. B. | Cantate a voce sola, Op. 1 | Micheletti | Bologna |
| 1688 | Bassani, G. B. | Cantate a voce sola, Op. 7 | Monti | Bologna |
| 1688 | Perti, G. A. | Cantate morali a 1 e 2 voci, Op. 1 | Monti | Bologna |
| 1688 | Tosi, G. F. | Cantate a voce sola, Op. 2 | Micheletti | Bologna |
| 1689 | Viviani, G. B. | Cantate a voce sola, Op. 1 | Monti | Bologna |
| 1690 | Degli Antonii, P. | Cantate a voce sola, Op. 6 | Monti | Bologna |
| 1691 | Brevi, G. B. | Cantate a voce sola, Op. 1 | Monti | Bologna |
| 1691 | Gabrielli, D. | Cantate a voce sola, Op. 2 | Monti | Bologna |
| 1692 | Porfirii, P. | Cantate a voce sola, Op. 1 | Monti | Bologna |

| Year | Composer | Short description | Publisher | City |
|------|----------|------------------|-----------|------|
| 1694* | Alghisi, P. | Cantate | Monti? | Bologna |
| 1695 | Bassani, G. B. | Cantate a voce sola, Op. 16 | Monti | Bologna |
| 1696 | Predieri, G. C. | Cantate morali a 2 e 3 voci, Op. 1 | Silvani | Bologna |
| 1697 | Bassani, P. A. | Cantate a voce sola, Op. 1 | Silvani | Bologna |
| 1698 | Bassani, G. B. | Cantate a voce sola, Op. 19 | Silvani | Bologna |
| 1698 | Cherici, S. | Ariete o cantate, Op. 5 | Silvani | Bologna |
| 1698 | Pistocchi, F. A. | Cantate, Op. 1 | Silvani | Bologna |
| 1701 | Aldrovandini, G. | Cantate a voce sola, Op. 2 | Silvani | Bologna |
| 1703 | Bassani, G. B. | Cantate a voce sola con violini unisoni, Op. 31 | Silvani | Bologna |
| 1703 | Braibanzi, F. | Cantate a voce sola, Op. 2 | Silvani | Bologna |
| 1704 | Motta, A. | Cantate a voce sola, Op. 2 | Silvani | Bologna |
| 1707 | Silvani, G. A. | Cantate morali a 1, 2, e 3 voci, Op. 5 | Silvani | Bologna |
| 1714 | Albergati, P. | Cantate e oratorii a 1, 2, e 3 voci, Op. 10 | Silvani | Bologna |
| 1717 | Albergati, P. | *Corona de preggi di M.V.*, Op. 13 | Silvani | Bologna |
| 1720 | Montuoli, C. etc. | Cantate a voce sola e basso continuo | Montuoli | Bologna |
| 1686 | Del Ricco, A. | Cantate a voce sola | — | Florence |
| 1690 | Viviani, G. B. | *Veglie armoniche*, Op. 7 | — | Florence |
| 1713 | Keiser, R. | *Divertimenti serenissimi* | Greflinger | Hamburg |
| 1715 | Stricker, A. R. | Cantate a voce sola, Op. 1 | — | Köthen |
| 1726 | D'Astorga, E. | Cantate a voce sola | — | Lisbon |
| 1721 | Bononcini, G. | Cantate e duetti | — | London |
| 1727 | Kelleri, F. | Cantate e arie con strumenti | Smith | London |
| 1727* | Sandoni, P. G. | Cantate da camera . . . | — | London |
| 1728 | Ariosti, A. | [Six cantatas and six lessons] | — | London |
| 1728 | D'Alay, M. | Cantate e suonate | — | London |
| 1732 | Arrigoni, C. | Cantate da camera | Atkins | London |
| 1735 | Porpora, N. | Cantate, Op. 1 | — | London |
| 1735* | Duni, A. | Cantate da camera | Smith | London |
| 1735* | Roseingrave T. | VI Italian cantatas | Cooke | London |
| 1699 | Coletti, A. B. | Cantate a voce sola | Gregori | Lucca |
| 1699 | Gregori, G. L. | Cantate a voce sola, Op. 3 | Gregori | Lucca |
| 1701 | Della Ciaia, A. B. | Cantate da camera a voce sola | Gregori | Lucca |
| 1704 | Canuti, G. A. | Cantate da camera a voce sola | Gregori | Lucca |
| 1679* | Coya, S. | *L'amante impazzito*, Op. 1 | Camagni | Milan |
| 1695 | Brevi, G. B. | *I deliri d'amor divino*, Op. 5 | Rosati | Modena |
| 1696 | Brevi, G. B. | Cantate a voce sola, Op. 7 | Rosati | Modena |
| 1702 | Albergati, P. | Cantate spirituali, Op. 9 | Rosati? | Modena |
| 1685 | Amodei, C. | Cantate a voce sola | De Bonis | Naples |
| 1699* | Badia, C. A. | *Tributi armonici* | — | Nuremberg |
| 1695 | Gasparini, F. | Cantate a voce sola, Op. 1 | Mascardi | Rome |
| 1700 | Gaffi, B. | Cantate da camera a voce sola | Mascardi | Rome |
| 1673 | Grossi, C. | *La cetra d'Apollo*, Op. 6 | Gardano | Venice |
| 1675 | Grossi, C. | *L'Anfione*, Op. 7 | Gardano | Venice |
| 1681 | Grossi, C. | *Il divertimento de grandi*, Op. 19 | Sala | Venice |
| 1688 | Vinaccesi, B. | *Il consiglio degli amanti*, Op. 3 | Sala? | Venice |
| 1689 | Paulato, A. | Cantate a voce sola, Op. 1 | Sala | Venice |
| 1693 | Bassani, G. B. | Cantate a voce sola, Op. 14 | Sala | Venice |

| Year | Composer | Short description | Publisher | City |
|------|----------|------------------|-----------|------|
| 1694 | Bassani, G. B. | Cantate a voce sola, Op. 15 | Sala | Venice |
| 1695 | Marino, C. A. | Cantate a voce sola, Op. 4 | Sala | Venice |
| 1695 | Zanata, D. | Cantate a voce sola, Op. 2 | Sala | Venice |
| 1696 | Zanata, D. | Cantate a voce sola, Op. 4 | Sala | Venice |
| 1698 | Zanata, D. | Cantate a voce sola, Op. 6 | Sala | Venice |
| 1699 | Bassani, G. B. | Cantate a voce sola, Op. 17 | Sala | Venice |
| 1699 | Caldara, A. | Cantate a voce sola, Op. 3 | Sala | Venice |
| 1701 | Bassani, G. B. | Cantate a voce sola, Op. 28 | Sala | Venice |
| 1702 | Albinoni, T. | Cantate a voce sola, Op. 4 | Sala | Venice |
| 1705* | Altogiri, Abate | Cantate a voce sola | Sala | Venice |
| 1706 | Ruggieri, G. M. | Cantate a voce sola, Op. 5 | Sala | Venice |
| 1708 | Marcello, A. | Cantate da camera a voce sola | Bortoli | Venice |

*Note: starred years are approximate.*

Italian composers of instrumental music addressed the crisis by sending their new works directly to Roger, as Corelli did with his reissued Op. 5 (the version with the ornamented Adagios) and Op. 6, Albinoni with his Op. 6, and Vivaldi with his Op. 3. Indeed, the possible risks and drawbacks of dealing directly with a foreign publisher were offset by the quality of the result: the engraving process was tailor-made for a musical style that increasingly privileged long series of short notes and employed sophisticated slurring (contemporary typography was unable to beam notes together, and the fixed sizes and shapes of slurs in typeset music coped very badly with the varied needs).

But why, then, did these composers not do the same with their cantatas? Here, the answer is more elusive. It could well be that Roger's experiment with the issue of Italian cantatas around 1700 – at a time when his catalogue consisted, in its Italian department, mainly of works 'pirated' from their original publishers – was deemed by him a failure in commercial terms. It is significant that between 1702 and the onset of the crisis in Italian music publishing not a single cantata appeared from Roger. Whatever the reason for Roger's reluctance to publish Italian cantatas precisely in the years leading up to 1710, the window of opportunity soon narrowed drastically: cantatas in other languages (French and English) began to provide competition to their Italian models, and the general swing away from cantatas to free-standing arias, which will be discussed later, set in gradually.

Of the composers represented in Table 1.1, Gasparini (1695), Scarlatti (1701), and Albinoni (1702) were just in time to 'catch the boat', while Bononcini won his chance under very different conditions later in London (1721).[3] Unlike his elder brother Alessandro (1669–1747), Benedetto Marcello published no cantatas, although a collection of secular vocal music of different type, his *Canzoni madrigalesche*, Op. 4, appeared in Bologna in 1717. Vivaldi arrived on the scene a few years too late to profit from the opportunity.

---

3    Some arias from cantatas in Albinoni's Op. 4 gained even wider currency by being issued in London in the form of song-sheets with translated (more accurately: paraphrased) words.

However, the absence of printed cantatas was not the decisive issue for a composer's reputation within the genre. Had it been so, Marcello, for one, would not have earned his fame. More significant was the number of times the cantatas were re-copied after their initial use. The persons who desired to obtain copies were various. They included patrons who wished to acquire them for singers in their service, collectors of music both domestic and foreign, performers themselves, and tourists seeking souvenirs of a visit.

It is precisely from this secondary copying activity that Vivaldi appears to have benefited very little. Most of his surviving cantatas exist only in the form of an autograph score (or one by a member of his entourage made under his supervision) preserved among the Turin manuscripts – the composer's personal archive today housed at Turin in the Biblioteca Nazionale Universitaria.[4] Each of the thirteen authenticated cantatas preserved outside Turin (eleven in Dresden, one in Meiningen, and one in Oxford) can be linked directly to the Turin manuscripts either putatively – as a primary copy of a work originally present among them but today missing – or, as in five cases, through textual comparison.[5] In the single instance where two sources of the same cantata exist outside Turin (*Usignoletto bello*, RV 796), each can be related independently to Vivaldi's workshop in Venice. We have yet to discover an unequivocal instance where a contemporary copied a Vivaldi cantata from a manuscript not in the composer's possession. The inference is that, once delivered to their first destination, Vivaldi's cantatas were performed only once, or, if repeated, remained within the same locality. This factor alone would account for the lack of contemporary mention. The contrast with Vivaldi's concertos, which fanned out into all corners of Europe, could hardly be greater.

The nearest thing to a critical discussion of Vivaldi's cantatas by a contemporary that I have found occurs in Johann Mattheson's *Der vollkommene Capellmeister* of 1739.[6] Mattheson's comment refers to Vivaldi's writing for the voice in generic terms: that is, it applies just as much to his operas or motets as to his cantatas. The German critic praises Vivaldi, an instrumentalist by background, for his ability to adapt his style when writing vocal music:

> Vivaldi, albeit no singer, has had the sense to keep violin leaps out of his vocal compositions so completely that his arias have become a real thorn in the flesh to many a practised vocal composer.

An assumption underlying this evaluation deserves comment. In Vivaldi's day there was no pressure on composers to demonstrate versatility. Quite the

---

4    The twenty-eight cantatas are bound in the volumes Foà 27 (eleven works) and Foà 28 (seventeen works).

5    The four cantatas with RV numbers that today are considered spurious are the three in Florence (*Filli, di gioia vuoi farmi morir*, RV 672; *Ingrata Lidia, ha vinto il tuo rigor*, RV 673; *Piango, gemo, sospiro e peno*, RV 675), and *Prendea con man di latte*, RV 753, in Oxford.

6    Johann Mattheson, *Der vollkommene Capellmeister*, Hamburg: Herold, 1739, p. 205. Original text: 'Vivaldi, ob er gleich kein Sänger ist, hat doch aus seinen Sing-Sachen die Geigen-Sprünge so weit zu verbannen gewust, daß seine Arietten manchem geübten Vocal-Componisten ein rechter Stachel in den Augen geworden sind'.

contrary: the musician as performer was expected to reflect the musician as composer, and vice versa. This corresponded perfectly to the manner in which most music was placed in circulation, the composer himself giving the première. In an age when the guild mentality still held sway, specialization was the rule, universality the exception.[7] One respect in which Vivaldi shared the high ambition of J. S. Bach and Handel was his evident desire to be an all-round artist for whom no genre was in principle out of bounds. Only his failure to produce independent keyboard music betrays any hint of a limitation.

According to a report by the French traveller Charles de Brosses, who met Vivaldi in 1739 and provided a vivid pen-portrait of him, Tartini – motivated, perhaps, by envy – reasserted the traditional view that composers of instrumental music should stick to their last and not venture into the vocal domain, citing Vivaldi as a composer applauded in the first category but hissed in the second.[8] This judgement is inaccurate, at least as a record of Vivaldi's experience during his career, since his operas held the stage between 1713 and (posthumously!) 1742 and achieved a peak of success in the 1720s.

The earliest critical mention of cantatas by Vivaldi occurs in the fourth volume (1789) of Charles Burney's *General History of Music*, in the course of a section where the author reviews the history of the cantata genre from Carissimi onwards. To be accorded the honour of a separate paragraph, Vivaldi has already done well, since Burney treats only a handful of composers similarly. He writes:

D. ANTONIO VIVALDI merits a place among the candidates for fame in this species of composition: several are inserted in the collection mentioned above [that of Henry Aldrich at Christ Church, Oxford, mentioned in connection with Caldara's Op. 3]; but these, and all that I have seen elsewhere, are very common and quiet, notwithstanding he was so riotous in composing for violins. But he had been too long used to write for the voice, to treat it as an instrument.[9]

These few lines are pregnant with valuable information. We note, first, the remark on Vivaldi's skill and experience at writing for the voice, which echoes, and very likely was prompted by, Mattheson's evaluation. Burney's observation that in relation to Vivaldi's other compositions his cantatas are 'common and quiet' – which we should read as 'conventional and sober' – hits the nail on the head. In form they reveal none of the innovatory spirit and zest for experimentation that characterizes his concertos and sacred vocal music, and even to some extent his sonatas, and their musical language, though never staid, shows a sense of restraint. However, such remarks should be placed in a wider context. As a genre, the late Baroque cantata tended towards conformity to shared norms and expectations. This convergence began with the poets, and the composers merely mirrored it at the next stage of the creative process. The consistency was, in a way, a boon

---

7 The absence of vocal music from Corelli's oeuvre, or of instrumental music (with trivial exceptions) from Lotti's, demonstrates the point.

8 Charles de Brosses, *Lettres historiques et critiques sur l'Italie*, 3 vols, Paris: Ponthieu, 1799, 2, p. 316. This is the work published in later editions under the description of *Lettres familières*.

9 Charles Burney, *A General History of Music from the Earliest Ages to the Present Period*, 4 vols, London: Becket and others, 1776–89, 4, p. 178.

for singers, since it enabled them, via their art of improvised embellishment, to personalize a musical performance in a way that would have been harder, had the 'product' on which they worked been less stable. So Vivaldi's cantatas would have been expected under any circumstances to be less adventurous than his concertos.

Most interesting of all is Burney's reference to Vivaldi cantatas examined in Aldrich's collection. Dr Henry Aldrich (1648–1710), who was made Dean of Christ Church in 1689, was an assiduous collector of music and included much recently composed Italian music in his library, which passed after his death to the college. If his collection once held cantatas by Vivaldi, as Burney asserts, these must have been acquired before his death in 1710 (no trace of them survives today). This would make them older by several years than any known cantatas by Vivaldi, the earliest of which appear to date from his Mantuan period (1718–20) or not long before. Such an early date is not in itself implausible, since Vivaldi's earliest known vocal work, the lost serenata *Le gare del dovere*, RV 688, dates from 1708. However, one cannot help feeling that there is some inaccuracy in Burney's report. Perhaps the cantatas were indeed in the Christ Church library but postdated Aldrich's time. Perhaps they were attributed to Vivaldi by mistake – a kind of error more prevalent in the cantata repertory than in any other. If and when these cantatas turn up, we will be able to form a view of their period and authenticity. Until then, caution is advisable.

Burney may have been able to gain knowledge of Vivaldi's cantatas from a separate source: a manuscript in his possession containing 'Cantate and Arie &c.' by 'Porpora, A. Scarlatti, Bononcini, Gasparini, Orlandini, d'Astorga, Vivaldi, Fiore, &c.' sold as lot 615 at the auction of his collection of music held in the year of his death, 1814.[10] No volume in a public collection conforming to that description appears to exist today. Seeing that cantata volumes of this kind, containing music by several authors, are very often 'binder's collections', which means that there is no necessary connection between the several items, it would be hazardous to estimate the date of the Vivaldi cantatas (if they were indeed cantatas rather than operatic arias), but the presence, within the group, of younger composers, in particular Porpora and Orlandini, makes it on balance more likely that these works belonged to Vivaldi's maturity.

When Burney published the fourth volume of his history, Vivaldi's music was about to reach the nadir of its fortunes. Performers of his music had died off or moved on to newer things. Unlike Corelli or Marcello, he had failed to achieve in any genre the status of a 'classic' whose music was known and respected, even if it rarely graced the concert platform. For the final decades of the eighteenth century and most of the nineteenth Vivaldi was of interest only to biographers, who made the most of his eccentricities and foibles, not to musicians. It is quite possible that between his death in 1741 and the 1940s no one sang a note of his chamber cantatas.

---

[10] A facsimile of the sale catalogue is reproduced in Alec Hyatt King, *Catalogue of the Music Library of Charles Burney, sold in London, 8 August 1814*, Amsterdam: Frits Knuf, 1973.

## How Modern Commentators have seen them

Although Vivaldi's instrumental music became a frequent item on concert programmes or in publishers' catalogues only after the First World War, a tiny sliver survived more or less continuously from the eighteenth century into the nineteenth in the shape of his once famous but today rather neglected 'Cuckoo' (or 'Cuckow') Concerto (RV 355), which was first published in 1717 by the London dealer Daniel Wright. It was a favourite 'party piece' of the Hereford innkeeper and violinist Thomas Woodcock (brother of the flautist-composer Robert Woodcock). In Burney's memoirs, preserved only in autograph fragments, the historian recalled c.1742:

[Vivaldi's] *Cuckoo Concerto*, during my youth, was the wonder and delight of all frequenters of country concerts; and *Woodcock*, one of the Hereford waits, was sent far and near to perform it.[11]

Within a few years the publisher John Walsh was advertising it, and new editions continued to come out at intervals in England up to at least 1896, when Henry Farmer arranged it for violin and piano for the London publisher Joseph Williams.[12]

But this was a sideshow, a freak of nature. The main story is that Vivaldi's concertos and (to a minimal extent) his sonatas re-entered the consciousness of musicians and critics very slowly, and initially only as a by-product of the Bach revival. Already in Forkel's ground-breaking biography of J. S. Bach (1802) Vivaldi had received a slightly grudging credit for his influence on Bach, especially in matters of form, and attention had been drawn to the transcriptions for keyboard that Bach had made of Vivaldi concertos. Bach scholars were thereby stimulated to track down the originals and compare them (usually to their detriment) with Bach's arrangements. It was in fact within the covers of the collected edition of the Bach-Gesellschaft that the first 'modern' editions of Vivaldi's music with a claim to completeness and accuracy came out.[13] Towards the end of the nineteenth century, and into the first years of the twentieth, a thin stream of instrumental works, always issued individually, emerged. These were drawn almost exclusively from the published collections (chiefly Op. 3, *L'estro armonico*), and the main criterion for selection seems to have been either their historical value (as in the editions by Alfred Einstein and Paul Graf Waldersee) or their pedagogical utility combined with novelty value (as in the editions by Sam Franko, Alfred Moffat, Emilio Pente, Tivadar Nachez, and Gustav Jensen); in the latter case, the accompaniment was invariably arranged for piano.

11 Transcribed in Slava Klima, Garry Bowers, and Kerry S. Grant (eds), *Memoirs of Dr Charles Burney, 1726–1769*, Lincoln and London: University of Nebraska Press, 1988, p. 32. The report resurfaced almost verbatim in Burney's *General History* (3, p. 561).
12 'Arranged' is perhaps a misnomer. In the intervening period the piece had been so maimed and disfigured by accretions (including a minuet pastiche) that virtually nothing survived of the original beyond a few simple figurations.
13 These were the tenth concerto of Vivaldi's Op. 3 (RV 580) and the second concerto of the second volume of his Op. 7 (RV 299).

Rather surprisingly, although the large collection of manuscript works by Vivaldi in Dresden was known to exist – Moritz Fürstenau mentioned it in his history of music at the Saxon court (1861–2), and Julius Rühlmann made a preliminary evaluation in an article of 1867 – nothing of it was seemingly published until well into the twentieth century, when Arnold Schering raided it for a Largo movement from a violin sonata.[14]

This same collection in Dresden, which has been inherited by the present-day Sächsische Landesbibliothek – Staats- und Universitätsbibliothek (to be referred to hereafter as 'the SLUB'), is home to the only group of Vivaldi cantatas preserved outside Turin, and perforce, until the 1920s, the sole known repository of Vivaldi's cantatas.[15] The contents of the part of the musical collection originating from the former *Hofkapelle* have in the past been hard for those not on the spot to ascertain, although the recent on-line publication of the card catalogue has greatly improved the situation. Already at the start of the twentieth century Robert Eitner's *Quellenlexikon* mentioned the presence of eleven Vivaldi cantatas in the then Royal Library in Dresden, opening the door to scholarly investigation.[16]

This did not take long to materialize. In 1905 the Leipzig publisher Breitkopf & Härtel inaugurated, under the general editorship of Hermann Kretzschmar, a series of 'Short Handbooks of Music History by Genres' (*Kleine Handbücher der Musikgeschichte nach Gattungen*). There was nothing short about the first volume, Arnold Schering's magisterial history of the concerto, which contains the first thorough (and the first appreciative) evaluation of Vivaldi's contribution to the genre.[17] Subsequent volumes maintained the serious tone and high scholarly standard. Fifth among them was Eugen Schmitz's *Geschichte der weltlichen Solokantate* (the first, and in the event only, part of a wider project that would have embraced also the *concerto sacro* under the general banner of *Geschichte der Kantate und des geistlichen Konzerts*), which came out in 1914.[18] Strangely, this extraordinary achievement is the only general survey in book form of the Baroque cantata as a whole to have appeared up to the present day. It is a child of its time and place in that it adopts what a recent author describes, not in a spirit of approval, as the 'organism model of history, complete with its periods of flowering, maturity, and decline'.[19] For Schmitz, the period of *Verfall* (decline) began

[14]  Moritz Fürstenau, *Zur Geschichte der Musik und des Theaters am Hofe zu Dresden*, 2 vols, Dresden: Kuntze, 1861–2, 1, p. 86; Julius Rühlmann, 'Antonio Vivaldi und sein Einfluss auf Joh. Seb. Bach', *Neue Zeitschrift für Musik*, lxiii (1867), 392–7, 401–5, and 413–16. Schering's edition was published c.1925 by C. F. Kahnt, Leipzig.

[15]  Not counting the isolated works in Meiningen, Oxford (formerly Tenbury), and Vienna.

[16]  Robert Eitner, *Biographisch-bibliographisches Quellenlexikon der Musiker und Musikgelehrten der christlichen Zeitrechnung bis zur Mitte des neunzehnten Jahrhunderts*, 10 vols, Leipzig: Breitkopf & Härtel, 1899–1904, 10, p. 113. As if presciently, Eitner included among the cantatas attributable to Vivaldi the cantata *Usignoletto bello*, RV 796, which in the Dresden source known to him (more recently, the library has acquired a second manuscript) lacks a composer's name.

[17]  Arnold Schering, *Geschichte des Instrumentalkonzerts bis auf die Gegenwart*, Leipzig: Breitkopf & Härtel, 1905.

[18]  Eugen Schmitz, *Geschichte der weltlichen Solokantate*, Leipzig: Breitkopf & Härtel, 1914.

[19]  W. Dean Sutcliffe, *The Keyboard Sonatas of Domenico Scarlatti and Eighteenth-Century Musical Style*, Cambridge: Cambridge University Press, 2003, p. 223.

at exactly the same time that the 'grand' *da capo* aria form (the expanded version of the form in which the 'A' text is sung through twice on each occasion) established its hegemony, thus close to the end of the seventeenth century.

It will be useful at this point to clarify, and to justify, the transition from *Blütezeit* to *Verfall* identified by Schmitz. He does not mean that the average musical quality of cantatas begins to sink at this point.[20] Clearly, it does not; and Schmitz pays due tribute to the artistic achievements of Scarlatti in his late years, Handel, Marcello, and many others. What he means – and this is objectively verifiable – is that the form in which cantatas are cast becomes progressively ossified: the options tend to narrow as the decades pass, and at the same time the cantata's generic distinctiveness vis-à-vis the operatic aria and *scena* weakens.[21] This loss of a strong generic identity proved fatal for the solo cantata, since as a literary form it was always more restricted in appeal than as a musical experience. One could express almost the same thought by saying that for the public, if not for the poet, arias enjoyed more popularity than recitatives.[22] The fall from favour of plain continuo accompaniment for cantata arias, following in the footsteps of operatic arias, from which accompaniment by continuo alone tends to disappear rapidly after c.1710, is a symptom of the same convergence. Inexorably, from the 1730s onwards, operatic arias, performed and sometimes even conceived from the start as concert pieces, began to displace the cantata genre from its last redoubts. It is no accident that, after a brief final efflorescence in London, the published solo cantata comes to such an absolute full stop around 1735, even though the market for published vocal music in general remains buoyant. Late examples of the genre, such as Haydn's *Arianna a Naxos* (1790), show the cantata imprisoned within the conventions of the dramatic *scena*.[23]

So, in this rather technical sense, Schmitz's perception of 'decline' seems justified. We could use a similar description for the madrigal after 1625 or the symphonic poem after 1918. Naturally, a 'technical' decline is apt to produce, in time, an artistic decline, as front-rank figures, with the approval of their patrons, redirect their efforts elsewhere. However, this did not happen quickly in the case of the Italian solo cantata, which during almost the whole length of Vivaldi's career retained its high status.

Schmitz discusses Vivaldi together with Albinoni and Marcello in a subsection devoted to Venetian composers within a chapter on the solo cantatas of the

---

[20] In this connection, it is interesting to note that Burney (*General History*, 4, p. 164), unshakeable in his fundamental belief in the continuous improvement of music, locates what he terms 'the golden age of cantatas in Italy' in the years around 1700 – the start of the decline, according to Schmitz.

[21] A partial exception could be made for Marcello's *Sujetkantaten*, which are unusually extended cantatas on 'heroic' themes taken from antiquity. But these are few in number and evoked little response from other composers.

[22] This point was conceded by the German librettist Carl Wilhelm Ramler when he wrote, in a letter of 29 June 1754 to J. W. L. Gleim, that arias were 'for the composer alone', whereas recitatives were 'for the poet' ('die Arien nur für den Musikus, die Recitatife aber für den Poeten sind').

[23] The dramatic cantata (serenata) for two or more singers proved more robust, since it had an organic connection with the ceremonial side of public life.

'Neapolitan' school.[24] By 'Neapolitan' he means simply 'post-Scarlattian'. Modern musicology is shy of using this label with too broad a meaning, especially when the composers in question have no obvious connection with Naples. However, a good case can be made for identifying as genuinely 'Neapolitan' the *galant* style in its early phase (the second half of the 1720s and the 1730s), when three masters trained in that city, Leo, Vinci, and Porpora, almost overnight achieved dominance over the Italian stage and by so doing imparted a new stylistic inflection to vocal music of all kinds, including the cantata. According to that criterion, Vivaldi's cantatas written before c.1725 may be regarded as 'pre-Neapolitan', and his later cantatas as 'Neapolitan'.

But this is to quibble over mere terminology. Although Schmitz did not have access to a broad cross-section of Vivaldi's cantatas, which reduces the usefulness of his generalization, he made several perceptive and valid points, which will be discussed at the appropriate place later in this book. It is interesting that, just as Arthur Hutchings was to do in his survey of the Baroque concerto, Schmitz 'twins' Vivaldi with Albinoni and structures his discussion of each around a direct comparison of their cantatas.[25] The honours are fairly evenly distributed. If Albinoni is judged the better melodist, Vivaldi receives credit for his inventive and expressive recitative.

The quantity and variety of Vivaldi cantatas available for inspection was naturally transformed by the recovery, during the 1920s, of Vivaldi's personal archive of musical manuscripts in a state that, while doubtless not complete (it is suspiciously deficient in sonatas), gives us a fairly accurate conspectus of his work as a composer from about 1712 onwards. The incredible story of its preservation and acquisition for the Biblioteca Nazionale Universitaria, Turin, has been told many times and need only be summarized here.[26] At some time between 27/28 July 1741, when the composer died in Vienna, and 1745 this hoard of manuscripts, perhaps purchased from Vivaldi's heirs, entered the library of the Venetian bibliophile Jacopo Soranzo. Under Soranzo's ownership it was bound into twenty-seven volumes, organized according to content and/or format. Later in the century it passed to Count Giacomo Durazzo, presumably during the period when this famous figure, best known for his patronage of Gluck, served as imperial ambassador to Venice between 1764 and 1794. Inherited by successive generations of the Durazzo family, the volumes were at one point divided into two almost equal portions, comprising respectively fourteen and thirteen volumes, each becoming the property of a different son. The larger portion, which was to become the major component of the Foà donation, was located in 1926 and acquired for the library in 1927. The complementary volumes making up the Giordano donation arrived in 1930.

The main credit for the discovery and purchase of the reunited collection must go to the perspicacity and tenacity of Alberto Gentili, who lectured in the history

[24] Schmitz, *Geschichte*, pp. 150–1.

[25] Arthur Hutchings, *The Baroque Concerto*, London: Faber, 1961. Schmitz's main source of reference for Albinoni's cantatas was a volume containing eighteen of them that is preserved today in Berlin, Staatsbibliothek 'Preußischer Kulturbesitz', Mus. ms. 447.

[26] For an account in English, see Michael Talbot, *The Sacred Vocal Music of Antonio Vivaldi*, Florence: Olschki, 1995, pp. 11–14.

of music at the University of Turin. Soon after the library received the Foà volumes, Gentili wrote an article in which he summarized and evaluated their contents.[27] He mentioned that two of them were headed 'Cantate' (being respectively Tomo I and Tomo II) and together contained twenty-four cantatas (he miscounted: there are twenty-eight), both with and without instruments in addition to continuo. His pronouncement on their value is worth quoting:

> The cantatas are of very variable quality. However, they include some that tend to confirm what we have said with regard to the oratorio *Iuditha* [referring to his earlier plaudits for this work]. Indeed, certain of them contain passages so compelling that they take us back to the golden age of the cantata in the previous century [Gentili shares Schmitz's concept of a *Blütezeit*] and elevate Vivaldi above composers of cantatas of his own time such as Ariosti and Bononcini. Especially notable for their departure from the norm are a few cantatas containing arioso passages, accompanied recitatives and obbligato writing for violin.[28]

It is disappointing that between 1927 and 1938 (when Mussolini's so-called Racial Laws removed Gentili, who was Jewish, from public life) the writer of those lines did not follow them up with a more extended discussion. Although Gentili did not impede access to the Turin manuscripts by other scholars, he did not actively further it, and since his own involvement with the collection was limited, so far as the outside world was concerned, to the edition of a few heavily arranged concertos, momentum was inevitably lost. In 1938 leadership of the Vivaldian cause passed to a circle of musicians (plus the poet Ezra Pound) associated with the Accademia Musicale Chigiana in Siena. The 'Vivaldi Week' promoted by this circle in Siena in September 1939 is recognized as the decisive historical breakthrough in the campaign to present the composer as a major musical figure. Yet traditional biases remained. The concert programmes included operatic music, sacred music, a serenata, a sinfonia and concertos galore – but not a single chamber cantata. This pattern continued in the Accademia's later programmes of Vivaldi's music.

When the first generation of studies of Vivaldi's life and works appeared shortly afterwards, this marginalization persisted. Mario Rinaldi's pioneering book *Antonio Vivaldi* (1943) hardly mentions them, and Marc Pincherle's massively influential *Antonio Vivaldi et la musique instrumentale* (1948) maintains a similar silence, albeit more legitimately in view of its declared emphasis on the instrumental music.[29] The disadvantage suffered by the cantatas was in

---

[27] Alberto Gentili, 'La raccolta di rarità musicali "Mauro Foà" alla Biblioteca Nazionale di Torino', *Accademie e Biblioteche d'Italia*, i (1927–8), 36–50.

[28] Ibid., p. 48. Original text: 'Le Cantate sono di valore molto vario; non mancano però quelle che portano a confermare quanto abbiamo asserito a proposito dell'Oratorio *Iuditha*; inoltre qualcuna ha delle pagine così intense da riportarci all'epoca aurea della Cantata, nel secolo antecedente, e di porre il Vivaldi al di sopra degli autori di Cantate suoi contemporanei, siano essi pure un Ariosti o un Bononcini. Notevoli, per la forma che esce dai quadri divenuti usuali, alcune Cantate comprendenti Ariosi, Recitativi accompagnati, Violino obbligato'.

[29] Mario Rinaldi, *Antonio Vivaldi*, Milan: Istituto Alto Cultura, 1943; Marc Pincherle, *Antonio Vivaldi et la musique instrumentale*, 2 vols, Paris: Floury, 1948.

essence the same as that of the sonatas (likewise neglected by Pincherle), only writ large. They were short, lacked perceived historical significance and – equally important – could not be linked to events in Vivaldi's life. Pincherle's later, more compact study entitled simply *Vivaldi* (1955) manages to find space for the operas and sacred vocal music but continues to leave the cantatas out in the cold.[30] The situation improves very slightly in Walter Kolneder's *Antonio Vivaldi: Leben und Werk* (1965), where one page of text is allotted to the cantatas and one such work, *Cessate, omai cessate* (RV 684), is mentioned by name.[31] Ironically, Kolneder overstates the number of cantatas surviving from Vivaldi's pen, giving their number as fifty-nine when their true total (ignoring more recent discoveries and counting as genuine certain works today regarded as spurious) ought to have been thirty-nine.[32] His mistake arose simply from an uncritical reading of the catalogues and inventories then available.

A major step forward was achieved by Meneve Dunham's doctoral dissertation on the Vivaldi cantatas in the Foà collection (1969).[33] This study today shows its age in many ways, not least in its excessive reliance on quantitative analysis of a kind familiar to readers of William S. Newman's history of the sonata idea and in its insufficient attention to the cantata as a literary genre. Against this may be set its methodical approach and attention to detail. At last, Vivaldi's cantatas had emerged as an object worthy of sustained consideration. It should be pointed out, however, that Dunham's research was driven as much by the rehabilitation of the Baroque cantata in general, which during the 1960s was in full swing in American universities, as by a wish to fill a particular void within Vivaldi studies.[34]

---

30  Marc Pincherle, *Vivaldi*, Paris: Plon, 1955. Translated into English as *Vivaldi: Genius of the Baroque*, New York: Norton, 1957. Pincherle does, however, quote Burney's comments on the cantatas.

31  Walter Kolneder, *Vivaldi: Leben und Werk*, Wiesbaden: Breitkopf & Härtel, 1965. Translated into English as *Antonio Vivaldi: His Life and Work*, London: Faber & Faber, 1970.

32  Kolneder, *Antonio Vivaldi, His Life and Work*, p. 189.

33  Mary Meneve Dunham, 'The Secular Cantatas of Antonio Vivaldi in the Foà Collection', unpublished doctoral dissertation, University of Michigan, 1969.

34  Examples of North American doctoral dissertations completed before 1980 that, like Dunham's, focus on the cantata output of a single composer are: Gloria Rose, 'The Cantatas of Giacomo Carissimi', Yale University, 1959; Caroline O. Sites, 'Benedetto Marcello's Chamber Cantatas', University of North Carolina, 1959; David L. Burrows, 'The Cantatas of Antonio Cesti', Brandeis University, 1961; Edwin Hanley, 'Alessandro Scarlatti's Cantate da Camera: A Bibliographical Study', Yale University, 1963; Irving R. Eisley, 'The Secular Cantatas of Mario Savioni (1608–1685)', University of California at Los Angeles, 1965; Kathleen Ann Chaikin, 'The Solo Soprano Cantatas of Alessandro Stradella (1644–1682)', Stanford University, 1975; Josephine R. B. Wright, 'The Secular Cantatas of Francesco Mancini (1672–1736)', New York University, 1975; Kathryn Jane O'Donnell, 'The Secular Solo Cantatas of Antonio Lotti', University of Iowa, 1975; John Mayo, 'Handel's Italian Cantatas', University of Toronto, 1977; Cecilia Kathryn Van de Kamp Freund, 'A Study of the Duet Cantatas and Solo Cantatas with Obbligato Instrumental Accompaniment of Alessandro Scarlatti', North-Western University, 1979. This list is indebted to Teresa M. Gialdroni, 'Bibliografia della cantata da camera italiana (1620–1740 ca.)', *Le fonti musicali in Italia. Studi e ricerche*, iv (1990), 31–131. Addenda to Gialdroni's list and further items published on the Italian cantata between 1990 and 1997 appear in Colin Timms, 'The Italian Cantata since 1945: Progress and Prospects', in Francesco Fanna and Michael Talbot (eds), *Cinquant'anni di produzioni e consumi della musica dell'età di Vivaldi, 1947–1997*, Florence: Olschki, 1998, pp. 75–94.

Alongside the moves made to evaluate Vivaldi's cantatas – indeed, their necessary complement – came their location, authentication, and cataloguing. A start had been made in 1936, when the violinist Olga Rudge, Ezra Pound's companion, drew up a manuscript thematic catalogue of Vivaldi's secular vocal works. This was published in photographic reproduction in 1941 and used in the preparation of Mario Rinaldi's general catalogue (1945).[35] However, the inadequacies of all existing Vivaldi catalogues – including that of Marc Pincherle for the concertos and sinfonias – were becoming embarrassingly evident by the 1960s: they were too incomplete, too unsystematic and too liable to simple error. It was then that the Danish scholar Peter Ryom set himself the task of compiling for Vivaldi a *catalogue raisonné* comparable in its rigour and scope with those of, say, Wolfgang Schmieder for J. S. Bach or Anthony van Hoboken for Haydn.

The preparation of this catalogue took several years. On his way, Ryom produced several articles justifying the need for such a catalogue (principally by showing up the faults of those existing at the time) and explaining the principles on which the new catalogue would be based. One of these was an article concerned specifically with the cantatas (1972).[36] This was a good advertisement for the catalogue to come. If one leaves aside the four cantatas that have since become regarded generally as spurious and the two new ones that have been identified only in recent years, Ryom's list will serve almost as well today as when it was originally compiled.[37]

The manner in which Ryom's catalogue passed into the public domain was highly unusual (a reversal, in fact, of the stages through which such catalogues normally pass), and the resulting effects persist today. There was initially considerable resistance to the idea of creating yet another Vivaldi catalogue, since there were already three in existence (by Rinaldi, Pincherle, and Fanna), each of which had its adherents. Finding a publisher for the catalogue in its full form was not immediately possible, and as a stop-gap measure a 'short' edition (*Kleine Ausgabe*) was chosen as the vehicle for its official introduction. In the meantime, Ryom, together with a small group of scholars collaborating with him on the newly founded multilingual journal *Vivaldi informations*, softened up the market by using 'RV' numbers at every opportunity.[38] As RV numbers passed piecemeal

[35] 'Catalogo delle opere vocali inedite e dei microfilms della B[iblioteca] Chigi Saracini', in Sebastiano A. Luciani (ed.), *La scuola veneziana (secoli xvi–xviii). Note e documenti raccolti in occasione della settimana celebrativa (5–10 settembre 1941)*, Siena: Accademia Musicale Chigiana, 1941, pp. 74–80; Mario Rinaldi, *Catalogo numerico tematico delle composizioni di A. Vivaldi*, Rome: Cultura Moderna, [1945].

[36] Peter Ryom, 'Le recensement des cantates d'Antonio Vivaldi', *Dansk Aarbog for Musikforskning*, vi (1968–72), 81–100.

[37] It does, however, mix up the folios attributable to two cantatas, RV 658 (*Il povero mio cor*) and RV 653 (*Del suo natio rigore*), some of which have accidentally become exchanged in the Turin volume. The mistake was not recognized and corrected until the second edition (1979) of the 'short' edition of Ryom's catalogue.

[38] Only two volumes (1971–1972 and 1973) of *Vivaldi Informations* appeared. The second volume contains (pp. 61–100) an inventory of the contents of the fourteen Foà volumes ('Inventaire de la documentation manuscrite des œuvres de Vivaldi: I. Biblioteca Nazionale di Torino. Première Partie: le fonds Foà'), which includes the cantatas contained in Foà 27 and 28. Contrary to popular belief, 'RV' is not short for 'Ryom-Verzeichnis' (by analogy with, say, 'Köchel-

into general circulation and it became increasingly vital, for the sake of a be-wildered and increasingly irritated public, to establish their relationship to existing numbers in the Rinaldi, Pincherle, and Fanna catalogues, the pressure grew to produce a usable catalogue even in advance of the appearance of the *Kleine Ausgabe*. In 1973 this materialized in the form of a *Table de concordances*, which is in effect an 'extra-short' catalogue.[39]

RV numbers are divided into a main series, which in recent years has topped 800, and a supplement, or *Anhang*. In principle, the first contains authenticated works, while the second gathers up works that have been attributed to Vivaldi (in some source, at some point in history) but are reckoned spurious. It goes without saying that individual cases are contested, in the sense that any Vivaldi scholar (the present writer is no exception) might wish an item in one category to be trans-ferred to the other. By and large, however, Ryom's verdicts on authenticity are accepted. The catalogue numbers are ordered not chronologically, as in Köchel numbers for Mozart or Deutsch numbers for Schubert, but according to genre and/or scoring. Most of the authenticated cantatas (and three of contested authen-ticity) are found in a bloc running from RV 649 (*All'ombra d'un bel faggio*) to RV 686 (*Qual in pioggia dorata i dolci rai*).[40] These subdivide into twenty-one cantatas for soprano and continuo (RV 649–669), eight for alto (contralto) and continuo (RV 670–677), five for soprano, instrument(s) and continuo (RV 678–682) and four for alto (contralto), instrument(s), and continuo (RV 683–686).[41] The *Table de concordances* already contains one 'late' entry, the soprano cantata *Prendea con man di latte*, RV 753 (which later research has shown to be spurious); the last few years have seen the addition of two further soprano cantatas: *Usignoletto bello*, RV 796, and *Tremori al braccio e lagrime al ciglio*, RV 799. The untidiness of having 'stragglers' widely separated from the main bloc, their numbers determined solely by the chronology of their discovery, is naturally a great inconvenience. With hindsight, it would have been better to leave vacant numbers at the end of each category in order to accommodate newcomers.

Ryom's *Anhang* is practically void of cantatas. Those that Burney claimed to have found in Dr Aldrich's collection are listed as RV Anh. 60. The practice of assigning a single number to a group of works of unknown size (and uncertain existence) is highly questionable – but the point need not be laboured, since to my knowledge this number has never passed into active use.

---

Verzeichnis'); it stands for 'Répertoire vivaldien'. However, the first interpretation is hard to resist, since the most widely circulated versions of the catalogue have been in the German language.

39  Peter Ryom, *Antonio Vivaldi: table de concordances des œuvres*, Copenhagen: Engstrøm & Sødring, 1973.

40  In a few cases the titles given in the present study differ slightly from those adopted by Ryom in his catalogue. My preference is to normalize (and in so doing modernize) spelling and punctua-tion, and to give text incipits, which have to serve also as titles, in the form of complete lines, whereas Ryom frequently stops short of the end of the line. Hence the longer title for RV 686 (Ryom ends at 'dorata').

41  RV 684 exists also in a variant, which Ryom distinguishes by appending 'a' to the numeral. Within each subgroup the cantatas appear in alphabetical order according to their text incipit.

In 1974 the *Kleine Ausgabe* finally appeared.[42] A second edition, updated and corrected, followed from the same German publisher in 1979. To date, it remains the only Vivaldi catalogue to cover the whole of the composer's output with reasonable accuracy. In 1986 a 'large' version of the catalogue covering only instrumental works in the main series appeared.[43] No counterpart exists, however, for the vocal music. At the time of writing, a 'large' version of the complete catalogue is in active preparation, and it is anticipated that, when this appears, there will be some changes to individual numbers. *Faute de mieux*, the revised 1979 edition of the *Kleine Ausgabe* remains the most convenient, if not always the most informative, source of quick reference on the cantatas.

The year 1978, in which the 300th anniversary of the composer's birth occurred, was a watershed in the history of Vivaldian studies. It witnessed the first-ever international conference on the composer, the absorption of the Istituto Italiano Antonio Vivaldi into the Fondazione Giorgio Cini (the Venetian foundation that also hosted that conference), the decision to publish a Vivaldi yearbook, *Informazioni e studi vivaldiani* (which first came out in 1980), and the formation of an editorial board for a 'New Critical Edition of the Works of Antonio Vivaldi' (*Nuova Edizione Critica delle Opere di Antonio Vivaldi*).[44] The proceedings of the conference became the first in a series of Vivaldi monographs (*Quaderni vivaldiani*), of which eleven have appeared to date.

Predictably, the cantatas have had relatively little part in the cornucopia of writings on Vivaldian subjects since that pivotal date. Nevertheless, their near-absolute neglect has finally been ended. The larger of my two general studies of the composer (1978) devotes a little space to them.[45] Peter Ryom's ever-valuable study *Les manuscrits de Vivaldi* contains much of direct relevance to them, including information on the physical structure of the manuscripts, the composer's notational habits, his handwriting, and his creative process.[46] A catalogue by Ortrun Landmann of all the eighteenth-century sources of Vivaldi's music in the SLUB adds significant bibliographical data.[47] The cantata texts set by Vivaldi have been transcribed in their near-entirety by Gianfranco Folena;[48] Francesco Degrada has commented on the texts of two cantatas: *T'intendo, sì, mio cor*, RV 668, and *Nel partir da te, mio caro*, RV 661.[49] From Colin Timms

---

[42] Peter Ryom, *Verzeichnis der Werke Antonio Vivaldis (RV): Kleine Ausgabe*, Leipzig: Deutscher Verlag für Musik, 1974.

[43] Peter Ryom, *Répertoire des œuvres d'Antonio Vivaldi: les compositions instrumentales*, Copenhagen: Engstrøm & Sødring, 1986.

[44] The title of the edition will be given hereafter as *NEC*.

[45] *Vivaldi*, London: Dent, 1978. The later revised and augmented edition (1993) is virtually unaltered in relation to the cantatas.

[46] Peter Ryom, *Les manuscrits de Vivaldi*, Copenhagen: Antonio Vivaldi Archives, 1977.

[47] Ortrun Landmann, 'Katalog der Dresdener Vivaldi-Handschriften und -Frühdrucke', in Wolfgang Reich (ed.), *Vivaldi-Studien: Referate des 3. Dresdner Vivaldi-Kolloquiums*, Dresden: Sächsische Landesbibliothek, 1981, pp. 101–67.

[48] Gianfranco Folena, 'La cantata e Vivaldi', in Lorenzo Bianconi and Giovanni Morelli (eds), *Antonio Vivaldi. Teatro musicale, cultura e società*, Florence: Olschki, 1982, pp. 131–90. Work on the *NEC* has revealed several errors in Folena's transcriptions, but their collection in a single location has meant that they remain invaluable for many purposes.

[49] Francesco Degrada, 'Note filologiche in margine all'edizione critica delle cantate di Antonio

there is a general analytical survey of the cantatas and also a dissection of *Prendea con man di latte*, RV 753, that establishes this work's non-authenticity.[50] An analysis of one technical aspect of Vivaldi's cantatas has been published by the present author.[51] Karl Heller probes Vivaldi's possible authorship of the anonymous Dresden cantata *Usignoletto bello*, RV 796, and comes up with a positive verdict (more recently confirmed by the discovery of an attributed source of the same work).[52] The recent discovery by Olivier Fourés of an undetected Vivaldi cantata in Vienna (RV 799) has resulted in an introductory article.[53] And, naturally: the Critical Notes in both Italian and English that follow every *NEC* volume collectively constitute an important contribution, albeit one strongly biased towards the bibliographical.

All things considered, this is a rather small haul. To some extent, it reflects the past paucity, or poor accessibility, of sources for scholars to consult. The concertos, for example, have had a head start of several decades, so far as accessible sources are concerned. Fortunately, the situation is today utterly transformed, as will be shown in the discussion that follows.

## Their Modern Revival

It would be too simple to say that the public reception of Baroque music, its availability in the form of modern editions, and its approval by scholars invariably move in step with each another. For a long time Telemann brought players pleasure and publishers profit without earning plaudits from mainstream musicology (indeed, Theodor Adorno reserved especial contempt for him). Gian Paolo Colonna has excited scholars for decades, but no *opera omnia* loom on the horizon, and his compositions are rarely heard. It is true, however, that a relationship of a kind does exist between these three factors, and that the typical outcome is self-reinforcing: either a virtuous spiral or a vicious circle.

Until the Early Music Movement reached maturity in the 1980s, there was really very little in the way of a suitable public 'forum' for the Baroque cantata. Unlike a solo sonata for violin and bass, which can 'work' at a basic level as a composition for violin and piano suitable for insertion in, say, a programme of Classical and Romantic pieces, a cantata performed by solo voice and piano

Vivaldi', in Antonio Fanna and Giovanni Morelli (eds), *Nuovi studi vivaldiani. Edizione e cronologia critica delle opere*, Florence: Olschki, 1988, pp. 355–85.

50  Colin Timms, 'The Dramatic in Vivaldi's Cantatas', in Lorenzo Bianconi and Giovanni Morelli (eds), *Antonio Vivaldi. Teatro musicale, cultura e società*, Florence: Olschki, 1982, pp. 97–129; idem, ' "Prendea con man di latte": A Vivaldi Spuriosity?', *Informazioni e studi vivaldiani*, vi (1985), 64–73.

51  Michael Talbot, 'How Recitatives End and Arias Begin in the Solo Cantatas of Antonio Vivaldi', *Journal of the Royal Musical Association*, cxxvi (2001), 170–92.

52  Karl Heller, 'Zu einigen Incerta im Werkbestand Vivaldis', in Antonio Fanna and Michael Talbot (eds), *Vivaldi. Vero e falso. Problemi di attribuzione*, Florence: Olschki, 1992, pp. 43–57, at 52–7.

53  Olivier Fourés and Michael Talbot, 'A New Vivaldi Cantata in Vienna', *Informazioni e studi vivaldiani*, xxi (2000), 99–108.

alongside songs by Schubert or Wolf fits awkwardly into a recital programme. There are too many obstacles: the accompaniment is wrong in terms of timbre, balance, and (perhaps most of all) atmosphere; the vocal technique demanded differs considerably from that required for Lieder and *mélodies*; the language of the text appears (especially outside Italy) archaic, precious, and far too full of such devices as elision and synaloepha that seem designed to trip up a foreigner. And what is true of the arias is multiplied in the recitatives, for which there seems no right solution: if they are sung in an overly 'dramatic' manner, the chamber-music character of the programme (in terms of the conventions governing song recitals) is compromised; if they are sung too dispassionately, the result is tedium.

This intractable problem about recitative explains why – even in the eighteenth century outside Italy – there has always been a temptation to domesticate cantatas by ignoring the recitative and making tuneful lollipops of the arias. This tendency is exemplified by the three collections of *Arie antiche* for voice and piano edited (and sometimes tacitly composed) by Alessandro Parisotti in the late nineteenth century, which remain staple fare for singing pupils and recitalists alike up to this day.[54] Needless to say, the distinctions between cantata aria and operatic aria, or between 'accompanied' aria and continuo aria, are obliterated in this context. It would be no exaggeration to claim that precisely because of this difficulty the modern publication and performance of cantatas in their integrity has until quite recently always needed a heavy dose of musicological mission. Hugo Riemann's anthology *Auserwählte Kammer-Kantaten der Zeit um 1700* ('Selected Chamber Cantatas from the Period around 1700') is a prime specimen of its rare breed.[55]

The dependence of professional performers specializing in early music on the availability of a published edition (or, at any rate, on an edition prepared by someone else), not so long ago taken for granted, is today rapidly becoming a thing of the past. For a present-day ensemble to be, to a high degree, self-sufficient in obtaining the scores and parts from which it performs is a matter both of professional pride and of financial convenience. Where performers have the opportunity to obtain photographic reproductions of the music, whether as print-outs from microfilm, photocopies, or facsimile editions, they often have the ability and confidence to do exactly as the first performers did and read from the unaltered original source. If they do not, they can always make a desktop edition of the music for themselves. This non-dependence on a published edition protected by copyright (or, to be less coy, this lack of a provable degree of dependence that would carry weight in a court of law) obviates the need to pay editor or publisher performance royalties or mechanical rights.[56] To an already

---

[54] Alessandro Parisotti (ed.), *Arie antiche*, 3 vols, Milan: Ricordi, 1895–8. The Vivaldi aria collected by Parisotti, 'Un certo non so che', is not from a cantata but from the opera *Ercole su'l Termodonte*, RV 710.

[55] Hugo Riemann (ed.), *Auserwählte Kammer-Kantaten der Zeit um 1700*, Leipzig: Breitkopf & Härtel, 1911.

[56] Rather ironically, a scrupulous modern edition has less chance than a licentious arrangement of earning royalties, since it is less distinguishable, aurally and visually, from the original source. The reason why recording artists so rarely use in an obvious manner the continuo realizations provided by the editors of published pieces is partly laudable and artistically desirable (it enables the continuo player to improvise genuinely and to adjust his part to such factors as instrumental

high, and still increasing, extent, a modern critical edition – even if it conscientiously aims at the same time to provide a convenient performing text – serves scholars rather than performers. Those relatively few people who use it just as it stands tend to be amateurs, musicians who perform mostly for private pleasure, or persons who come from corners of the world that the Early Music Movement has so far failed to penetrate.

Most of the foregoing was untrue only thirty years ago (one remembers that until the late 1960s photocopiers were unavailable in Britain, so that for music there was no middle way between preparing a single copy by hand and running off an entire printing). At that time, even the most accomplished performers required someone else to provide them with the text to sing or play. This normally took the form of a published edition, although in the case of a recording or broadcast it was sometimes possible to commission a scholar to prepare a special manuscript edition.[57] Until the 1980s, or thereabouts, the frequency with which a work was performed in concert or recorded depended crucially on its availability in print. This point can be brought out by first giving an account of Vivaldi cantata editions prior to the appearance, in 1984, of the first cantata volumes in the *NEC*, then listing the recordings of cantatas that were made during that period, and finally looking for connections between the two lists.[58]

The first modern edition of a Vivaldi cantata, from Carisch (Milan), came out c.1947. Ironically enough, it was of a work that is regarded today as spurious: *Ingrata Lidia, ha vinto il tuo rigor,* RV 673. The editor, Virgilio Mortari, was a member of the Siena circle – it was he who, in 1939, had prepared the material for the earliest modern performance of a Vivaldi opera (*L'Olimpiade,* RV 725). In 1956 John Edmonds edited for R. D. Row Music Co. (Boston, USA) five of the six arias contained in the three spurious Florentine cantatas: RV 673 (again), RV 672 (*Filli, di gioia vuoi farmi morir*), and RV 675 (*Piango, gemo, sospiro e piango*). This compilation continued the old practice of extracting single arias for use as 'lollipops'. In 1958 Franco Floris edited for Zanibon (Padua) complete versions of the same three cantatas, to be followed c.1970 by an edition by Mortari of RV 675, again for Carisch. This episode illustrates the inertia that can so easily set in when performers and their audiences 'know what they like and like what they know'.

In 1976 the first genuinely Vivaldian cantatas came out: a group of six edited by Roger Blanchard for the Parisian publisher Mario Bois.[59] Taken without exception from the Foà collection, they comprised RV 651, 654, 657, 659, 660, and 670. In the same year Manfred Fechner produced an exemplary critical edition for Deutscher Verlag für Musik of the lone cantata with obbligato flute,

---

timbre, balance, the room acoustic, and tempo), but is also motivated by a wish to avoid anything that could make the performance traceable back to one particular published edition and therefore legally liable for the payment of royalties.

[57] A case in point is the complete recording of Vivaldi's sacred music undertaken by Vittorio Negri for Philips in the late 1970s and early 1980s, for which Franz Giegling supplied handwritten scores.

[58] A list of these *NEC* volumes, with dates, is included as an appendix to the present volume.

[59] This edition was reissued in Italy by Edizioni Curci (Milan) in 1981.

*All'ombra di sospetto*, RV 678. The first – and, to date, only – facsimile edition of Vivaldi cantatas was printed in Milan by Tip. U. Allegretti di Campi in 1978; these were *Allor che lo sguardo*, RV 650, and *La farfalletta s'aggira al lume*, RV 660, edited by Vanni Scheiwiller with a preface by Massimo Mila. In 1979 a major landmark was at last reached: a critical edition (albeit in some respects an imperfect one) of a representative portion of Vivaldi's cantatas. The first of the two volumes contained eight works for soprano (RV 651, 656, 657, 662, 667, 678, 680, and 682); the second, seven works for alto (RV 670, 671, 674, 676, 677, 683, and 684). The editor was Meneve Dunham, author of the doctoral dissertation mentioned earlier, and the publisher was A-R Editions (Madison, Wisconsin).

The recordings made during this period follow a similar trajectory.[60] First, in 1952, came a recording, sung by Giancola Borelli, of the orchestrally accompanied cantata *Qual in pioggia dorata i dolci rai*, RV 686, for which the conductor, Angelo Ephrikian, created the performance material.[61] In 1963 Edwin Loehrer supplied the baritone Laerte Malaguti with the material used for recordings of RV 675 and RV 684 (*Cessate, omai cessate*).[62] Small groups of cantatas were then recorded in 1977 by Ana-Maria Miranda under Roger Blanchard (RV 651, 654, 659, 660);[63] in 1979 by René Jacobs (RV 677, 683, 684, 685);[64] and in 1982 by Nella Anfuso (RV 651, 684, 684a). The 'lollipop' tradition continued with a recording by Frederica von Stade in 1982 of an aria from RV 672, and with the importation of an aria from RV 656 by Claudio Scimone for his 1980 version of the opera *Orlando furioso*, RV 728.

What this comparison tells us is that although the level of interest in Vivaldi was comparable in the two spheres, there was initially a partial mismatch between what editions could supply and musicians wished to record. This arose from the special favour in which instrumentally accompanied cantatas (beginning at RV 678) were held by recording artists. There has long been a distinct bias, observable generally in modern performances of Baroque cantatas, in favour of pieces displaying 'counterpoint' and/or instrumental colour: in other words, cantatas *con strumenti*. However, these are the most expensive to publish and the most difficult to market to amateurs. So on the comparatively frequent occasions when artists recorded thickly scored cantatas, performance material was of necessity prepared specially. For continuo cantatas, in contrast, performers hardly ever looked beyond what was published.

From its publication until the present day Dunham's edition has been the most widely used, overtly or surreptitiously, in recorded performances and doubtless

---

[60] For information on recordings of Vivaldi's cantatas, I am indebted to the reports by Roger-Claude Travers on Vivaldi recordings issued during the previous year ('Discographie vivaldienne'), published annually since 1980 in *Informazioni e studi vivaldiani* and its successor, *Studi vivaldiani*. Dr Travers also very kindly supplied me privately with information on recordings of cantatas prior to 1979.

[61] Period Renaissance LP RN X58.

[62] Accord CD 330 642 (transferred from a recording of 1963).

[63] Solstice LP Sol 5.

[64] Archiv 2533.385. From this point onwards, recordings will not be identified by label and number, since those details are retrievable from Travers' annual discography.

also in live performances. In comparison, the *NEC* volumes have not made the public impact for which one would have hoped. This is not because musicians – least of all, specialists in early music – are indifferent to the qualities of accuracy, fidelity, and informativeness valued by scholars. It is, rather, that they are pragmatists. An edition that comes out before another edition is today nearly always the early bird that catches the worm. Those who are interested invest in a copy, and they are accustomed to remain faithful to it without a special reason for turning elsewhere. But the advantages of a more scrupulous or competent edition may not be immediately clear, especially if a well-thumbed edition has apparently served the performer well in the past, while its disadvantages, if it is expensive or hard to obtain (qualities not uncommon in critical editions), may be only too evident.

Since 1984 the 'supply problem' with published Vivaldi cantatas has grown ever smaller, and has in any case been overtaken by the increasing self-sufficiency of performers noted earlier. A new threshold was reached in 1990, when the Ensemble Concerto under Roberto Gini issued the first of what was evidently to have been a multi-volume 'edition' of Vivaldi chamber cantatas. This did not proceed beyond the first CD, but similar later projects have had more success. In 1997 Cecilia Gasdia recorded, with Barocco Veneziano under Claudio Ferrarini, all twenty-six cantatas for soprano (minus the then undiscovered RV 799). A similar project was undertaken between 1997 and 2001 by Modo Antiquo under Federico Maria Sardelli.[65] A third collected edition of these cantatas, sung by Roberta Invernizzi, yielded two CDs with eleven works in 1998 and may not yet have been abandoned. In contrast, the much less numerous but equally meritorious alto cantatas have so far failed to stimulate a comparable project.

'Two cheers' would be the right response to this showing on the twin fronts of publication and recording. Every Vivaldi cantata so far uncovered can now be consulted in at least one adequate modern edition and listened to in at least one adequate recorded performance. This is an achievement scarcely conceivable thirty years ago. All the same, congratulation has its proper limits. As programme and sleeve notes inadvertently reveal time and again, this is a repertory less well understood than any other within Vivaldi's oeuvre. It shares in the general public diffidence towards the Baroque cantata as an art-form that is not merely musical but also literary. Before we go any further, therefore, we have to examine the literary premises of this genre.

---

[65] Sardelli's recording includes RV 799 but at the time of writing lacks RV 649, 650, 663, and 666.

# CHAPTER TWO

# The Cantata Genre

## *Its Historical Development*

Much confusion is liable to arise from the fact that a generic label applied to musical compositions (sonata, symphony, cantata, etc.) as part of their title is rarely perfectly coextensive with the same word operating as a modern historical or analytical category. In other words, some pieces originally entitled 'cantata' manifest a set of characteristics untypical of the genre – to the extent that one may perhaps wish to exclude them altogether from discussion – whereas, conversely, other pieces not so titled may display cantata characteristics in abundance and legitimately be taken into account. In the opening volume of his history of what he termed 'the sonata idea' William S. Newman adopted a so-called semantic approach designed to produce 'the history of a single term, by whatever principles it might be governed'.[1] Such an approach has the virtues of clarity and expediency, but is in the end less rewarding than one based on musical realities rather than on a choice of title that may be arbitrary, whimsical, or even inauthentic. On the other hand, these musical realities must not be conceived too inflexibly. Probably the best basis for assigning a work to a generic category is its conformity to most – but not necessarily all – items in a list of criteria, in which the generic title appears only as one item among several. For the Italian chamber cantata, this list might look as follows:

1.  The composition is described or headed 'cantata'.
2.  It is for a single voice. Compositions for two or three voices on a common text are normally regarded as chamber duets, terzets, or madrigals, while compositions for two or more voices with individual texts are classed as dialogues or serenatas (alternatively known as 'dramatic' cantatas).
3.  There is instrumental accompaniment. 'Continuo' cantatas have only a simple bass for performance by one or more melody or harmony instruments, while 'accompanied' cantatas use additional instruments, ranging from a single obbligato instrument to a full orchestra.
4.  The composition is multi-sectional or in several discrete movements. Musical divisions follow the poetical divisions, the fundamental structural principle of which is the alternation of 'recitative' verse with 'aria' verse (to be explained later). Single-movement compositions are likely to be simple arias.

---

[1]  William S. Newman, *The Sonata in the Baroque Era*, Chapel Hill: University of North Carolina Press, 1959, pp. 5–6.

5.  The poetic text is purpose-written for a musical setting. In this respect, it has more in common with an opera libretto, despite the disparity of length, than with a sonnet, which, in the first instance, is self-sufficient as poetry.
6.  The poetic theme is secular (pastoral, heroic, or historical). It may also be devotional (as in the *cantata morale*) or didactic (as in the *lezione amorosa*) but is never suitable for performance at a religious service.[2]

Some explanatory remarks on the criteria are relevant at this point. The word 'cantata' (which means, literally, no more than 'sung piece') makes its first appearance in the late sixteenth century.[3] In this formative period its significance is not yet generic in the narrow sense: the word serves merely to distinguish sung verse from spoken verse, or sung music from played music. The sister terms 'sonata' and 'concerto', it is interesting to note, both went through comparable pre-generic phases before crystallizing as generic terms. The first recorded use of 'cantata' to distinguish one kind of vocal music from another occurs in the first book of *Cantade et arie* by Alessandro Grandi, published in Venice in 1620. Since the edition in question is not a first edition, the putative date should be brought forward by a few years – and, in any case, one would expect this use of the term in manuscript sources to have predated its appearance in print. The new genre takes at least a couple of decades to establish itself firmly and develop a profile that is the common property of composers.[4] By the sixth decade of the century it has achieved maturity in the hands of such composers as Luigi Rossi (c.1598–1653) and Giacomo Carissimi (1605–74), and it then becomes possible to speak of a cantata 'mainstream' to which composers conform with or without the addition of a personal inflection.

The distinction made in the second criterion between 'dramatic' and 'non-dramatic' presentation is crucial. In seventeenth-century terms, which are rooted in concepts established in classical antiquity by such authorities as Aristotle, a sung work is dramatic whenever two or more singers engage in dialogue and therefore have different texts, irrespective of whether they act and memorize their parts or merely stand (or sit) and read from music. Similarly irrelevant is whether or not the work is dramatic in the modern, secondary sense of 'gripping'. On this basis, operas, oratorios, serenatas, and dialogues are equally dramatic genres. A work for a single singer may adopt, wholly or in part, a dramatic 'voice', in that the singer takes on the persona of a character distinct from that of the poet in either his 'lyric' voice (when he addresses the audience with his own thoughts) or his 'epic' voice (when he narrates or describes what he sees).[5] But this does not suffice to make the work itself dramatic, as understood by contemporaries.

---

2   *Lezione amorosa* means 'lesson in love' or 'advice to lovers'. Such cantatas take the form of a monologue addressed by the poet (in the guise of an older, wiser person) to a young lover.

3   The second edition of the *New Grove* (art. 'Cantata', 5, p. 9) gives as the first recorded instance of the word a *Cantata pastorale fatta per Calen di Maggio* performed in Siena (Siena: Bonetti, 1589).

4   The early history of the cantata (and of the uses of the word 'cantata') is explored very thoroughly in Robert R. Holzer, 'Music and Poetry in Seventeenth Century Rome: Settings of the Canzonetta and Cantata Texts of Francesco Balducci, Domenico Benigni, Francesco Melosio and Antonio Abate', 2 vols, unpublished doctoral dissertation, University of Pennsylvania, 1990, pp. 226–77.

5   Telemann's *Ino* (1765), which is from start to finish a monologue in the mouth of the named

Conversely, a work entitled 'cantata a due voci' may, or may not, be a chamber cantata. If the two parts (which will usually bear the names of two characters) have distinct texts, it is quite clearly a dramatic cantata. If, however, the texts are identical (except that certain portions may be reserved for only a single voice), it is a chamber cantata – unless the lack of any clear separation into distinct movements makes the description of chamber duet more apt for ordinary analytical purposes.

A pedant might argue that employing the analytical term 'continuo cantata' begs the question of whether the notated bass line is performed by a melody instrument alone, without any realization of the implied harmonies, or by a harmony instrument (supported, or not, by a melody instrument) that supplies a realization of this kind. But the point is too fine to persuade one to seek an alternative term, especially since in the eighteenth century one occasionally sees 'basso continuo' used to describe a purely melodic part, as in the definition of the expression by Sébastien de Brossard in his *Dictionnaire de musique* (Paris, 1703), where the author remarks that such a line is sometimes played simply ('simplement') and without figures ('sans chiffres') on the bass violin and other instruments, or in the 'basso continuo per violoncello o cembalo' prescribed by Benedettc Marcello for his recorder sonatas, Op. 2, of 1712.

The distinction between a multi-sectional and a multi-movement work is so fundamental and rich in consequences that it is surprising how little attention has so far been paid to the question in studies of the cantata – as opposed, notably, to ones of the sonata.[6] One has to begin, naturally, by defining 'section' and 'movement'. In ordinary musicological discourse the boundary between the two terms is rather hazy, so what one is seeking is a distinction that is sufficiently clear-cut to be analytically useful but not so rigid as to appear artificial or contrary to everyday perception. I drew up a set of criteria for establishing their separate identities in another context, and it will be appropriate to reproduce them here:[7]

| *Sections* | *Movements* |
|---|---|
| Tonally open or closed | Tonally closed |
| Connected to surrounding material | Disconnected from surrounding material |
| Monothematic | Polythematic |
| Progressive or rounded form | Rounded form |

Once again, to qualify as a section or a movement a group of bars need not correspond to each single criterion, provided that its overall profile is congruent.

The most interesting of the criteria is the last. One could express the difference

---

heroine, conforms analytically to the profile of a 'solo' cantata rather than to that of a 'dramatic' cantata by virtue of the lack of dialogue with other characters.

6   On the distinction between sections and movements in sonatas, see especially Andrea Dell'Antonio, *Syntax, Form and Genre in Sonatas and Canzonas, 1621–1635*, Lucca: Libreria Musicale Italiana, 1997.

7   Michael Talbot, *The Finale in Western Instrumental Music*, Oxford: Oxford University Press, 2001, p. 19.

between a multi-sectional and a multi-movement composition by saying that the first is syntactic in its macrostructure and paratactic in its microstructure, while the second is exactly the reverse. To explain: a syntactic structure is one in which the components are organized hierarchically and in a patterned manner. In a musical context, typical expressions of syntactic organization are tonal rounding (the opening key returns at the end) and thematic rounding (the opening theme returns at the end). A paratactic structure is one in which the units have a simple additive relationship – like the carriages making up a train. A musical unit that is wholly through-composed and tonally open is fully compatible with paratactic organization. By 'macrostructure' is meant the overall structure of the complete work, while 'microstructure' represents the form at the level of an individual section or movement.

Like sonatas, cantatas moved from multi-sectional to multi-movement design in the mid-seventeenth century.[8] A 'movement' structure is at best only incipient in the cantatas of the Rossi-Carissimi generation and is not yet evident in those of Barbara Strozzi (1619–77), but it emerges clearly in the cantatas of Alessandro Stradella (1639–82). This is not the first occasion on which we will find the structural evolution of cantatas and sonatas proceeding almost in parallel. Schmitz saw this process, rightly, not as the renunciation of unity but as its achievement by alternative means.[9] The most important outcome of the change was the delineation of recitatives and arias as more or less self-contained movements. Whereas recitatives are through-composed and usually tonally open (so that in a different context the same music could be held equally well to constitute a section of a larger unit), the arias with which they alternate possess a clearly syntactic structure that marks them out as movements. Pursuing the analogy of a train, one could liken arias to the carriages, recitatives to the short corridors through which one passes from one carriage to the next.

The fifth criterion is no less fundamental to the identity of the cantata. Vocal music can be divided, from the very beginning of the Western art music tradition up to the present day, between music using poetic texts originally conceived quite independently of music (for silent reading or recitation) and music based on texts designed from the outset for a musical setting (and therefore unsatisfactory without musical presentation). Where the poetry exists independently, composers have no automatic way of setting it. They will generally respect its division into stanzas and internal patterns (such as the use of a refrain), but most decisions relating to musical structure have to be made autonomously, a situation that produces a great diversity of possible results. Where the verse is expressly *poesia per musica*, however, the poet's handiwork is apt to be more prescriptive and to restrict the composer's structure-related choices very firmly. This tight regulation of musical structure is seen at its most extreme in the *formes fixes* of the Middle

8    Willi Apel even attempted to identify a 'first' instrumental work to display multi-movement characteristics – the *Canzoni a tre*, Op. 2 (1642) of Maurizio Cazzati – although most commentators will prefer to remain more cautious. See Talbot, *The Finale in Western Instrumental Music*, p. 26.
9    Schmitz, *Geschichte der weltlichen Solokantate*, pp. 68–9.

Ages – the ballade, virelai, and rondeau. In the case of the chamber cantata, the variables are more numerous (for example, the number of movements is free, provided that the alternation of recitative and aria is observed, and recitative verse can be set in special ways – as accompagnato, arioso, or cavata – in special circumstances), but the general principle holds.

The inevitable outcome of a music-dependent poetry is a poetry-dependent music. Neither can evolve autonomously: what occurs instead is a slow co-evolution like that in nature between a plant and a pollinating insect. What is remarkable, indeed unique, about the period 1650–1750 in Italy is that virtually all its secular vocal music, across the whole spectrum from an aria to an opera, is set to purpose-written texts. If cantatas are easily distinguishable from arias by virtue of their complex (multi-sectional or multi-movement) form, they diverge equally strongly from madrigals, even in the early period (1620–40) when both genres existed side by side, simply by using these special texts in preference to the sonnets, octaves, *canzoni*, and the rest that make up the promiscuous diet of the latter.

Whether the cantata, as a musical genre, gained or lost on balance from this dependence is a moot point. Certainly, the literary and aesthetic quality of the poetry to which it was yoked was often no better than mediocre and frequently worse. One would not expect poets normally to include cantata texts, given their expressly musical destination, in their published *rime*, but the infrequency of poetic attributions in the musical sources tells its own story. Many of the poets were doubtless inexperienced poetasters writing for personal satisfaction rather than public recognition; in those instances (probably more frequent than one imagines) where the poets were recognized names, the perceived ephemerality and marginality of their contribution generally prevented them both from giving of their best and from seeking credit by claiming authorship. It is no coincidence that cantata texts collected as part of their author's *opera omnia* (such as those by Metastasio and Antonio Ottoboni) are invariably of superior quality, capable of standing with credit alongside their author's 'non-musical' verse.

It is true that the standardization of their texts results in a corresponding stan-dardization of the music for cantatas. Touches of originality and boldness are therefore to be sought not at the 'macro' but at the 'micro' level – for instance, in a well-judged arioso passage in the middle of a recitative or in an 'inessential' ritornello making a retransition from the end of a 'B' section to the start of a restated 'A' section. On occasion, one encounters self-consciously experimental cantatas, such as Marcello's *Sujetkantaten*, that break the mould. But even in these cases, the retention of the principle of alternating aria and recitative reduces the room for manoeuvre: the train simply acquires more carriages.

Undeniably, the Baroque cantata possessed the virtue of its defects in being such an easy type of composition to mass-produce. This mattered in an age when topicality was so desirable a quality and when the occasions at which cantatas were performed, such as the weekly *accademie* of a patron, succeeded one another so closely. A kind of composition that required more prior reflection on the part of either poet or composer would have served its social purpose less well.

The secular context of chamber cantatas – evident even when their theme is spiritual or moral – needs emphasis because of the contrary example of J. S.

Bach's cantatas. It is ironic that many of these works by Bach, particularly the early ones, were not originally called cantatas at all (they were sacred concertos or merely 'pieces'), while those that bore the title were settings of religious verse (supplemented by chorale texts) closely modelled on the 'standard' – i.e., secular – cantata. Actually, to describe a piece as a 'secular' cantata already concedes too much, since the qualification implies that this genre was an adaptation of a sacred model rather than the reverse.

The general features just discussed remained remarkably constant during the *Blütezeit* of the cantata (1650–1700) and its period of decline (1700 onwards). However, in one respect affecting poetry and music alike the cantata underwent a steady, unidirectional development over this period: its overall structure tended over time towards a simpler pattern based on fewer units and towards the primacy of aria over recitative.

The regular alternation between recitative and aria was deeply ingrained: it is very rare to find two adjacent arias not separated by recitative, and the concept of two adjacent recitatives is hardly sustainable, given the through-composed nature of the style. Consequently, recitatives and arias are either exactly equal in number (as in the RARA scheme) or differ by no more than one (as in the ARA and RARAR schemes).

Where recitatives and arias coexist, the former is always preparatory to the latter – never the reverse. This is demonstrated in musical terms by the fact that it is normal for the opening chord of a recitative following an aria to establish its tonal (and emotional) distance from the latter by moving to a new scale-degree, and very likely a new key. The poetic rationale for the relationship between the two movement-types is well summed up in Willi Flemming's dictum (originally applied to opera but equally relevant to the cantata) that 'the recitative loads the gun, the aria fires it'.[10] The standard modular unit of a cantata is therefore the RA pair. An eighteenth-century literary theorist, Ireneo Affò, recognised this when he characterized an RA structure as a 'simple' cantata (*cantata semplice*), a 'double' cantata (*cantata doppia*) being the more familiar RARA structure.[11] It was always possible to vary the structure by having a free-standing aria at the head of the cantata (as in ARA), comparable with an 'entry' aria (*uscita*) in an operatic scene, or a free-standing recitative at its close. Ending with an unadorned setting of recitative was normally avoided, since the result would have been too perfunctory, but the option of setting the last line or pair of lines as an arioso or a cavata – both types of treatment introducing a more patterned, melodious style – provided a simple means of achieving a climax comparable with that afforded by an aria.

From the poet's point of view, the recitative was the more important component. It was the vehicle for description and narration, and employed metres – seven-syllable (*settenario*) and eleven-syllable (*endecasillabo*) lines – widely

---

[10]  Quoted in Donald Jay Grout, *A Short History of Opera*, 2nd edn, New York: Columbia University Press, 1965, p. 187.

[11]  Ireneo Affò, *Dizionario precettivo, critico ed istorico della poesia volgare*, Parma: Carmignani, 1777, p. 114.

used in ordinary poetry, where they were associated with the most prestigious forms such as the *canzone* and the epic. However, audiences, singers, and composers alike regarded the aria as more important, exerting a persistent pressure to reduce the number and length of recitatives. Francesco Saverio Quadrio, whose massive history of Italian poetry is a valuable source of information on contemporary perceptions of the cantata, observed that recitatives risked boring audiences (for which reason he recommended that they should not exceed six lines in length) and tended to be skated over by singers, impatient to begin their next aria.[12] This prejudice favoured schemes framed by a pair of arias (ARA, ARARA, etc.) over ones in which recitatives formed either one (as in RARA) or both (as in RARAR) of the framing movements. For some listeners, of course, even a single recitative was excessive. In a letter of 15 December 1751 to C. H. Graun, Telemann blamed the presence of recitative for the unfashionability of cantatas and their replacement by arias. The steadily growing rejection of recitative in the domain of chamber music can be gauged by comparing the incidence of cantatas and separate arias in manuscript collections containing both. In seventeenth-century collections cantatas tend to outnumber arias, but in those of the following century the balance inexorably shifts in favour of the latter.

Favoured though they were, arias in cantatas tended to become fewer as time went on. This was partly in compensation for their increased length, the product of a more complex form and a more ornate style. In a letter of 14 February 1755 to Ranieri de' Calzabigi, Metastasio expressed his view that cantatas with four arias were too taxing for a singer. This was good advice for its time but would not have carried weight seventy years earlier.

Over and above the specific reasons why the structure of the cantata became more streamlined in the eighteenth century lies a more general one that David Burrows has identified as a major shift in 'cultural style' around 1700.[13] Taking Vivaldi's published concertos, Zeno's opera librettos, and Marco Ricci's landscape paintings as exemplars of their respective art-forms, Burrows shows how, in each case, a system of construction using a large number of small units was replaced by one in which the units were larger but fewer. In music, this is manifested in a reduction in the number of movements; in opera librettos, by a reduction in the number of scenes (and, correspondingly, of arias) per act; in painting, by a reduction in the 'clutter' of objects in view. This revolt against fussiness in favour of clear outlines is a feature that marks off the *Settecento* as a whole from the *Seicento*. First concertos and then sonatas follow the same path as the cantata. In fact, if one equates cantata recitatives with sonata slow movements (S), and cantata arias (in any tempo) with sonata fast movements (F), one can draw an exact parallel between the replacement of the SFSF by the FSF scheme in sonatas and the replacement (albeit less fully realized) of the RARA by the ARA scheme in cantatas.

---

12  Francesco Saverio Quadrio, *Della storia e della ragione d'ogni poesia*, 7 vols, Bologna/Milan: Pisarri/Agnelli, 1739–52, 2, pp. 333–4. On p. 336 Quadrio reproaches composers for having capitulated to the prejudice of the multitude (*volgo*) in order to spare themselves the effort of writing an opening recitative.

13  David Burrows, 'Style in Culture: Vivaldi, Zeno and Ricci', *The Journal of Interdisciplinary History*, iv (1973–74), 1–23.

Table 2.1 Cantata structures employed by Antonio Ottoboni and Pietro Metastasio

| Structure | A. Ottoboni | P. Metastasio |
|-----------|-------------|---------------|
| RA        | 4           | 5             |
| RAR       | 5           | –             |
| RARA      | 20          | 19            |
| RARAR     | 41          | –             |
| RARARA    | 15          | 2             |
| RARARAR   | 18          | –             |
| AR        | 1           | –             |
| ARA       | 5           | 8             |
| ARAR      | 28          | –             |
| ARARA     | 27          | 2             |
| ARARAR    | 30          | –             |

The working out of this general tendency can be illustrated by a comparison (shown in Table 2.1) between the schemes adopted by two producers of cantata texts: Antonio Ottoboni (1646–1720) and Pietro Metastasio (1698–1782).[14] Most of Ottoboni's texts date from the period 1670–1720, with a peak around 1700; those by Metastasio occupy the time-frame 1720–70, the bulk having been composed before the poet's removal to Vienna in 1729.

In Ottoboni's texts two arias and three arias occur with approximately equal frequency (94 and 90 times, respectively). Slightly more texts open with a recitative than with an aria (103 as against 91), while distinctly more close with a recitative than with an aria (123 as against 71). Ottoboni's 'classic' scheme is therefore RARAR, which, with 41 examples, is by a long way more common than any other. His texts are noteworthy for their variety: no permutation of R and A up to three arias is ignored.

In Metastasio's texts two arias (27 examples) are encountered much more often than three (4 examples). There is a numerically significant group of 'simple' cantatas (RA) resembling operatic *scene*. Special circumstances apply here: Metastasio wrote several celebratory works for birthdays or name-days of members of the imperial family, the singers for which were sometimes the archdukes or archduchesses themselves – hence the desirability of brevity. Considerably more of his texts open with a recitative than with an aria (26 as against 10), but – a sign of the times – not a single one closes with a recitative. Malcolm Boyd

---

[14]  The statistics for Ottoboni's cantatas are taken from Michael Talbot and Colin Timms, 'Music and the Poetry of Antonio Ottoboni (1646–1720)', in Nino Pirrotta and Agostino Ziino (eds), *Händel e gli Scarlatti a Roma. Atti del convegno internazionale di studi (Roma, 12–14 giugno 1985)*, Florence: Olschki, 1987, pp. 367–438, at p. 387; for greater simplicity, texts in which the division between recitative and aria portions is unclear, in which the arias number more than three, or in which arias stand in adjacent position are excluded from consideration. The details for Metastasio are based on the cantatas included in Bruno Brunelli's collected edition of the poet's works (*Tutte le opere di Pietro Metastasio*, 5 vols, Milan: Mondadori, 1947–54).

dates the beginning of the reluctance among Italian composers to have a recitative in final position to c.1700, and his observation seems to be borne out by the evidence, whichever composer (or poet) one takes.[15] Metastasio's 'classic' scheme is, therefore, RARA.[16] As we will see when we consider the texts set by Vivaldi, Metastasio is quite conservative in his general preference for an opening recitative. Quadrio observed that recitative had a special usefulness at the start of a cantata, where it could explain the situation and establish the dominant mood.[17] Moreover, its presence there brought an important musical advantage, in that it liberated the first aria from the need to remain in the home key. Where tonal closure was desired for the composition as a whole – and very few composers (Handel and Alessandro Marcello are the best-known) were prepared to sacrifice it – adopting the ARA plan condemned composers willy-nilly to place both arias in the same key, thereby renouncing an important means of contrast. The fact that they were so often willing to do so only underlines the irresistibility of the trend just described.

The table also illustrates in stark fashion the narrowing of macrostructural options in the later phases of the solo cantata's existence. Leaving aside the texts for 'simple' cantatas, RARA and ARA schemes account together for almost 90 per cent of Metastasio's total. Small wonder that Vivaldi and the poets who served him remained so firmly wedded to these two plans, which had by then become as standard for the cantata as the familiar three-movement and four-movement schemes were in instrumental music.

## Its Literary Nature

The basic unit of the poetry making up a cantata text is the stanza (strophe). A recitative stanza may contain any number of lines greater than one. Notwithstanding Quadrio's recommendation of six lines as the effective limit, much longer stanzas are commonly encountered: for instance, the opening recitative of the cantata *Là nelle verdi spiagge* by Benedetto Vinaccesi (c.1666–1719) comprises a single sentence stretching over eighteen lines. For arias, the number of lines is more circumscribed. Four lines is the lower limit, while twelve lines represents the practical upper limit.

Recitative verse is formed from freely mixed *endecasillabi* (hendecasyllables, or eleven-syllable lines) and *settenari* (heptasyllables, or seven-syllable lines). These are the two metres canonized in the poetry of Petrarch (1304–74) and ever since dominant in Italian poetry. The two metres are closely related, since an *endecasillabo* can be viewed as a *settenario* either preceded or followed by a 'lesser' hemistich containing the remaining four or (with synaloepha, to be

---

[15] Malcolm Boyd, 'Form and Style in Scarlatti's Chamber Cantatas', *Music Review*, xxv (1964), 17–26, at 23.

[16] According to Boyd (ibid., 22–3), 60 per cent of Alessandro Scarlatti's mature (post-1696) cantatas adopt RARA form – a clear sign of its growing pre-eminence around the turn of the century.

[17] Quadrio, *Della storia e della ragione d'ogni poesia*, 2, p. 336.

described on p. 35) five syllables. The great attraction of hendecasyllables and heptasyllables for Italian poetry – especially when used repetitively – is the great variety of stress pattern they permit. As a Romance language, Italian has a prosody governed by syllable count rather than, as in Germanic languages, by stress count. So the metrical flexibility that English iambic pentameter achieves through varying the nature of the foot (as iamb, trochee, etc.) is available to an *endecasillabo* (and to many other Italian metres, though predominantly ones with an odd number of syllables) through varied placement of the stress.

Aria verse may also employ *settenario* and *endecasillabo* but tends to prefer 'shorter' (sometimes called 'quicker') metres with six syllables or fewer and/or metres containing an even number of syllables. Lines with three (*ternario*), four (*quaternario*), five (*quinario*), six (*senario*), eight (*ottonario*), nine (*novenario*), ten (*decasillabo*), and even twelve (*dodecasillabo*) syllables may be employed. Even-numbered metres, especially the ever-popular *quaternario* and *ottonario*, enjoy special favour, since their relative regularity of stress (more comparable with the metres of Germanic poetry) contrasts with recitative verse and also conforms well to the regular musical accents that characterize arias, but not recitatives. Aria stanzas may be either monometric (employing a single metre throughout) or polymetric (employing more than one metre in either symmetrical or asymmetrical fashion).

A fundamental characteristic of aria stanzas during the entire life of the cantata is their division into two semistrophes.[18] The semistrophes are syntactically well separated – they often comprise different sentences – and they are often distinct in meaning and imagery. Typically, the first semistrophe expresses a thought that the second semistrophe illustrates, extends, modifies, or contradicts. Irrespective of what musical form is chosen for the stanza, its division into two sections has always forced composers into making difficult decisions. Should the musical treatment of the stanza be uniform, making little of the textual difference between the two semistrophes, or should this difference be accentuated through musical contrasts? There is no universal recommendation to follow: all depends on context and individual preference.

This binary division of aria verse can be illustrated by quoting the text of the opening aria of Vivaldi's *Vengo a voi, luci adorate*, RV 682. In the quotation, and in later quotations of aria verse, the opening lines of the two semistrophes are left unindented, while the remainder are indented.

| | |
|---|---|
| Vengo a voi, luci adorate, | I come before you, beloved eyes, |
| per dar tregua a tante pene, | to offer a truce after so much pain, |
| e ritorno ad adorarvi. | and I am returning to love you. |
| Benché siate tanto ingrate, | Although you are so ungrateful, |

---

18 Some writers regard the semistrophe as a self-contained stanza, making the full aria text bi-stanzaic. That this is really inaccurate is shown, however, by the frequent practice, observable during most of the seventeenth century, of repeating the music of an aria to new words. It is obviously far less cumbersome to speak of an aria employing successive stanzas than of one employing successive stanza-pairs.

care luci del mio bene,                     dear eyes of my beloved,
io non lasciar vo' d'amarvi.                I will never cease to adore you.[19]

Here, the first semistrophe explains that the lover (female) is returning to the object of her affections, having suffered greatly during her estrangement. It is left to the second semistrophe, however, to explain that ingratitude (normally to be equated with the non-reciprocation of amorous feelings or even with infidelity) was the cause of that estrangement. The poet leaves the composer the option of emphasizing the negativity of the first line of the second semistrophe (perhaps by a turn to minor tonality and/or the use of dissonance or chromaticism) or of setting the two stanzas in similar style throughout in order to underline the overall positive mood.

How the syllables of Italian verse are to be counted – this knowledge is vital for the reconstruction of the poem, if it exists only in the form of an underlaid text – is not an easy matter for the uninitiated, especially if they are not native speakers. The standard kind of line is called 'plain' (*piano*): its final syllable is unstressed, and its penultimate syllable is stressed. All the lines of the aria quoted above conform to the *piano* model. Recitative verse hardly ever employs any other type. If the final unstressed syllable is suppressed, leaving a stressed syllable to end the line, the latter is said to be 'truncated' (*tronco*). The two opening lines of the second aria of *Era la notte, quando i suoi splendori*, RV 655, follow this model: 'Se non potei mirar | le luci del mio sol'. It is important to remember that when a line is *tronco*, its metre is described as if the missing final unstressed syllable were actually present. So the quoted lines are *settenari*, not *senari*. (When metre is described using figures, the expression '7t' can be used for a *settenario tronco*.) A *tronco* line is especially valued as the closing line of an aria semistrophe, where it facilitates the composer's task of placing the final syllable on a suitably accented note. The third kind of line, called 'sliding' (*sdrucciolo*), adds an extra unstressed syllable to the single unaccented syllable ending a *piano* line. This supernumerary syllable is similarly ignored when classifying the metre. *Sdrucciolo* lines, the least common of the three types, are encountered most often in aria verse in short metres, particularly where a comic effect is desired (as with *buffo* characters in opera). It is seen in the opening two lines of Vivaldi's cantata RV 669: 'Tra l'erbe i zeffiri | placidi spirino'. Here, the effect is deliberately playful (the highly appropriate word *scherzino* appears at the end of the first line of the second semistrophe). The suffix 's' identifies a *sdrucciolo* line in descriptions of metre, so the two above lines would be described as '5s'.

The identification of the metre is complicated further by the operation of poetic devices that effectively knock two (or more) syllables into one or, conversely, resist doing this in contexts where coalescence would be expected. The most important of these are synaeresis (*sineresi*) and synaloepha (*sinalefe*). In *sineresi*, adjacent vowels in the same word are treated as one syllable; in *sinalefe*, adjacent vowels belonging to two or more adjacent words are treated similarly. Consider the following *endecasillabo*, which opens the central recitative of *Alla caccia, dell'alme e de' cori*, RV 670:

---

[19]  All translations of cantata texts are by the author.

Ma sia crudele o infida, oh Dio, mi piace.
1   |2   |3  |4 |5      |6|7      |8    |9  |10|11

If one counts up all the syllables individually, they total a surprising sixteen. But *sineresi* operates in two instances, causing *sia* and *Dio* to be treated as monosyllables. *Sinalefe* also takes its toll, reducing the trisyllable '-le o in-' and the bisyllable '-da, oh' to effective monosyllables. (In the underlaid text of a modern, printed musical score such coalescence is conventionally shown with so-called 'elision slurs'.) So the final result is a metrically orthodox line of eleven syllables.

More radically, vowels in collision with other vowels may simply be omitted, producing the familiar effect of elision, shown in such forms as *vostr'ombre* (for *vostre ombre*). Elision never causes problems for those seeking to identify metre, since the 'extra' vowels are not present in the first place. Some difficulty may be experienced, however, in recognizing the effects of diaeresis (*dieresi*) and dialoepha (*dialefe*), which can be described as the intentional non-application of *sineresi* and *sinalefe*, respectively. There is usually a good poetic reason for eschewing the normal coalescence-producing devices: the syllables may be the last two in the line (where coalescence is excluded *a priori*); the adjacent vowels may belong to words located in different clauses or simply sound unpleasant together. Just occasionally, one suspects the poet of using *dieresi* or *dialefe* merely to get himself out of a metrical fix. For their part, composers are apt to introduce these devices casually in defiance of the poet's intention, and with the inevitable result that the line becomes hypermetric. But this was a permitted licence: so long as listeners did not become spontaneously aware of the violation of prosody, composers felt free to tailor lines of poetry in this way to their musical intentions.

The use of end-rhyme in recitative and in aria stanzas is different. Most recitative is cast in the form of *versi sciolti* (unrhymed lines). A few poets – Antonio Ottoboni, discussed earlier, is among them – resisted the facility of blank verse, but these were in a tiny minority. In a recitative stanza, it is conventional, however, to rhyme the closing line with the penultimate or the antepenultimate line (rather as in the 'rhyming couplets' of Shakespearean verse). This acts as a signal of closure and can give the final line an attractively epigrammic quality.

In arias, most lines are rhymed, using patterns such as the following:

| | |
|---|---|
| *rime baciate* | AABB |
| *rime alternate* | ABAB |
| *rime intrecciate* | ABBA |
| *rime incatenate* | ABA BCB CDC |

With rare exceptions, end-rhymes are not shared between the two semistrophes, except for the so-called 'key rhyme' (*rima chiave*) that customarily links the final line of each semistrophe. It is not obligatory to match every line with a rhyming line. 'Singletons' are, in fact, very common, and have great salience in Metastasian verse.

Part of the poet's art in arias is to establish sufficient, but not excessive, regularity. There are four principal parameters that may be treated in either a tightly patterned or a loosely patterned way:

1. The two semistrophes may have an identical or divergent number of lines.
2. The metre of the two semistrophes may be identical or divergent.
3. The stanza may be monometric or polymetric.
4. End-rhyme may be pervasive or incomplete.

As a rule of thumb, loose patterning in one or two of these parameters can be compensated for by tight patterning in the others. Consider the following three examples:

> O di tua man mi svena
>   o con un guardo il mio morir consola.
> Quest'alma senza pena
>   con tal mercede ai rai del dì s'invola.

In this aria, taken from the cantata *Ingrata Lidia*, RV 673 (attributed to Vivaldi but no longer considered authentic), the metrical structure of each semistrophe is 7–11. This irregularity must, however, be set against the total symmetry between the semistrophes. The rhyme occurs in this instance between, rather than within, the semistrophes (AB|AB) – less unusual when these consist only of a couplet or tercet.

> Mentiti contenti
>   son veri tormenti
>   d'amante fedel.
> Gran male è quel bene,
>   son dardi quei guardi
>   che vibra per pene
>   bellezza crudel.

This is the second aria of *All'ombra del sospetto*, RV 678. It is asymmetrical in its number of lines (3 + 4) and its inclusion of one unrhymed line (the fifth). A compensatory regularity is provided by the uniformity of its *senari* (6–6–6t | 6–6–6–6t), the line bearing the key rhyme being *tronco*.

> Le fresche vïolette
>   e le vezzose erbette
>   in voi fioriscano,
>   liete gioiscano
>   al mio partir.
> So che tra lor diranno:
>   'Lungi sarem d'affanno
>   se quel partì da noi
>   che coi lamenti suoi
>   sempre ne' fe' languir'.

This aria closes *Perché son molli*, RV 681. The two semistrophes have an equal number of lines and a matching rhyme scheme (AABBC|DDEEC), but their lines are of very diverse length and nature: 7–7–5s–5s–5t | 7–7–7–7–7t.

The poetic themes of cantata texts depended intimately on their social and cultural context, which was dominated on the one hand by the institution of the *accademia*, which determined the nature of their audience, and on the other by the convention of pastoralism, which governed their style and expression.

At its simplest, an 'academy' was merely a private concert or recitation of poetry. Burney defines it *tout court* as a concert.[20] More accurate is Edward Wright's characterization of it as 'a general Word us'd among them [Italians] for publick Assemblies and Performances, whether of Musick, or of *Belles-Lettres*'.[21] (Wright's 'publick', needless to say, has to be understood in its contemporary sense of 'pertaining to respectable society'.) Even more specifically, academies could be societies at which any combination of music, poetry, and drama could be cultivated but whose main business was scholarly investigation (in the manner of a learned society), open discussion (in the manner of a debating club), or simple ceremony. Such societies had formal constitutions and a list of identified members, who most commonly adopted 'academic' names on entry.[22] Intermediate between the most informal and the most formal kinds of academy were the regular – for example, weekly – meetings of a small but not necessarily fixed group of persons at the home of a patron, where music and poetry were heard (and refreshments, naturally, were served). Such were the celebrated *conversazioni* held in the late seventeenth and early eighteenth centuries in the *palazzi* of Benedetto Pamphilij, Pietro Ottoboni, and Francesco Maria Ruspoli in Rome. A revealing description of an Italian academy around the middle of the eighteenth century is provided in Giorgio Antoniotto's *L'arte armonica*, published in London in the 1760s.[23] As an Italian immigrant (a cellist) working in England, Antoniotto (c.1690–1776) saw it as his task to describe for his readers the settings and occasions of musical performance in his native country, which he often does with an attention to detail lacking in similar accounts written by Italians for other Italians. The extract quoted below follows the description of a *conversazione* with pertinent comments on its most characteristic musical genre, the cantata:

> The simple vocal [chamber music] without instruments [other than those of the basso continuo] is only used in *Italy*, and very seldom in other countries, and it is used in some particular assemblies of lords and ladies, who pass the long winter evenings in singing some cantatas or duettos, only with the harpsichord and violoncello, when the rest of the assembly pass the time in playing at cards or otherwise. These cantatas are performed only by the ladies of quality, and sometimes by some young lords, in which assembly are not admitted the professors of music, but only some stranger[s] of the best sort, and that but very

20  Charles Burney, *The Present State of Music in France and Italy*, London: Becket, 1771, p. [iii].

21  Edward Wright, *Some Observations made in Travelling through France, Italy [. . .] in the Years 1720, 1721, and 1722*, 2 vols, London: Ward and Wicksteed, 1730, 2, 450n.

22  For a discussion of academies in general, and of the rôle of music within them, see Michael Talbot, 'Musical Academies in Eighteenth-Century Venice', *Note d'archivio per la storia musicale*, nuova serie, 2 (1984), 21–50, reproduced in facsimile in: idem, *Venetian Music in the Age of Vivaldi*, Aldershot: Ashgate, 1999.

23  On Antoniotto and his treatise, see Emilia Zanetti, 'Giorgio Antoniotto, il suo trattato "L'arte armonica" (London, 1760) e l'Opera V di Corelli', in Pierluigi Petrobelli and Gloria Staffieri (eds), *Studi corelliani IV. Atti del Quarto Congresso Internazionale (Fusignano, 4–7 settembre 1986)*, Florence: Olschki, 1990, pp. 381–404.

seldom. This simple music is of the best sort, composed by the best poets, and masters of music; and sometimes by the same lords the poetry and music, or also the music by the ladies, among whom are not only many excellent singers, but also composers. These sort of compositions being deprived of the help of the instrumental [*sic*], and of all action, consequently there must be used all the most expressive combinations, and properest progressions, in composing not only the recitative part, but also the airs; the melody of which must be extremely proper to the words. The bass for the violoncello, when it is separated from that for the harpsichord, must be composed in the best and most melodious manner, by imitation or some different melody, proper to help the expression of the vocal part: The harmony of the harpsichord, particularly in pathetic airs and recitatives, must be in as full combination as possible, with its accicaturas [*sic*], more proper for the strongest expression. These cantatas are very studious, and give the greatest pleasure with their moving affections: But in some ordinary cantatas, a voice [*sic*] sola, composed by [*sic*] an indifferent poetic style, the music cannot be of the moving sort, but only proper to the insignificant sense of the poetry; and these sort of cantatas are those which commonly run in every country, but the best sort very seldom, because the persons keep them zealously close for their own use.[24]

We will return to Antoniotti's account later, but what is interesting for present purposes is his statement that professional musicians, the 'professors of music', were excluded from the gatherings. Doubtless, this was true in circumstances where it was considered that professionals would sully the 'politeness' of the assembly or where the noble amateurs wished to exercise their poetic or musical talent unobserved by the multitude, but it was at least as common – particularly when the same musicians were in the employ of noble households – to make use of their services. Indeed, the liberality and 'conspicuous consumption' of a patron would shine all the more brightly if he went to such expense.

What academies could be at their most elaborate is shown by the description for his English readers by another Italian émigré living in London, Giuseppe Baretti (1719–89), of the Arcadian Academy in Rome.[25] As well turned and witty as Antoniotto's commentary is awkward and ponderous, Baretti's text can be allowed to run on a little, since he continues with a description, laced with hilarious satire, of the aesthetics of Arcadia.

Next to the academy *Della Crusca*, that of the *Arcadia Romana* rose in repute. The business of this Arcadia was to correct, encrease and beautify our poetry, as that of the Crusca to purify, illustrate, and fix our language.

The Arcadian life, as fabulous history represents it, was altogether innocent and simple. The inhabitants of that country lived on the mere products of their lands and flocks, and cultivated only those arts that are conducive to rural elegance and guiltless pleasure.

Upon this foundation Jacopo Sanazzaro [Sannazaro], who lived in the beginning of the sixteenth century, composed in Italian a pastoral romance intitled

---

[24] Giorgio Antoniotto, *L'arte armonica*, 2 vols, London: Johnson, 1760, 1, p. 109.
[25] Strictly speaking, 'Arcadian Academy' is a misleading expression, since the second word does not appear in the society's official name, Adunanza degli Arcadi. A good way to circumvent the problem is to call it the 'Roman Arcadia'.

*L'Arcadia*, which in Italy did him no less honour than his Latin poem *De Partu Virginis*, and out of Italy procured him several imitators, amongst whom the celebrated Sir Philip Sidney did not disdain to be numbered.

Sanazzaro's Arcadia is in prose, intermixed with eclogues in verse; and both his prose and his eclogues are so crouded with pastoral images and sentiments, that one would think the subject quite exhausted. Yet the Italians did not think so towards the middle of the last age, where some few verse-mongers of Rome took it into their heads again to cultivate that imaginary rural region.

If we credit Maria [*recte*, Michel Giuseppe] Morei, who published lately the history of this academy, those who first clubbed together to form it [in October 1690] were no more than *fourteen*, whose names Morei has thought proper to preserve. But such is the fondness of the Italians for verse and rhyme, that it soon consisted of as many thousands.

These fourteen people joined in a friendly body, to which they gave the effective title of *Arcadia Romana*; and amongst the few laws, written for them in very elegant Latin by the learned Vincenzo Gravina, there was one, by which it was enacted, that no person should be admitted into this society without first assuming a pastoral name.

It is impossible to conceive the eagerness with which this whimsical scheme of turning all sorts of men into imaginary shepherds was adopted both in Rome and out of Rome; and how the inflammable imaginations of my countrymen were fired by it! The very pope then reigning, with many cardinals and principal monsignori's, suffered themselves to be persuaded, that this poetical establishment would prove infinitely advantageous to literature in general, and poetry in particular; nor did they disdain to be listed in the catalogue of these Arcadian swains, befriending their union with several privileges, assigning them a place to hold their assemblies in, and attending frequently at their meetings.

The fame of this new academy was soon spread all over Italy, and the rural compositions produced on their first outset by the Arcadians, met with so great and general a favour with a nation always eager after every novelty, especially poetical novelty, that all became ambitious of being admitted into such an academy. But as this wish could not instantly be gratified, no less than *fifty-eight* towns of Italy, according to Morei's account, resolved on a sudden to have like academies of their own, which they unanimously called *Colonies of the Roman Arcadia*.[26]

The madness of pastoral now became universal. Every body who had the least knack for poetry, was metamorphosed into a shepherd, and fell directly upon composing rustic sonnets, eclogues, ydylliums, and bucolics. Nothing was heard from the foot of the Alps to the farthermost end of Calabria but descriptions of purling streams rolling gently along flowering meadows situated by the sides of verdant hills shaded by spreading trees, among whose leafy branches the sad Progne with her melancholy sister Philomela warbled their chaste loves, or murmured their doleful lamentations.

Rome being thus transformed by a poetical magic into a province of Greece, saw her capital turned to a cottage, the favourite habitation of Pan and Volumnus; and the charming Flora did not scruple to walk hand in hand with

---

[26] It should be pointed out, in correction of Baretti's implication, that many of these colonies, including the Accademia degli Animosi in Venice, were pre-existing literary societies that merely needed to affiliate to the Roman Arcadia to earn the status of colonies.

the lovely Pomona about the Vatican and Saint Peter. No body was to be found in the streets but coy nymphs and frolicksome satyrs, or amorous fauns and buxom dryads. No body was now called by his christian or family name; all our Antonio's, Francesco's, and Bartolommeo's were turned into Ergasto's, Dameta's, and Silvano's: and as neither the Arcadia nor her colonies refused admittance to the other sex, it may easily be guessed that every fair would now be a handsome nymph or an artless shepherdess, and that our Maria's, Orsola's, and Margherita's became on a sudden all Egle's, Licori's, and Glicera's. None of our cicisbeo's dared now to peep out of his hut, but with a hook in one hand, and a flute in the other.[27]

There are many reasons for the vogue for the pastoral that Baretti does not give. In the first place, the genre paid homage to the prototype of an academy: the garden near Athens named after the hero Academus used by Plato and his followers from c.387 BC for their meetings. The location of the mythical realm within the heartland of the Ancient World, in the Peloponnese, made this historical connection ever-present. Second, it provided opportunities for the display of erudition that no alternative *mise-en-scène* (for instance, that of the medieval Romance) could equal and referred to a corpus of literature with which most members of academies had – or would claim to have – at least a little acquaintance. Third, its portrayal of an egalitarian world of shepherds and nymphs corresponded neatly to the oasis of social familiarity between noble and non-noble lovers of music and poetry that academies were intended to provide; the Arcadian names adopted by members made it all the easier to introduce veiled topical reference without giving offence or causing embarrassment.[28] An Arcadian disguise rendered palatable, even amusing, many a sharp and personal point or a controversial statement of political allegiance.

At this point, it is appropriate to digress briefly in order to comment on the view advanced by the distinguished Handel scholar Ellen Harris that academies and the cantatas performed at them formed a locus for the expression of homoerotic feeling.[29] It is true that Arcadianism accepted, as part of its classical inheritance, portrayals of close bonds between members of the same sex. But whereas Homer's Achilles and Patroclus or Virgil's Nisus and Euryalus were presented to societies in which homosexual displays and practices were acceptable in certain situations (as the strange institution of the *cicisbeo* was in seventeenth-century Italy), the revived classicism of Arcadia existed within a society nominally

---

[27]  Joseph [Giuseppe] Baretti, *An Account of the Manners and Customs of Italy*, 2 vols, London: Davies, 1769, 1, pp. 247–52. The 'cicisbeo's' (*cicisbei*) of the last sentence were young single men who, according to Italian upper-class custom, were allowed to befriend and accompany married women openly and – one imagines – usually innocently.

[28]  Writing in the nineteenth century about Venetian academies in the last decades of the Republic, the historian Giovanni Rossi observed that 'in the majority [of academies], where nobles and priests mixed with diverse kinds of people, it was thought fitting that all should fraternise and abandon distinctions of birth and rank, while remembering nevertheless to address each other correctly' (for the original Italian text and source details, see Talbot, 'Musical Academies', p. 29).

[29]  Ellen T. Harris, *Handel as Orpheus: Voice and Desire in the Chamber Cantata*, Cambridge (MA) and London: Harvard University Press, 2001.

accepting official Christian morals. The big question is whether such expressions are to be taken as fantasy sanctioned by convention (in the manner of references to pagan gods) or as allusions to reality. Even if the second conclusion is drawn, we still have to disentangle the respective relationships of the patron, the poet, and the composer to the homoerotic representation. Harris sidesteps this problem to some extent by focusing on the milieu itself: homoeroticism, she argues, was something that permeated the world of the academy and of the cantata and in that way drew in even those who had no special affinity for it. One would not seek to deny that there is a historical connection between intense collective interest in the arts and homoerotic currents – as evident in the nineteenth-century salon and perhaps in the modern 'readers' group' as in the academies of the Baroque period. And it is equally true that Arcadian texts, steeped in sly allusion, provided the perfect cover for risqué comment or sentiment. But one always has to beware of reading too much into texts and music that were intended first and foremost as entertainment, not as a manifesto. In Vivaldi's case, the question never surfaces directly. None of the cantata texts he set appears to have even the slightest homo-erotic content, and one must assume that the Red Priest, notorious for having women in his entourage (the Girò sisters), was not minded to introduce it on his own initiative.

To some extent, the authors of cantata texts must have regarded Arcadian convention as an amusing form of game-playing. A cheerful cynicism emerges from a portion of text from a cantata by Bernardo Pasquini (1637–1710) quoted almost a hundred years ago by Edward Dent:

| | |
|---|---|
| Eh che non è possibile | How impossible it is |
| scrivere e non parlar di Filli e Clori! | to write without mentioning Phyllis and Chloris! |
| Il mondo vuole amori, | The world wants to hear about love, |
| vuol sentir dolci pene, | to experience sweet suffering, |
| vuol parlar di catene, | to hear talk of chains, |
| vuol suono di piacer, non di rigori.[30] | to hear the sound of pleasure, not of pain. |

The poetic themes of cantatas crystallized around a few *topoi*, each with its favourite set of keywords inviting musical illustration. Schmitz recognized this narrowness when he wrote of older Italian lyric poetry in general:

In fact, Italian lyric verse, whether popular or literary, has made the subject of love pre-eminent from the very beginning, although it gradually became treated in a tasteless and monotonously mannered way in texts from our time [the Baroque period] and musical genre [the cantata]. Here, one encounters the traditional recitation of woes in phrases sated with tragic pathos or of witty conceits delving into stereotyped figures of speech already used for centuries in Italian poetry – delightfully rhymed, cleverly expressed, but also inexpressibly tedious. Whether a lover moans because he must depart from his lady-love or because she resists his advances, one cannot escape the same finely tuned pleas to the supremely beautiful and supremely cruel object of desire: always the

---

[30] Edward J. Dent, 'Italian Chamber Cantatas', *The Musical Antiquary*, ii (1910–11), 142–53 and 185–99, at 191.

same outbursts and exquisitely tooled cries of pain, always the 'io moro' [I am dying] or the 'morirò' [I shall die] as the final remedy for interminable grief – the never-changing expression of a passion in whose reality no one believes, least of all the poet who puts the words into the mouth of the lover.[31]

Of course, Schmitz's distaste for this kind of poetry was rooted in the belief widely held in his age (also by Italians themselves) that, after the Renaissance, Italian letters had entered a period of decadence, from which they had to be rescued by Romanticism. Nevertheless, his criticisms continue to strike home, even when one has grown to accept many of these *topoi* as convenient starting points, rather than final destinations, of poetic invention – at least, where the better poets are concerned.

The texts of Vivaldi's thirty-seven cantatas are a sample-card of these *topoi*. Eleven deal with the subject of separation between lovers, the central keyword being *lontano* (distant) and its cognates.[32] Ten, including one text set twice, deal with the non-reciprocation of love, for which such keywords as *crudele* (cruel) and *rigore* (harshness) are apposite.[33] Two introduce the related theme of the beloved's infidelity, real or alleged.[34] As many as four describe a timid lover, initially unable to confess his feelings, drawing on such keywords as *confuso* (confused) and *tacere* (to be silent).[35] Then there are two texts that vent a non-specific *Weltschmerz*.[36] More positive feelings are expressed in one cantata (RV 660) that is a declaration of love, another celebrating a long-delayed reciprocation of love (RV 669), another recounting the act of falling in love (RV 653), another singing the praises of Arcadia as a refuge from a hostile world (RV 671), and two (RV 685 and 686) that are encomiums of identified persons. This leaves three *cantate morali* that are not specifically Arcadian in locale: RV 670, a *lezione amorosa*, cautions male lovers against female snares, while RV 676 and RV 678 offer wistful meditations on the nature of love.

To treat these themes, the author has the choice of four poetic 'voices'.[37] The

---

31 Schmitz, *Geschichte der weltlichen Solokantate*, pp. 19–20: 'In der Tat hat in der italienischen Lyrik, in der volkstümlichen wie in der kunstgemäßen, die Liebesdichtung von jeher eine absolut prävalierende Rolle gespielt, die in der Textliteratur unserer Zeit und Musikgattung allmählich zu geschmackloser, eintöniger Manier geworden war. Das ist jener "herkömmliche Liebes-jammer["] in Phrasen voll tragischen Pathos oder in witzigen Concetti mit getreuer Wieder-holung der in der italienischen Poesie seit Jahrhunderten stereotyp gewordenen Redensarten, ganz zierlich gereimt, ganz artig ausgedrückt, aber auch von unaussprechlicher Langweiligkeit. Ob der Liebende jammert, weil er von der Geliebten scheiden muß oder weil sie ihm unerbittlich bleibt – es kommen immer dieselben wohltönenden Apostrophen an den unerhört schönen und unerhört grausamen Gegenstand der Herzensflammen, immer dieselben Ausrufungen und edel stilisierten Schmerzensschreie, immer das "io moro" oder "morirò" als letztes Mittel gegen die endlose Pein – der stets gleiche Ausdruck der Leidenschaft, an deren Wahrheit niemand glaubt und der im Namen des Liebenden sprechenden Dichter am allerwenigsten.'

32 RV 652, 653, 654, 655, 657, 658, 659, 661, 662, 665, and 680.

33 RV 650, 651/683, 656, 664, 666, 667, 677, 682, 684(a), and 679.

34 RV 674 and 676.

35 RV 649, 663, 668, and 799.

36 RV 681 and 796.

37 This typology is introduced and discussed in Michael Talbot, *Benedetto Vinaccesi: A Musician in Brescia and Venice in the Age of Corelli*, Oxford: Clarendon Press, 1994, pp. 166–7.

first is the familiar 'lyric' voice in which the poet addresses his audience directly *qua* poet. This is the voice normally adopted for *cantate morali*. The second is the narrative (or 'epic') voice, in which the poet describes a scene or narrates an event in the manner of a witness. It is preferred for the opening recitative of a cantata in RARA form, but is found quite often in later recitatives as well. The third is the 'quoting' voice. Here, the poet reproduces, in direct speech, the words of one or both of the protagonists (i.e., the lover and the beloved); this voice appears, logically, only in subordination to another voice. The fourth is the 'dramatic' voice, which is where the poet assumes from the start the identity of the protagonist, as in Marcello's *Cassandra* or Telemann's *Ino*. This voice is not limited to historical or mythological subjects already familiar to the audience: it can be used just as effectively for the words of an invented protagonist.[38] It enjoys prominence in Vivaldi's cantatas, although this is partly due to the high incidence of the ARA plan, which does not permit an initial narration. The boundary between the lyric and dramatic voices can sometimes be hard to establish. Does the voice that eulogizes Arcadia in *Care selve, amici prati* (RV 671) belong to the poet himself or to an imaginary shepherd? Since the practical import is nil, this is not a question to agonize over.

### Its Musical Nature

Looking through the text in front of him, a cantata composer of Vivaldi's time must have had a very clear idea of how to set it. The first movement, if an aria, would be in the home key; if a recitative, it would start from the tonic chord and then modulate to a different key for the following aria. If the cantata was *con strumenti*, there might be an introductory sinfonia, which would similarly relieve whatever movement followed from the task of establishing the tonic. The last movement, if an aria, would again be in the home key; if a recitative, it would start in a different key and work its way back to the tonic, ending with an extended passage of music, perhaps in the form of a cavata or an extended arioso passage, in that key.

The keys of the two or more arias were probably planned at an early stage, clarifying the tonal points between which the connecting recitatives had to navigate. Recitatives were likened earlier to the corridors forming the slightly flexible articulation between the carriages of a train. A strict analogy breaks down, however, when we consider in detail the manner in which recitatives are connected (or not) to the surrounding arias. A harmonic and even tonal disjunction after the aria is normal; it was suggested earlier that this helps to establish the pair RA (rather than AR) as the basic module from which a cantata (or operatic scene) is constructed. Composers vary greatly in the form of

[38] Timms, 'The Dramatic in Vivaldi's Cantatas', pp. 101–4, outlines the discourse around the 'voices' of the cantata in eighteenth-century German writings by Mattheson, Scheibe, and Krause. He draws a useful distinction (pp. 107–10) between 'soliloquy' (when the speaker's words are directed inward) and 'address', when they are directed outward at some person or thing. Arias tend towards the 'address' subtype, recitatives towards the 'soliloquy'.

connection they make between a recitative and a succeeding aria. What I like to call the 'zero' progression (from a final tonic chord to an identical initial tonic chord) is common, even standard, in seventeenth-century music, which in any case operates within a narrower tonal framework than eighteenth-century music.[39] This 'zero' progression has the effect of allowing the recitative to 'glide' smoothly into the aria – to make it seem a spontaneous continuation or expansion. However, if a recitative ends with a chord that is not the tonic chord of the following aria, this introduces an attractive element of uncertainty and, through the specific chord progression made at the point of connection, enables the composer to establish a mood (*affetto*) with the very first chord of the aria.

More than any other Baroque composer I have observed, Vivaldi makes a point of keeping the two chords, and the keys they represent, distinct. In so doing, he sets up a change (interpretable as intensification, mitigation, or negation) of *affetto* right at the start of the aria, which will be consolidated as the movement proceeds. The clearest example of this is the juxtaposition of a minor tonic chord and the major tonic chord a major third lower (as in E minor and C major). When the two chords occur in this order at the point of junction between a recitative and an aria, the effect is one of relief and relaxation. An example occurs in the first recitative–aria pair of *All'ombra di sospetto*, RV 678, where the two keys concerned are B minor and G major. Conversely, when their order is reversed, the effect changes to one of tension or even grimness. This is the case with the move from C major to E minor at the same point in *Qual per ignoto calle*, RV 677. In many instances, the content of the literary text both supports the description of the change of *affetto* given above and lends plausibility to the idea that Vivaldi did not leave such transitions to chance.

So the connection is not necessarily a 'tight fit' at either end. Common sense would nevertheless suggest that the prime task of a recitative is to negotiate the tonal passage from one aria key (or at least its environs) to the next. In opera, where the keys of successive arias are often very distinct, this function can be very evident. In chamber cantatas containing few arias, however, these keys normally remain close (within the *ambitus*, the theorist Johann David Heinichen's term for a group of related keys that in modern notation are no more than one accidental apart in their key signatures). This means that there is so little tonal ground to cover that a recitative threatens to 'walk on the spot' tediously. Fortunately, modulation is used in recitatives not only for functional but also for expressive reasons. Within late Baroque recitatives one finds bold and elaborate forms of modulation hardly encountered in any other type of movement prior to the development sections of sonata-form movements in the Classical period. For instance, there are 'modulation chains', my term for series of modulations in which each modulation is modelled exactly on the one preceding it. If the restraints of the *ambitus* are observed, as one progresses stepwise upwards in C major, one arrives successively at D minor, E minor, F major, and G major. The changes of mode and the variation between tone and semitone steps suffice to keep the music at all times within the orbit of C major. Now, if one progresses

---

[39] Talbot, 'How Recitatives End and Arias Begin', 171.

from C major to D major, and then by exact analogy from D major to E major, from E major to F sharp major, and so forth, one widens the field of modulation enormously and breaks free from the orbit of the home key. Naturally, the direction of such progressions can be reversed to bring one back. Thus one can travel flatwards along the circle of fifths from F sharp major to C major, passing on the way through B, E, A, D, and G major. Another helpful resource is the modal shift, whereby one replaces the major tonality on a given keynote by the minor tonality, or the reverse – moving three degrees along the circle of fifths at a stroke.[40] So the tonal 'curve' of a late-Baroque recitative of at least moderate length is likely to be not a smooth arc but a complex, zigzagging shape whose final destination becomes clear only at the very end.

Once again, we can illustrate this by taking an example from Vivaldi's music. His cantata *Sorge vermiglio in ciel*, RV 667, is cast in RARA form. The opening recitative starts on an A minor chord but begins to modulate in the third bar and finds its way eventually to a concluding cadence in E flat major. The aria that follows is in G minor (this is the 'mediant' relationship discussed two paragraphs earlier). Reversing the progression, Vivaldi begins the longer second recitative ('Ah Silvia, tu sei quella') in E flat major. Some listeners will hear, or sense, the identity of this harmony with the one closing the first recitative and perceive the second recitative as a linear continuation of the first, with the obvious implication that the aria sandwiched between them is an interpolation. This reading of the structure of a cantata, which carries the implication that recitative is more fundamental than aria, may seem at variance with common sense, but it has deep roots and can be seen operating time and again in Baroque opera, where arias are routinely removed, inserted, or exchanged in the course of a typical work's performance history. The final aria is, inevitably, in A minor, so the linking recitative, twenty-one bars long, has a relatively small tonal space to traverse (from G minor to A minor). The trajectory that it follows is, however, far from straightforward (upper-case letters represent major keys; lower-case ones, minor keys):

Bars 1–6:     $E\flat \to c \to d \to$
Bars 7–12:    $a \to C \to d \to e \to$
Bars 13–21:   $b \to G \to a \to e$

Bars 1–6 remain comfortably within the *ambitus* of G minor established in the preceding aria. In bar 7 the music breaks out of these confines and moves distinctly sharpwards, remaining until bar 12 in the *ambitus* of C major. In bar 13 it strikes out again (but less dramatically) in a sharpward direction; the last four modulations are to keys within the *ambitus* of G major. Overall, therefore, the movement performs the sharpward movement needed to bring it within striking distance of the key of the next aria, but the tonal curve is heavily 'kinked' and filled with incidental modulations that are, strictly speaking, redundant to the main purpose. The high density of modulation and the high incidence of 'deceptive' cadences that evade, by one means or another, the expected perfect cadence

---

[40] On modal shifts in Baroque music, see Michael Talbot, 'Modal Shifts in the Sonatas of Domenico Scarlatti', *Chigiana*, nuova serie, xx (1985), 25–43.

correspond extremely well to the emotional climate of the recitative, which depicts the lover's pursuit of Sylvia, who flees him. Note, however, that amid the apparently chaotic stream of modulations elements of regular patterning emerge. All three phases of the recitative accord a prominent place to modulation to the key a tone higher. In phase 1 this is $c$–$d$; in phase 2, $C$–$d$–$e$; in phase 3, $G$–$a$.

Regulating the incidence and nature of modulation is only one means among many of controlling the emotional temperature of a recitative. Single chord progressions themselves have a strong affective value. To the stability of a root-position chord can be contraposed the instability of an inverted chord; to the transparency of a simple triad, the gently dissonant richness of a seventh chord. The smoothness or angularity of the bass line also builds up a mood. Leaps convey restlessness; augmented or diminished intervals, harshness. An unexpected chord can be a way of representing shock or surprise in the text. The rate at which the chords succeed one another can also hold significance. If a single harmony is sustained – typically, with a string of tied semibreves or minims in the bass – over several bars, the general effect is restful; if chords succeed one another at the interval of a crotchet, it is agitated. In the section 'Vom Styl im Recitativ' ('On the Style of Recitatives') in his famous treatise on composition *Gradus ad Parnassum* (which is so much more than a mere counterpoint primer!) Johann Joseph Fux noted that where the text is impassioned, the bass should constantly change ('beständig den Baß dabei ändern'), whereas in reverential passages it should change little ('wenig zu verändern ist').[41]

Naturally, the shape and rhythm of the vocal line play a major part in setting the mood. The choice of wide or chromatically altered intervals for the singer has an effect similar to that already described for the bass line. In late Baroque 'simple' recitative accompanied only by continuo the singer is expected – true to the conception of recitative as 'heightened speech' – to exercise great rhythmic freedom, lending considerable plasticity to the square-cut series of crotchets, quavers, and semiquavers from which his or her line is formed. Example 2.1 shows the first six bars of a particularly arresting opening recitative by Vivaldi (that of *Perfidissimo cor! Iniquo fato!*, RV 674). Here, in typical fashion, rests are used not only to demarcate the lines of poetry, variously of eleven and seven syllables, but also the divisions within those lines.[42] The two *endecasillabi* with which the quoted passage opens, and that with which it closes, are all interrupted in this manner before the second hemistich (i.e., before *Iniquo*, *Tirsi*, and *si*), and the rhetorical repetition of *Dov'è* in the *settenario* forming the third line (on this occasion, not the composer's decision but prescribed by the literary text) is given added emphasis by an intervening rest. Highly characteristic of early eighteenth-century recitative are the cadences in bars 4 and 6. The second, a form of imperfect (or 'Phrygian') cadence in which the bass falls from submediant to dominant, while the voice rises from subdominant to dominant, is a *topos* to end all *topoi*:

---

[41] Johann Joseph Fux, *Gradus ad Parnassum oder Anführung zur regelmäßigen musikalischen Composition*, Leipzig: Mizler, 1742, p. 193. This edition is a German translation of the Latin original (1725).

[42] It sometimes happens that there are no rests separating the settings of adjacent lines. In such cases, the break is usually marked in an alternative way: by a deceleration (a move to minims or crotchets) at the close of the first vocal phrase.

Ex. 2.1  Vivaldi, *Perfidissimo cor! Iniquo fato!*, RV 674: opening

the standard method, adopted by all composers, of representing a question. The first is a *cadenza tronca*, or truncated ('foreshortened') cadence. The foreshortening in question is the closure of the singer's phrase on the dominant, leaving the bass to effect the move to the tonic and clinch the perfect cadence. The first note in bar 3 is written, in accordance with convention, as a C sharp – the pitch of the following quaver – but should be performed as an appoggiatura, taking its pitch, F sharp, from the previous note.

The *cadenza tronca* is perhaps statistically the most frequent variety of perfect cadence encountered in Baroque recitative after c.1680. The singer, composer, and author Pier Francesco Tosi (1654–1732) opined that such 'broken' cadences (the term is that of his translator, John Ernest Galliard) were ten times as numerous as they ought to be, but this remark only betrays his age and conservatism.[43] The blatant friction between tonic (in the appoggiatura of the vocal part) and dominant (in the bass) harmony has made this cadence a *cause célèbre*. In the later eighteenth century, the clash was averted by delaying the advent of the dominant note in the bass – at some cost to the music's flow. Until Winton Dean in 1977 produced decisive arguments in favour of the validity of foreshortened cadences, most performances of recitative in opera, oratorio, solo motet, and cantata alike followed (contrary to the notation of the sources) the 'delayed' model – transferring back to the earlier part of the eighteenth century a practice known to be valid for the later part.[44]

---

[43]  Pier Francesco Tosi, *Observations on the Florid Song*, London: Wilcox, 1742, § 5.13. This was the second edition of John Ernest Galliard's translation (with extra footnotes) of Tosi's *Opinioni de' cantori antichi e moderni*, Bologna: Lelio della Volpe, 1723. A German translation of the same treatise, greatly expanded, appeared as Johann Friedrich Agricola's *Anleitung zur Singkunst*, Berlin: Winter, 1757.

[44]  Winton Dean, 'The Performance of Recitative in Late Baroque Opera', *Music & Letters*, lviii (1977), 389–402. No article more influential for performance practice can ever have appeared.

The acceptance at face value of the *cadenza tronca* naturally compels the accompanist to find a solution that mitigates the harmonic clash. One easy solution is simply to add an acciaccatura on the same dissonant note as the appoggiatura to the dominant chord.[45] Less radically, one can introduce the suspension or appoggiatura of a fourth at the start of the chord, resolving it to the third on the last note of the vocal phrase. Where tempo permits, one can even use a 'Cadential Six-Four', the most euphonious solution of all. Whichever option is selected, a light, detached accompaniment will always produce less friction than a heavy, sustained one.

In his *Gradus ad Parnassum* Fux proposed a kind of grammar for the cadence-types used in recitative.[46] Each was matched with a punctuation mark: comma, full stop, question mark, exclamation mark, etc. This attempt to treat music and language as alternative expressions of the same ideas was characteristic of the German tradition, which, ever since the establishment of the *Lateinschule* in the sixteenth century, had attempted to legitimize music's place in the academic curriculum by demonstrating its close conformity to rhetorical and grammatical principles. In a similar spirit, Mattheson 'analysed' a cantata aria by Benedetto Marcello to reveal how its structure followed that of a classical oration, complete with *exordium, propositio, peroratio,* and the rest.[47] In a very broad sense, of course, Fux was right. The coincidences between the punctuation marks present (or implicit) in cantata texts and the designated types of cadence shown in his treatise are legion. But Italian composers worked from experience (or imitation of precedent) and instinct rather than from a prescriptive rule-book. In this light, the modern scholar should always beware of too readily carrying over the full weight of German theory (grammatical, rhetorical, aesthetic) to a coeval Italian context.

Tosi distinguishes between 'chamber', 'church', and 'theatrical' varieties of recitative, following the three-way division of music according to performance context normal in the period.[48] His distinction has little to do with the composer's art and mainly concerns the type of expression that the singer should bring to the music. More relevant for our purposes (but ignored by Tosi) is the difference in mode of performance between music memorized and sung during action on stage (in opera and some serenatas) and music read from the page and sung without action (in cantatas, oratorios, and most serenatas). Operatic recitative is conceived so as not to impose an impossible burden on the singer's memory and concentration. It is in the main formulaic – centonized from a stockpot of familiar fragments – and swift-moving. It is intended for the masses and avoids ostentation and complexity. Cantata recitative, intended for an elite audience, can be recherché and unusual: indeed, the quality of *bizzarria* was highly prized among musical connoisseurs in Italy. Being a short episode in a short composition,

---

45 'Acciaccatura' is used here in the sense employed by Antoniotto earlier: an added dissonant note, quickly released, that 'spices' the plain chord. Francesco Gasparini's primer *L'armonico pratico al cimbalo* (Venice: Bortoli, 1708) deals extensively with the device.

46 Fux, *Gradus ad Parnassum,* pp. 194–5.

47 Mattheson, *Der vollkommene Capellmeister,* pp. 237–9.

48 Tosi, *Observations on the Florid Song,* § V, 1–9.

cantata recitative does not need to hurry along: it can dwell on, and develop at leisure, selected passages. Since it does not have to be memorized, it revels in complication of every kind. Johann Adolph Scheibe recognized clearly the special opportunities available to recitative in chamber cantatas when he wrote in 1745:

> All species of interval – the diatonic, chromatic, and enharmonic alike – can be used to contribute to the refinement and beauty of a recitative of this kind [. . .] Recitatives in the chamber style and most especially in cantatas, about which I am now writing, confer on [the composer] in particular the freedom to obey the bidding of his imagination, to expand his thoughts in an impressive manner, to use all the resources of art and industry, and, finally, to introduce many kinds of harmonic beauty that the nature of other musical genres does not always permit.[49]

In addition to ordinary ('simple') recitative, 'accompanied' recitative was available to composers of cantatas *con strumenti*. Rousseau, in his *Dictionnaire de musique*, recognized a distinction between *récitatif accompagné* (accompanied recitative) and *récitatif obligé* (obbligato recitative) that, although not commonly made in present-day commentaries, aids clarity.[50] The first retains the traditional long, frequently tied, bass notes of simple recitative and simply adds to them the upper parts. This produces a 'halo' effect familiar from the passages for Jesus in Bach's *St Matthew Passion*. The second has more in common with arioso treatment, since strongly rhythmicized notes, usually in much shorter note-values, are assigned to the orchestra. The rhythmic freedom required for the singer in any kind of recitative prevents this orchestral texture from intruding to any great extent into the sung passages, but it is used to punctuate and connect vocal phrases.

In accompanied recitative, more than anywhere else, the Baroque cantata comes close to the world of opera. Just as in opera, the addition of the 'instruments' (generally comprising just the three upper string parts) is carefully rationed. Many passages remain in simple recitative, accompanied recitative taking over at moments of exceptional drama or poignancy.

For its part, the continuo cantata could always achieve greater weight and memorability in the setting of recitative verse by substituting an arioso section or a cavata for ordinary recitative. *Arioso* means 'aria-like'; it entails a switch to a style that is virtually indistinguishable from that of an aria except by its greater simplicity and its through-composed structure. Such sections, if placed at the end of a recitative, lend *gravitas* and reinforce closure. Short passages of arioso can

---

49   Johann Adolph Scheibe, *Critischer Musikus*, rev. edn, Leipzig: Breitkopf, 1745, pp. 399–400: 'Alle Arten der Intervallen, so wohl der diatonischen, chromatischen, als enarmonischen, sind es, die zur Auszierung und Schönheit eines solchen Rezitativs nicht wenig beytragen [. . .] Das Rezitativ im Kammerstil, vornehmlich aber in der Art von Cantaten, die ich anitzo beschreibe, erlaubet insonderheit die Freyheit, seiner Einbildungskraft zu folgen, auf edle Art aus-zuschweifen, Kunst und Arbeitsamkeit zu folgen, und endlich mancherley harmonische Schönheiten anzubringen, die die Eigenschaften anderer Musikstücke nicht allemahl zulassen.'
50   Jean-Jacques Rousseau, *Dictionnaire de musique*, Paris: Veuve Duchesne, 1768, art. 'Récitatif', pp. 399–405, at pp. 403–5.

also be used to excellent effect in the middle of a recitative whenever passing illustration of a keyword is desired. Vivaldi employed full-blown arioso only twice in his cantatas (in RV 677 and RV 680), but left many more examples in the recitatives of his solo motets and *introduzioni*.

A 'cavata' is so called because the words set are not destined automatically for this kind of setting but have to be extracted (*ricavato*) by the composer for the purpose. Its history and character have been examined minutely by Colin Timms.[51] The words selected were normally the last line, the last half-line, or the last two lines of a recitative stanza. The most common type of cavata – the kind cultivated with distinction by Vivaldi's older Venetian contemporaries Biffi, Albinoni, and Caldara – takes the form of a section of moderate length in a flowing two-part counterpoint that draws freely on the devices of fugato, canon, and invertible counterpoint. Such sections appear nowhere in Vivaldi's cantatas, and it is interesting to consider why.

In the first place, the *locus classicus* for a cavata was at the end of a final recitative. Since all Vivaldi's cantatas end with an aria, this opportunity is denied. It may also be that he, or the singers for whom he wrote, considered the cavata obsolete. Vivaldi was practised at imitative counterpoint, as the many superb fugues in his *concerti a quattro* prove, but he did not often make a show of it where it was not required. A hint of what a cavata by Vivaldi might have looked like is provided by the opening of the *Preludio* of the ninth sonata of his Op. 2 (1709), shown as Example 2.2. Were one to fit the words of a concluding *settenario* (e.g., 'Lontananza crudele') to the opening phrase, and to make the treble line more singable by compressing some of the 'violin leaps', one would have the perfect material for a typical cavata.

Ex. 2.2 Vivaldi, Violin Sonata in E minor, Op. 2 no. 9 (RV 16): *Preludio*, opening

Discussion of the structure of cantata arias must begin with a reminder of the bipartite structure of their text, a feature regularly encountered from the middle of the seventeenth century onwards. How this division is reflected is not uniform: what remains constant is that it always translates clearly into musical terms. During the middle third of the seventeenth century, the period of Carissimi and Cesti, binary form is preferred. The form is either simple (AB) or what

---

51  Timms, 'The Cavata at the Time of Vivaldi', in Antonio Fanna and Giovanni Morelli (eds), *Nuovi studi vivaldiani*, 1988, pp. 451–77. Albinoni's cantatas include some of exceptional length and contrapuntal complexity.

musicologists commonly term 'extended' binary form (ABB'), where the musical setting privileges the second semistrophe. In the last third of the century ternary form (ABA) swiftly assumed dominance. Initially, the 'A' section stated the complete text of the first semistrophe only once (discounting immediate repetition of individual words or phrases), so that it was equivalent in length and weight to the 'B' section. The reprised 'A' section was normally written out in full, which encouraged the presence of small variations vis-à-vis the first statement, and the dimensions were often compact enough for the entire ABA structure to be treated strophically.

Some time around 1690 a new trend (applying equally to operatic arias) set in. Two complete statements of the text of the first semistrophe instead of one were allowed in the 'A' section. This innovation radically modified the balance of the aria, transferring the weight decisively to the 'A' section. The imbalance carried the ever-present risk that the 'B' section would atrophy or become subject to purely routine treatment (as is so often the case with the 'middle eight' section in modern popular music). The anonymous author (believed to be Josse de Villeneuve) of a *Lettre sur le méchanisme de l'opéra italien* published in 1756 suggests that all too many composers succumbed. Explaining the structure of the Italian aria for his French readers, the author observes:

> This aria [. . .] is divided into two unequal parts: the first, the more elaborately worked, is the one in which the composer deploys all his art; the second is a kind of repose inserted to give the singer a breathing space.[52]

Good composers, of course, continued to fire on all cylinders during the 'B' section.

The expansion of the 'A' section went hand in hand with a general enlargement of scale, due in part to the increased cultivation and ever more extravagant character of melismatic writing. If there is a name that deserves to be attached to this cult of floridity, it is that of the highly influential and respected singer, singing teacher, and composer Francesco Antonio Pistocchi (1659–1726), an almost exact contemporary of Alessandro Scarlatti. The cantatas in Pistocchi's *Scherzi musicali*, Op. [2], published in Amsterdam in 1698, are a straw in the wind. Example 2.3 shows how the voice concludes the 'A' section of the first aria, 'Vedo Zeffiro con l'aura', of the fourth cantata (*Dolorosa partenza, oh Dio, che l'alma*) from this collection. In this case, the two melismas aptly illustrate the words of which the syllables concerned form part: the semiquavers for *scherzar* conjure up the sound of laughter, while the protracted undulations of the second melisma are a good visual and aural representation of *onde*. Less skilled, or less scrupulous, composers did not fail to abuse melisma, as did singers when improvising cadenzas. Benedetto Marcello flails the practice mercilessly in his satire *Il teatro alla moda* (1720), writing:

> If, in the aria, one finds proper nouns, such as *padre*, *impero*, *amore*, *arena*, *regno*, *beltà*, *lena*, *core*, etc., etc., or adverbs, such as *no*, *senza*, and *già*, the *modern* composer will write a *very long melisma* on them, in the style *paaaa* . . .

---

52  [Josse de Villeneuve], *Lettre sur le méchanisme de l'opéra italien*, Naples, 1756, p. 22.

Ex. 2.3  Pistocchi, *Dolorosa partenza, oh Dio, che l'alma*: 'Vedo Zeffiro con l'aura', bars 11–16

*impeeee . . . amoooo . . . areeee . . . reeee . . . beltaaaa . . . lenaaaa . . . coooo . . .* etc., *noooo . . . seeen . . . giaaaa . . .* etc. And this in order to make a break with the *old style*, where such melismas were not used on *proper* nouns or *adverbs*, but only on words denoting some *passion* or *emotion*, such as *tormento*, *affanno, canto, volar, cader*, etc., etc., etc.[53]

For better or for worse, however, this melismatic style was part and parcel of the late Baroque aria in all genres. If theorists hated it, singers loved it. Poets tried to accommodate it as best they could by placing expressive keywords strategically at convenient points – which generally meant in the middle of lines rather than at their extremities.

One consequence of the expansion of ternary form in arias was that it put an end to strophic repetition of the music. Another was that it forced composers to make specific decisions about the thematic relationship between the 'A' and 'B' sections. In the older version of the form the 'B' section was perceived as the continuation and pendant of the 'A' section, so the two sections could be related thematically in rather the same easy manner as the two halves of an allemanda or corrente. In the newer version the two sections were syntactically less dependent on one another (indeed, cuts sometimes took the form of suppressing the 'B' section and the reprised 'A') and therefore could, in principle, follow different

<hr />

[53]  Translated from the edited version by Andrea d'Angeli (Milan: Ricordi, 1956), which presents the text (p. 18) as: 'Se nelle *arie* vi entrassero nomi propri, verbigrazia *padre, impero, amore, arena, regno, beltà, lena, core*, etc., etc., *no, senza, già*, ed altri avverbi, dovrà il compositore *moderno* comporvi sopra un *ben lungo passaggio*: v.g. *paaaa . . . impeeee . . . amoooo . . . areeee . . . reeee . . . beltaaaa . . . lenaaaa . . . coooo . . .* etc., *noooo . . . seeen . . . giaaaa . . .* etc. E ciò per allontanarsi dall'*antico stile*, che non usava il passaggio su nomi *propri* o sopra *avverbi*, ma bensì sopra parole solamente significanti qualche *passione* o *moto*, v.g. *tormento, affanno, canto, volar, cader*, etc., etc., etc.'

paths, especially if the sense of the text encouraged this. The choice lay, essentially, between a 'monothematic' (Ellen Harris's term) approach, whereby the 'B' section would resemble the development section in sonata form, and a 'polythematic' one, for which an apt comparator would be the Trio alternating with a Minuet. Different composers inclined towards different models (Vivaldi is definitely to be counted among the partisans of monothematicism), but most retained a degree of flexibility. If anything, the general bias shifted towards polythematicism as the Baroque period drew to its close – a harbinger of advancing Classicism. One clear symptom of polythematicism is the choice of a different metre and/or tempo for the 'B' section. Fredrick Millner has noted how this feature becomes increasingly common in Johann Adolf Hasse's operatic arias after 1745, and there is good reason to suppose that his finding has equal validity for the cantata and solo motet.[54]

With increased length came a growing inclination to keep the reprised 'A' section identical in notation to the first statement (in performance, of course, the singer would ornament it elaborately). No direct cause-and-effect relationship between the two tendencies can be discerned, and it could well have been pressure from singers, who wished to improvise on – and to demonstrate to audiences their improvisation on – material already heard in simpler form, coupled with an understandable impatience to progress to the next task, that induced composers to finish writing out the aria at the end of the 'B' section, to which they appended 'Da capo' (from the top). If any alterations were to be made, these were usually cuts, which could be indicated in the notation of the original 'A' section by means of special signs (Vivaldi liked to use a large 'hash' shape). A few arias, particularly ones with orchestral accompaniment, add 'al segno #' to 'Da capo', thereby instructing performers to begin the reprise at the sign. In modern commentary such an aria is known as a *dal segno* aria.[55]

The standard layout of a cantata aria in the period 1700–50 is the following:

### 'A' Section

1   Introductory ritornello, starting and finishing in the tonic key.
2   First vocal period, ending with a cadence in a secondary key, which for major tonalities is normally the dominant (minor keys display more variety).
3.   Brief link passage or ritornello.
4.   Second vocal period, returning to the home key.
5.   Concluding ritornello, usually identical with the introductory ritornello.

### 'B' Section

6.   Third vocal period, visiting further related keys and always cadencing in a foreign key.

### Reprise of the entire 'A' section

---

[54] Fredrick L. Millner, *The Operas of Johann Adolf Hasse*, Ann Arbor: UMI Research Press, 1979, p. 41.

[55] In the original Italian the repeat is usually expressed as 'at' (*al*) rather than 'from' (*dal*) the sign.

There are many variables that lend diversity to this outline. The opening ritornello is not mandatory, except in an aria opening a cantata, where it serves to fix the pitch for the singer. In opera, arias in which the singer enters directly are often used to express interruption, as when a recitative by one singer leads to an aria by another, but in solo cantatas the omission of the introduction has more the effect of informality or simplicity, appropriate for dance-like movements. Vivaldi never dispenses with the opening ritornello in his cantatas, as opposed to his operas; the reason is perhaps not so much a lack of imagination as a positive, protective attitude towards the instrumental component.

Cantata composers who were also noted instrumentalists, such as the harpsichordists Marcello and Gasparini or the cellists Bononcini and Porpora, usually betray this affinity in their cantatas. A string player, for example, has a tendency to 'skew' the character of the bass line towards the cello, while a harpsichord player may favour his own instrument similarly. Instrumentalists may seek additional opportunities for obbligato participation, as when the bass part divides into a simple, accompanying line and an elaborate obbligato line (one for cello, one for harpsichord), or a keyboardist or violinist borrows the vacant bars on the singer's stave during a ritornello to insert an obbligato treble line. Both practices occur in Gasparini's *Cantate da camera a voce sola*, Op. 1 (1695), a collection with which Vivaldi presumably became acquainted during the years (1703–13) when the two men served side by side at the Pietà. Vivaldi does not introduce obbligato writing casually, as do many other composers – there is either an extra obbligato instrument or there is not – but he constantly reveals his instrumental background through the memorability and high level of activity of his bass lines, especially during ritornellos.

In designing the ritornello, composers had two main options. The first, favoured in continuo arias, was to give the bass a theme, often emphatically 'bass-like' in character, which, although it might well paraphrase the opening of the first vocal period in harmonic respects, preserved its independent identity throughout. Such a theme, broken down into its component fragments, could be used in accompaniment to the voice – or it could be replaced by simpler, more neutral material. The second option, the more common choice for orchestrally accompanied arias, was to model the ritornello melody on that of the voice, making it a 'pre-echo' of the following vocal material. This could also be done, albeit with greater difficulty, in continuo arias. The problem there was that a 'treble' melody is often hard to harmonize satisfactorily if transferred to the bass of the texture. In fact, composers rarely replicated vocal phrases from start to finish when quoting them in the bass: they started similarly but at some point switched to the more jagged shapes, in fourths, fifths, and octaves, that characterize cadential progressions in Baroque bass parts.[56] When a ritornello was too close in design to the first vocal period, the risk of tedium easily arose. In a highly interesting but little-known critique of the contemporary (1758) opera by another Italian émigré in London, Vincenzo Martinelli, we read:

---

[56] The subject of ritornello design is discussed at length in Michael Talbot, 'The Function and Character of the Instrumental Ritornello in the Solo Cantatas of Tomaso Albinoni (1671–1751)', *Quaderni della Civica Scuola di Musica* [Milan], xix–xx (1990), 77–90.

The reason why – speaking of arias, which are the singer's main business – even the most beautiful musical inventions often bore the listener, is the ritornellos, which pursue the singer from start to finish, their excessive length, their excessive repetition, and, finally, those blessed cadenzas in which singers [Martinelli uses the word *musici*, which refers principally to castratos] sometimes vomit forth in one gush the entire wealth of their art.[57]

Between the opening ritornello and the first vocal period it became fashionable during the approximate period 1690 to 1715 to insert an extra period, termed the *Devise* period. 'Devise' is the German word for heraldic device, and it was used by Hugo Riemann to denote a brief motto opening stated separately and leading to a cadence in the home key via an instrumental continuation. In most cases, the motto was identical with the opening phrase of the first vocal period, and the continuation with the closing phrase or phrases of the opening ritornello. This 'false start' formula, which can easily become wearisome if used routinely, lost currency swiftly during the 1710s. After 1720 only Albinoni, among composers active in Italy, remained attached to it. Vivaldi, apparently, never favoured it: it rarely appears even in his earliest surviving vocal compositions, such as the *Stabat Mater*, RV 621, of 1712 or the operas *Ottone in villa* (1713) and *Orlando finto pazzo* (1714).[58]

Between the first and second vocal periods there is nearly always a link-passage that allows the singer to catch his or her breath. In 'accompanied' arias this can amount to an intermediate ritornello, while in continuo cantatas it rarely extends beyond a phrase or two.

The second vocal period is commonly longer than the first. Not infrequently, it continues beyond the first cadence reaffirming the tonic with a passage leading to a second, even more decisive, cadence. This tailpiece often resembles the *petite reprise* used in some instrumental music and may be identical to the closing portion of the main, first section of the period. The most elaborate *fioritura* of the whole aria is likely to be contained in this passage.

In lighter arias around 1700, the first, and sometimes the second, vocal period may be repeated. This borrowing from binary form – a throwback to the early cantata (albeit now using the 'A' text alone rather than the complete text) – was usually coupled with the adoption of a dance metre, or at least a dance lilt. Venetian composers, who were known for their propensity to strait-jacket operatic arias into dance rhythms, participated gladly in this fashion, and the cantatas of Vinaccesi and Albinoni contain many such examples. This feature quite soon

---

57  Vincenzo Martinelli, *Lettere familiari e critiche*, London: Nourse, 1758, pp. 372–3: 'La ragione perché anco le cose più belle della Musica, parlando delle arie, che fanno il maggior negozio del canto, tediano spesse volte l'udienza, sono le zinfonie, che perseguitano il Cantore dal principio fino alla fine, l'esser troppo lunghe, le tante ripetizioni, e poi le benedette cadenze, nelle quali vomitano i Musici talvolta tutto in un colpo l'intero capitale dell'arte loro'. The significance of the word *perseguitano* ('pursue') is ambiguous: it could refer either to the common practice of using one of the violin parts to play *colla parte*, or to the echoing and pre-echoing of the voice by the orchestra. In an ensuing remark, Martinelli regrets that the orchestra has been used, since Pistocchi's time, to accompany the voice instead of just sounding alternately with it.

58  One example occurs in 'L'alma del forte' (*Orlando finto pazzo*, II.13), which has no introductory ritornello (the singer, Grifone, interrupts Ersilla).

petered out. The known examples by Vivaldi come, with one exception (RV 681), not from his cantatas but from his early operas and the motets of the same period – thus from the time just before he started to write cantatas in bulk.

The third vocal period, which constitutes the entire 'B' section, gives the composer his first opportunity for modal contrast. In major-key arias, the minor keys most likely to be visited are the submediant and mediant, often in that order. There are usually two cadences in different keys, the second bringing to a close the kind of tailpiece discussed just now in connection with the second vocal period. Such tailpieces are often set off from the preceding material – again, with the pragmatic object of providing a breathing space – by a short instrumental interpolation. The passage leading to the second cadence is sometimes long enough to accommodate the complete 'B' text, although this is rather exceptional.

Most often, the return from the final cadence of the 'B' section to the reprised 'A' section is direct, producing the effect of hiatus. This unmediated transition from, say, a mediant chord to a tonic chord can have the same powerful affective force as the equivalent progression at the junction of recitative and aria, discussed earlier. Just occasionally, one finds what, using the language of sonata-form analysis, would be described as a 'retransition', which steers the music smoothly back to the tonic before the 'A' section resumes. If the opening of a reprised 'A' section is modified in ways too complex to be shown with the familiar *segni*, the substituted bars may be written after the conventional thin-thin double barline ending the 'B' section. Late seventeenth-century cantatas often show great inventiveness in their reintroduction of the 'A' section – an inventiveness stimulated by the custom of writing out the reprise in full. Cantata composers of Vivaldi's time are more content to do the obvious, and Vivaldi himself is a prime case. Here, once again, one suspects pressure from singers – and perhaps also a production-line mentality inherited from operatic composition.

As well as being the 'Age of Thorough Bass', the Baroque period was the 'Age of Ground Bass'. Indeed, the use of this device, both learned and popular in its associations, permeates aria composition in the cantata genre, although it tended over time to become more sporadic and more dilute. In very early arias, free-standing or within cantatas, ground bass (*basso ostinato*) most often appears in its pure form, in which all repetitions occur at the same pitch.[59] The tonal plan of arias in the mature cantata did not allow for such stasis, so one finds movements in which the bass theme migrates from key to key, following the course of the modulations: a procedure very familiar from Purcell's songs. It is not always possible or desirable simply to repeat the theme unaltered at various pitch-levels. The solution is to employ, where necessary, 'altered' statements, in which the theme starts normally but then diverges, or even to insert on occasion a 'free' section that plays with fragments of the theme but does not state it in literal form. How sophisticated such a design can become is illustrated by a wonderful aria by Vinaccesi, 'Che pena è il vivere', from his cantata *Belve, se mai provaste*, which

---

[59] One encounters as well the 'strophic bass', in which the note-values of the bass theme vary from repetition to repetition.

Table 2.2  Treatment of the ostinato bass theme in Benedetto Vinaccesi's aria 'Che pena è il vivere' from *Belve, se mai provaste*

| Bars | Section | Form of theme | Key |
|------|---------|---------------|-----|
| $1_1$–$4_1$ | opening ritornello | basic | c |
| $5_2$–$8_2$ | *Devise* period | basic | c |
| $9_2$–$12_2$ | first vocal period (1) | basic | c |
| $13_2$–$16_2$ | first vocal period (2) | basic | g |
| $17_1$–$19_1$ | second vocal period (1) | derived motives | g, f, E♭, c |
| $19_2$–$22_2$ | second vocal period (2) | basic | c |
| $23_1$–$24_1$ | second vocal period, tailpiece | second half | c |
| $24_2$–$27_2$ | closing ritornello | basic | E♭ |
| $28_2$–$31_1$ | third vocal period (1) | basic | E♭ |
| $32_2$–$34_2$ | third vocal period (2) | derived motives | c, g |
| $35_2$–$38_2$ | third vocal period (3) | basic | g |
| $40_2$ → | section 'A' minus closing ritornello | | |

dates from c.1700.[60] Its plan is shown in Table 2.2. Vinaccesi very artfully uses rests in the bass part, while the vocal phrases continue normally above, in order to articulate repetitions of the theme and at the same time to smooth out harmonic transitions that might otherwise have been too abrupt. After about 1710 such parading of a *basso ostinato* dwindles to almost nothing in cantatas.

Vivaldi introduces the device occasionally in the arias of his earlier operas – 'D'un bel viso in un momento' in *L'incoronazione di Dario* (I.5) is a good example – but he is far less interested in it in his vocal music than in his concertos (especially his 'ripieno' and 'chamber' concertos), where it often derives from the chaconne.[61] Fundamentally, Vivaldi is a 'bottom up' composer: he forms themes from motives, not motives from themes. This is why his themes and theme-complexes are so protean, while his germinal motives remain so constant. His music is saturated by the ostinato principle, even where actual ostinato themes are missing. The contrast with Albinoni could not be greater: Albinoni is a 'top down' composer for whom the complete theme, often complex in its motivic make-up, is primary. One is not surprised, therefore, to find that ostinato basses are quite common in the arias of Albinoni's cantatas.[62]

Our last general reflection on the form of late Baroque cantatas concerns their overall tonal shape. In ARA cantatas, the placement of both outer movements, the

---

[60]  Paris, Bibliothèque du Conservatoire National Supérieur, Rés. 1451, ff. 94v–101v. This cantata, edited by the present writer, is available from Edition HH (Launton).

[61]  'D'un bel viso' itself employs a typical 'chaconne' progression, albeit transmuted into 2/4 metre.

[62]  The fifth and twelfth cantatas of Albinoni's Op. 4 (1702) each contain one aria over a modulating *basso ostinato*.

arias, in the home key guarantees a symmetrical, well-balanced tonal shape. Indeed, the central recitative has to work hard to establish any tonal variety at all. In RARA cantatas, however, imbalance is the rule. The home key may have been established in the opening recitative by no more than a single phrase, even a single chord. When the first aria arrives, its key is liable to be taken by the listener – usually incorrectly – as the primary tonality of the work. The contrast with the otherwise so similar four-movement (SFSF) sonata is striking, since the latter likes to place both fast movements, in addition to the opening slow movement, in the home key.

For Vivaldi – perhaps because he was steeped in the tradition of the chamber sonata, in which all the movements are commonly in the same key – tonal unity was always more important than tonal variety. More than any other composer of his generation, he was prepared to place the internal slow movements of concertos and sonatas not in the relative key (the quasi-automatic choice for Bach and Handel), nor in a remote key (like Valentini and Locatelli), but in the tonic key itself, sometimes with modal variation. Nor was he always greatly concerned to compensate for tonal sameness with metrical variety: in the concerto for two flutes RV 533 all three movements are in C major and in common time. Surprisingly many instances of this homotonality and homometricality, presumably inspired by his practice in instrumental music, occur in the arias of Vivaldi's cantatas. Timms notes that four of his RARA cantatas (RV 652, 676, 678, and 686) place the first aria in the home key, while as many as twenty cantatas overall employ the same metre for both arias.[63] This does not mean, of course, that Vivaldi was indifferent to the need for contrast: it means, simply, that he often sought it by other means.

In recitatives and arias alike, the presence of words imposes special tasks on the composer. The first is to reflect the natural accentuation of words, as they would be declaimed in spoken poetry. 'Reflect' is not the same as 'reproduce': syllables become unnaturally elongated or compressed in any style that employs a great variety of note-values and admits melisma. Italian is more forgiving of deviations from standard accentuation than German or English, and therefore more pliable in this respect. Many are the instances where, standing at the head of a line or hemistich, a normally unaccented particle such as 'di' or 'a' is placed on a strong beat. There is little variation between Italian composers in the tolerance that they show for deviations from natural accentuation, and surprisingly little contemporary criticism concerned with word-setting, the abuse of extended melisma excepted.

All Italian composers subscribed to the idea of expressing the general mood of a text, the *affetto*, in the general features of a movement. The choice of tempo, metre, rhythm, mode, and key set the initial parameters, which were then reinforced by the style of writing selected for the voice and its accompaniment. However, composers were equally keen to illustrate individual words and phrases, especially the ones with special expressive force that are called 'keywords' in this study. Sometimes, the two principles come into collision: the

---

63 Timms, 'The Dramatic in Vivaldi's Cantatas', p. 119.

keyword contradicts, rather than supports, the overall *affetto*. I have quoted else-where the case of an aria in Albinoni's opera *Statira* (1726) in which the heroine's words expressing fortitude in the face of a threat of imprisonment ('Non creder, no, che sia ld'orrore all'alma mia') are accompanied by 'horrific' diminished seventh chords.[64] The problem is that keywords cannot be illustrated as negatives, only as positives.

As a composer with a background in instrumental music and a tendency to develop musical material autonomously, without reference to specific features of the sung text, Vivaldi did not always capture the *affetto* of a text impeccably, although on balance he was more successful in this than most around him. Where he excelled, however, was in keyword illustration. Unlike many contemporaries, he nearly always avoided using extended melisma on neutral, inexpressive words and instead homed in on the keywords, which he highlighted not only through melisma but also by inventive use of the instruments – of which he, naturally, was a past master.[65] We will see this mastery demonstrated over and over again in his cantatas.

---

[64] Talbot, *Tomaso Albinoni: the Venetian Composer and his World*, Oxford, Clarendon Press, 1990, p. 240.

[65] Vivaldi's use of melisma in *La costanza trionfante degl'amori e de gl'odii* (1716) is compared favourably with that of Lotti and Porta in Faun Tanenbaum Tiedge and Michael Talbot, 'The Berkeley Castle Manuscript: Arias and Cantatas by Vivaldi and his Italian Contemporaries', *Studi vivaldiani*, iii (2003), 33–86. Francesco Degrada expresses the same contrast between Vivaldi the setter of texts and Vivaldi the illustrator of individual words when he writes ('Note filologiche', 359): 'È indubbio che in Vivaldi c'è una grande attenzione per la parola come portatrice di affetto, ma altresì una relativa indifferenza ai valori specificamente stilistici dei testi da lui musicati' ('It is undeniable that Vivaldi is very attentive to the word as bearer of an *affetto*, but at the same time he shows a relative indifference towards the specific stylistic characteristics of the texts that he set').

# CHAPTER THREE

# Vivaldi and the Voice

## The Composer and the Text

Whether or not he had been much exposed to vocal music previously, Vivaldi became immersed in it from his teenage years onwards. He trained as a priest from 1693 to 1703, and this experience must have left him with a thorough knowledge of both *canto fermo* (plainsong) and *canto figurato* (figural music – the catch-all term for composed sacred vocal music). His work as a jobbing violinist alongside his father, Giovanni Battista Vivaldi (c.1655–1736), must have introduced him to countless sacred and operatic works; his first known public appearance as a violinist was at Christmas 1696, when he was engaged as a supernumerary player at the ducal church of S. Marco.[1] Giovanni Battista, if he is identical with the Giambattista Rossi who composed a short dramatic work, *La fedeltà sfortunata*, in 1688, may even have possessed a composer's under-standing of vocal music himself.[2] It cannot be stressed enough that until the 1710s – perhaps, more exactly, until the publication of Antonio's *L'estro armonico* concertos in 1711 – Giovanni Battista was the 'senior partner' of the two in status as well as in age. He must have been a massive formative influence. His loyalty to Antonio's interests – with which, of course, his own and those of the whole Vivaldi family were bound up – caused him later to serve his son almost until his death (which occurred not many years before Antonio's own) as a diligent and reliable copyist, and perhaps also as an accompanist and partner in performances.

A republican polity without a court in the accepted sense, Venice lacked a focal point for the cultivation of the cantata. But it possessed many other venues: the homes of patricians (such as Antonio Ottoboni) who had literary aspirations or musical inclinations; the residences of foreign ambassadors, who, forbidden by law to socialize with the Venetian nobility, made their own entertainment in private; the salons of leading singers. A good description of such a salon is provided in the biography of Johann David Heinichen (1683–1729) that appears in Johann Adam Hiller's *Lebensbeschreibungen berühmter Musikgelehrten und Tonkünstler neuerer Zeit*, a series of biographies of leading musicians, mainly

---

[1] For details, see Gastone Vio, 'Antonio Vivaldi violinista in San Marco?', *Informazioni e studi vivaldiani*, ii (1981), 51–9.

[2] 'Rossi' or 'Rosso' – a reference to red hair-colour – was a sobriquet frequently used in place of their real surname for the two Vivaldis, father and son.

German, which were in part based on information supplied by the subjects themselves. The relevant episode runs:

> Shortly after this time [1713], Heinichen had occasion to make the acquaintance of a fine singer, Angioletta, who had been raised in the Venetian *ospedale* of the Incurabili but had married a rich merchant [named Bianchi]. She took a liking to Heinichen's cantatas, some composed with an obbligato part for the harpsichord, which she played very well herself. The husband of this singer had the task of paying allowances for his needs to the crown prince of Saxony-Poland, the future elector of Saxony and king of Poland [Friedrich] August II, who was then staying in Venice. The prince sometimes came to his house, where Signora Angioletta often had the opportunity to sing and play to him. Not only did she sing some of Heinichen's cantatas, which the prince liked very much, and inform him that their composer was a Saxon by birth: her husband also laid on a grand *festa* in his own house to mark the prince's birthday [17 October 1716], for which Heinichen had to compose a serenata in great secrecy [. . .][3]

One must assume that for occasions such as these Vivaldi gained opportunities to play the violin (and also the cello?) for cantatas, if not also to compose some of his own. Documentary evidence is lacking, however. From Remo Giazotto we have a report that Vivaldi, together with the singers Giovanni Paita and Santa Marchesini, performed in 1705 for the French ambassador, Henri de Pomponne, at a soirée held for the benefit of the Capuchin convent of S. Girolamo, which had suffered fire damage.[4] But the existence of the document that he cites has never been proven.

Vivaldi presumably learned something about cantata composition from his close contact with Francesco Gasparini, who, as *Maestro di coro* of the Ospedale della Pietà, a post to which he was appointed in 1701, recommended him for the post of *Maestro di violino* in 1703 and apparently worked harmoniously with him until his own departure in 1713. Gasparini, as we saw, was a specialist in cantata composition and in accompaniment at the keyboard. It is uncertain whether the *figlie di coro* of the Pietà (the female foundlings who constituted its choir and orchestra) learned or performed cantatas. There was certainly a large music salon

---

[3] Johann Adam Hiller, *Lebensbeschreibungen berühmter Musikgelehrten und Tonkünstler neuerer Zeit*, Leipzig: Dykische Buchhandlung, 1784, pp. 136–7: 'Bald hernach bekam Heinichen Gelegenheit, mit einer braven Sängerin, welche in dem venezianischen Hospitale *agli Incurabili* erzogen, jetzt aber an einen reichen Kaufmann verheyrathet war, und mit ihrem Vornahmen *Angioletta* hieß, bekannt zu werden. Diese fand an Heinichens Cantaten Geschmack, deren einige mit dem concertirenden Klaviere, welches sie selbst sehr gut spielte, gesetzt waren. Der Mann dieser Sängerin hatte an den damals in Venedig sich aufhaltenden königlichen Churprinzen, nachherigen König von Polen und Churfürsten von Sachsen, August II, die benöthigten Gelder auszuzahlen. Der Prinz kam bisweilen in sein Haus, und dabey hatte Signora Angioletta oft Gelegenheit vor ihm zu singen und zu spielen. Sie sang nicht nur etliche von Heinichens gedachten Cantaten, welche dem Prinzen sehr gefielen, und machte dabey demselben bekannt, daß der Verfasser der Cantaten ein geborner Sachse sey: sondern ihr Mann gab auch dem Prinzen, an desselben Geburtstage, in seinem Hause ein großes Fest, wozu Heinichen in aller Stille eine Serenade hatte componiren müssen [. . .]'.

[4] Remo Giazotto, *Antonio Vivaldi*, Turin: ERI, 1973, p. 62.

next to the governors' board room that would have served as the ideal venue for the performance of such works before an audience. Moreover, several of the older *figlie* possessed keyboard instruments of their own – we know this from dowry lists – and would therefore have been quite capable of giving self-accompanied performances in their own rooms. The Pietà could scarcely have objected on principle to music dealing with amorous or pagan subjects, when it was prepared to honour eminent visitors with serenatas from exactly the same stable.[5]

Even if Vivaldi had little occasion to write chamber cantatas before his move to Mantua in 1718, he gained considerable practical experience of writing in all the vocal forms cultivated in the genre. He was composing arias and recitatives by no later than 1708, the date of the lost serenata *Le gare del dovere*, RV 688.[6] It is a great shame that Vivaldi's private archive as preserved in Turin contains no manuscripts of his music datable to before 1712, the year of the *Stabat Mater*, RV 621. It may be that prior to that time he did not trouble to retain archival copies of his music, or perhaps some disaster such as fire or loss in transit caused his 'first' archive to disappear. After 1713, when Vivaldi composed the first of a long stream of operas, *Ottone in villa*, and succeeded Gasparini as main purveyor of new sacred vocal compositions to the Pietà, his surviving vocal compositions, both sacred and secular, become plentiful. Among the operas of the period up to 1718 we possess in complete or near-complete form *Orlando finto pazzo* (1714, autumn), *Arsilda, regina di Ponto* (1716, autumn), *L'incoronazione di Dario* (1717, carnival) and *Armida al campo d'Egitto* (1718, carnival), while substantial numbers of arias from *La costanza trionfante degli amori e de gl'odii* (1716, carnival) and *Tieteberga* (1717, autumn) are extant. Then we have the oratorio *Juditha triumphans* of 1716. Among the sacred works for solo voice there are, in addition to the *Stabat Mater* written for the Chiesa della Pace in Brescia, two settings of psalms (the *Laudate pueri Dominum* RV 600 and the *Nisi Dominus* RV 608), five motets (RV 624, 625, 630, 633, and probably RV 628) and five *introduzioni* (RV 635, 638, 639, 641, and 642). Most similar to cantatas are the motets, which could be described as ARA cantatas on sacred Latin texts concluding with an 'Alleluia' that resembles a concerto movement, with the voice as soloist. (The addition of the 'Alleluia' makes a vital difference, however, since it enables the second aria to be in a key other than the tonic.) The *introduzioni*, prefaces to longer works on liturgical texts (*Gloria*, *Dixit Dominus*, etc.), resemble motets except in having no 'Alleluia' and sometimes departing from the ARA plan. Finally, there are the *concertato* works, such as the *Gloria* RV 589, which contain individual movements for solo voice.

In his very earliest known vocal works, Vivaldi betrays his inexperience by the sometimes rather chaotic delivery of the text, of which fragments appear in

---

5   Examples are Giovanni Porta's *Il ritratto dell'eroe* (1726: in honour of Pietro Ottoboni), Vivaldi's *Il Mopso* (c.1716: in honour of Duke Ferdinand Maria of Bavaria) and Gennaro D'Alessandro's *Il coro delle Muse* (1740: in honour of Friedrich Christian, prince of Saxony-Poland).

6   On Vivaldi's serenatas, see Michael Talbot, 'Vivaldi's Serenatas: Long Cantatas or Short Operas?', in Lorenzo Bianconi and Giovanni Morelli (eds), *Antonio Vivaldi. Teatro musicale, cultura e società*, pp. 67–96.

seemingly random order. The words seem to be there to 'clothe' the notes, not the other way round. In addition, Vivaldi, in the liturgical works, makes a habit of troping: interpolating portions of text taken from elsewhere. A striking instance occurs in the penultimate movement of the psalm *Laudate pueri Dominum*, RV 600, which dates from around 1715. Like most movements in psalm settings, this is a 'church aria' – a movement for solo voice structured like the 'A' section of a *da capo* aria.[7] The words that are supposed to be set are those of the second verse of the Lesser Doxology: 'Sicut erat in principio, et nunc, et semper, et in saecula saeculorum. Amen'. What emerges instead is the following mélange:

> *Laudate pueri, laudate Dominum.* Sicut erat in principio, et nunc, et nunc, et semper, et semper, et in saecula saeculorum. Amen. *A solis ortu usque ad occasum. Laudabile nomen Domini*, et nunc, et nunc, et semper. *Laudabile nomen Domini*, et nunc, et semper, et in saecula saeculorum. Amen. *Sit nomen, nomen Domini, sit benedictum, sit benedictum*, et nunc, et nunc, et semper, et in saecula, in saecula saeculorum. Amen. *Laudate nomen Domini, laudate nomen Domini.*

The italicized words are reprised, none too tidily, from vv. 1–3 of the psalm, which provide the text for movements I–III. Vivaldi is of course responding in the traditional punning way to the phrase 'Sicut erat in principio' ('Thus it was in the beginning') by bringing back the material of the first movement, and in that way rounding off the music in a satisfying way. Completely anomalous, however, is the reintroduction of actual text from 'the beginning' (and in fact from much further into the psalm than the beginning). No profound theological purpose informs Vivaldi's tropes: he is no Bach making a subtle connection or communing privately with God. Their spirit is casual, almost playful.

As with the very first works that Handel composed in Italy, it is difficult to know what is the boldness of youth, what is ignorance of convention, and what is sheer sloppiness. At all events, Vivaldi slowly civilized and regularized his text-setting as time went on. Some questionable features, such as the inversion of phrases on their repetition, never completely disappeared. But peccadillos of this kind abound among Italian composers generally.

Around the middle of the 1720s Vivaldi, like all Venetian composers, found it necessary to adjust his musical style to conform to the new fashion introduced by a group of Naples-trained composers, among whom Leo, Vinci, and especially Porpora were prominent. The first sign of the 'new wave' was the production of Leo's *Timocrate* at the Teatro S. Angelo in 1723. By 1725 Neapolitan composers and Neapolitan style ruled the roost in Venice.[8] The main novelties of this Neapolitan style are the following:

---

7    Since psalm texts and other liturgical texts are not designed for textual reprises, the full ABA form is inappropriate.

8    On the impact of Neapolitan composers on Venice, see Reinhard Strohm, 'The Neapolitans in Venice', in Iain Fenlon and Tim Carter (eds), *Con che soavità: Studies in Italian Opera, Song and Dance, 1580–1740*, Oxford: Clarendon Press, 1995, pp. 249–74. The same essay is reprinted in Reinhard Strohm, *Dramma per musica: Italian Opera Seria of the Eighteenth Century*, New Haven and London: Yale University Press, 1997, pp. 61–80.

1. The music is more treble-dominated than before. Basses are slower-moving (or use simple devices such as repeated notes to achieve animation) and highly functional. The harmonic rhythm is generally slower.
2. The melodic line (in the voice or the violins) is rhythmically very diverse and fussy in its details. The 'sewing-machine' style of the 1710s is abandoned.
3. Specific melodic and rhythmic devices are favoured: trills, appoggiaturas, Lombardic rhythms (inverted dotted groups), and triplet semiquavers are especially prominent.
4. Points are specifically created (the end of the second vocal section is a favourite spot) for the performance of vocal cadenzas (as opposed to the instrumental cadenzas that Vivaldi tried to introduce during the previous decade).
5. The phrase structure tends to four-squareness, and the word-setting is highly rational and disciplined.

Ironically, Vivaldi himself received credit for the introduction and popularization of Lombardic rhythms during his operatic sojourns in Rome of 1723 and 1724 from no less an authority than Quantz.[9] Otherwise, however, there was much for our composer to absorb. He quickly conformed to the new taste in all respects except the last. His 'bottom up', additive method of musical construction always preferred asymmetry to the straightforwardly quadratic phrase structures of the Neapolitans. Symptomatic is the fact that 'ternary' phrase-groups (A + B + C) abound in his music, the 'C' being either a foreshortened consequent to 'A' and 'B' combined or a restatement, usually varied, of 'B'. This idiosyncrasy remained with him till the end.

Recitatives are found regularly in his motets and *introduzioni*, and there are even some quasi-recitatives in the psalm settings and the hymn *Stabat Mater*, where Vivaldi, for the sake of brevity and variety, chose to employ an approximation to accompanied recitative. In some of these movements he achieves dramatic effects and touches of originality that place him among the best writers of recitative of his time. The motet *Nulla in mundo pax sincera*, RV 630, has a ravishing central recitative that uses arioso passages in a variety of tempi to underline keywords. *Corda* ('hearts') inspires a slow melisma over a diminished seventh; *fuggiamus* ('let us flee'), a rapid succession of semiquavers; *vitemus* ('let us evade'), a twisting and turning line; *ostentando* ('showing off'), a mock-pedantic passage of two-part imitation.[10] For dramatic realism there is little to equal the recitative in *Juditha triumphans* in which Vagaus, Holofernes' steward, discovers his master's headless trunk. Here, Vivaldi's pacing and choice of modulation and chord-change are masterly.[11] Sadly, but perhaps also predictably, there is also much recitative of a humdrum, unmemorable (and even, on occasion, clumsy) kind in Vivaldi's vocal music. In recitative he needed, perhaps, something particularly vivid to illustrate before he could rise to his full potential. This unevenness exists also in his cantatas.

---

9 Johann Joachim Quantz, *Versuch einer Anweisung die Flöte traversiere zu spielen*, Berlin: Voss, 1752, p. 309.
10 The complete recitative is transcribed in Talbot, *The Sacred Vocal Music*, pp. 293–4.
11 Transcribed ibid., pp. 439–41.

## *Vivaldi as Literary* Bricoleur

Where did composers obtain their cantata texts from? The question is less naïve than it appears. Whereas composers of madrigals or of nineteenth-century art songs could go straight to the poetry, usually available in published form, and make their choice, cantata composers relied almost exclusively on texts that had no independent existence outside the genre. When cantatas were produced for performance at *conversazioni* in a nobleman's residence, the poet or poets could be the nobleman himself, his secretary, the tutor to his children, his fellow academicians, or his guests. The poem would often be hurriedly composed and equally hurriedly set to music in a smooth, if hectic, line of transmission. Ottoboni's *Trattenimenti poetici* contain a piece by Angelo Farina entitled 'Duetto fatto per commando di due dame all'improviso a cavallo, messo subito in musica dal Signor Angelo Farina e cantato dalle medesime' ('Duet improvised on horseback at the behest of two ladies, set to music on the spot by Signor Angelo Farina, and sung by the same ladies').[12] The result of such collaboration was as much the property of the patron-poet as of the composer, and it is no surprise to see Antonio Ottoboni collecting the annual 'crop' of cantatas set to his texts in souvenir volumes.[13]

However, the texts for many cantatas were not set on a plate before the composer. They had to be borrowed or invented. This was especially true when composers presented cantatas on their own initiative to patrons, sold them to customers, or fulfilled commissions from persons who supplied no poetry for setting. Texts suitable for borrowing existed in great quantity in the manuscripts of cantatas by other composers. These were readily available, if through no other route, from the repertory of singers. Because of their itinerant existence, singers were the natural couriers of music in this period. Many surviving collections of cantatas for a single voice-type must be the relics of singers' own collections. Copying the text for a new cantata from that underlaid to the notes in an old cantata (rather than from a separate poem) was a recipe for minor errors arising from misreading, and it is therefore not surprising that the text in different settings of the same poem often diverges, apparently unintentionally, in trivial but revealing ways.

Four Vivaldi cantatas – RV 668, 670, 677, and 678 – exist in musically unrelated settings by other composers, and it is interesting to compare the readings of the underlaid text in the different versions. The direction of transmission frequently remains unclear, and is always complicated by the knowledge that extant sources for cantatas constitute only a fraction of the vast quantity that must once have existed. Nevertheless, a philological investigation into the text can sometimes help to date a cantata, or at least to place it within a particular orbit.

RV 668 is set to words that are a primitive version of the text by Metastasio first published, under the title *Amor timido*, by Quillau (Paris) in 1755. In its

---

[12]  Venice, Museo Civico Correr, Ms. Correr 466, pp. 577–8.
[13]  There are volumes for 1709 and 1710 in the British Library (Add. Mss. 34056 and 34057), and a volume for 1713 is on loan to the British Library as Loan 91.11.

revised version, the text acquired an introductory recitative (thus changing its form from ARA to RARA), and had its second recitative completely rewritten; the two arias were also polished up a little. Contemporary with Vivaldi, we find the following four settings of the original version, which must have been penned before Metastasio moved to Vienna in 1729:[14]

Leonardo Leo: Milan, Conservatorio di Musica 'Giuseppe Verdi', Fondo Noseda L 40–221.

Nicola Porpora: Hamburg, Staats- und Universitätsbibliothek 'Carl von Ossietzky', Musiksammlung, M A/833:2, pp. 320–3.

Giovanni Battista Pescetti: Hamburg, Staats- und Universitätsbibliothek 'Carl von Ossietzky', Musiksammlung, M A/833:2, pp. 384–9.

Diogenio Bigaglia: listed in Eitner, *Quellenlexicon*, 11, p. 28, as in the private collection of Hermann Springer (Berlin).

Metastasio's ties to Roman and Neapolitan composers were much stronger than those to Venetian ones, whom he had little opportunity to meet in person. A good working hypothesis would be that either Leo or Porpora, or both, set Metastasio's text in Naples, and that the three Venetians – Bigaglia, Vivaldi, and Pescetti – and possibly also one of the Neapolitans acquired it as a result of the inflow of Neapolitan musicians to Venice during the 1720s.[15] It is an interesting fact that the text set by Leo, Porpora, and Pescetti is concordant in every detail. Vivaldi's text is mostly concordant, but the deviations – for which one suspects that Vivaldi was personally responsible – are very revealing.[16]

In the first aria, there are no divergences between the text as transmitted by the four composers (Vivaldi, Leo, Porpora, Pescetti). Metastasio, however, later made two beneficial changes to the second and third lines of the first quatrain, altering 'Con tanto sospirar | forse ti vuoi lagnar' to 'Con tanto palpitar | so che ti vuoi lagnar'. In the following recitative, altered for Metastasio's published version, Vivaldi detaches himself from his three confrères. The two versions of the stanza are given below:

| *Leo, Porpora, Pescetti* | *Vivaldi* |
|---|---|
| Aure suavi e grate, | Aure suavi e grate, |
| garruli ruscelletti, ameni colli, | garruli ruscelletti, ameni colli, |
| voi *taciti* serbate | voi *placidi* serbate |
| d'un rispettoso amante il nobil foco. | d'un rispettoso amante il nobil foco. |

[14] I ignore for present purposes the much later settings of the poem by Hasse, Naumann, Gassmann, Paër, and Beethoven.

[15] The presence in the Hamburg manuscript of copies in the same hand of settings by both Porpora and the Venetian Pescetti of two cantatas, *T'intendo, sì, mio cor* and *Questo è il platano*, implies that the former's settings belong to one of his two periods of residence in Venice: either 1725–33, when he was *Maestro di coro* at the Incurabili, or 1741–47, when he held the same position first at the Pietà and then at the Ospedaletto.

[16] This interpretation – that Vivaldi modified an early version of Metastasio's text set in its 'pure' form by Leo – coincides with that advanced by Degrada in his previously cited article 'In margine all'edizione critica delle cantate di Antonio Vivaldi'. Degrada does not refer to the other contemporary settings, but their testimony only reinforces his original point.

| O se giammai per *gioco* | O se giammai per *poco* |
| a Filli dir la pena mia volete, | a Filli dir la pena mia volete, |
| il nome di chi l'ama almen tacete. | il nome di chi l'ama almen tacete. |

Since this is recitative, the opportunity to exploit the change of a single word for illustrative purposes is minimal. Leaving aside the rather remote possibility that two slightly different early versions of this text reached Venice separately, Vivaldi's changes seem petty in the extreme. The conversion of *taciti* ('silently') to *placidi* ('peacefully') is at least in keeping with what we know of Vivaldi's less than enthusiastic attitude towards Metastasio's verse.[17] This can be summed up as an indifference to the ethical and philosophical preoccupations of the poet and a dissatisfaction with the insufficiently vivid expression of his language. The change from *per gioco . . . volete* ('you wish in jest . . .') to *per poco . . . volete* ('you are on the point of wishing . . .') alters the meaning quite radically but has no impact on the music. One concludes – and many other cases will bear out this interpretation – that Vivaldi was a compulsive 'meddler', or *bricoleur*, where poetical texts were concerned. He always thought he knew best – and he certainly believed he knew what he, and the singers under his direction, needed in order to play to their strengths.

In the second aria text there is an interesting divergence between Vivaldi and the others where, for the first time, their reading coincides with Metastasio's final version and his does not: he has *s'incontri* ('if you meet'), whereas they have *se trovi* ('if you find'). This case suggests even more strongly than the others that Vivaldi made the alterations autonomously. Once again, the change is rather pointless.

The case of RV 670, *Alla caccia dell'alme e de' cori*, exemplifies perfectly how composers, or the poets who assisted them, modified texts to suit new requirements. Its text exists in three successive versions set, respectively, by Heinichen, Porpora, and Vivaldi; both the second and the third version radically amend the one immediately preceding it. One cannot be sure that there were not originally intermediate versions, today lost, but the line of transmission from Heinichen to Porpora, and then from Porpora to Vivaldi, is perfectly coherent as it stands. The three versions, laid out in such a way as to bring concordant lines level with one another as much as possible, run as follows, opposite (italics highlight changes).

Heinichen's setting presumably dates from his years in Venice around 1715;[18] it may even have been written for Angioletta Bianchi's *conversazioni*. In this, its original form, the poem is well proportioned. The text for the first aria consists of two quatrains, with the interesting complication that the two opening lines are *settenari* rather than *senari*. The central recitative has the substantial but not excessive length of ten lines. For the final aria, the poet provides two tercets of *ottonari*.

---

17  Francesco Degrada writes about Vivaldi's discomfort with Metastasio's dramas in 'Vivaldi e Metastasio: note in margine a una lettura dell'*Olimpiade*', in Francesco Degrada (ed.), *Vivaldi veneziano europeo*, Florence: Olschki, 1980, 155–81.

18  Dresden, SLUB, Mus. 2391-I-2, 27 (pp. 419–38).

| Heinichen | Porpora | Vivaldi |
|---|---|---|
| Alla caccia dell'alme, | Alla caccia dell'alme, | Alla caccia dell'alme, |
| | *e de' cori,* | e de' cori, |
| alla caccia de' cori, | | |
| la perfida Clori, | la *barbara* Clori, | la barbara Clori, |
| amanti, sen' va. | amanti, sen' va. | amanti, sen' va. |
| Già i lacci dispone, | Già i lacci dispone, | Già i lacci dispone, |
| le reti già stende; | le reti già stende; | le reti già stende; |
| al passo vi attende | al *varco* vi attende | al varco vi attende |
| l'ingrata beltà. | l'ingrata beltà. | *quell'empia* beltà. |
| | | |
| All'erta, all'erta, amanti, | All'erta, *amanti, all'erta,* | *Ma sia crudele o infida, oh Dio,* |
| da quel labro e da quel ciglio | *dal crin, dal sen, dagl'occhi* | *mi piace.* |
| ove stanno l'insidie, i strali e | ove stanno l'insidie, i strali e | *E sebben sia spietato,* |
| l'arco. | l'arco. | *da quel bel volto, o cor, tu sei* |
| Ma più ti guardi il Ciel da | | *legato.* |
| quel bel seno | | |
| ove hanno il trono i dispietati | | |
| amori. | | |
| E tu, cor mio, guardati ben da | E tu, cor mio, *la libertà, la vita* | |
| Clori, | | |
| | *salva se puoi, dico, se puoi, da* | |
| | *lei* | |
| che prigionier ti vuole. | *che sua preda* ti vuole *o vivo o* | |
| | *morto.* | |
| Guardati ben. Ma, oh Dio, non | *Salvati.* Oh Dio, non | |
| m'hai inteso, | m'hai inteso, | |
| povero incauto core? | povero incauto *cor? Tu* già sei | |
| | preso. | |
| E già, e già, sei preso. | | |
| | | |
| S'egli è ver, ah non sperar | *Preso sei, non sperar più* | Preso sei, *mio cor piagato,* |
| | | *non sperar,* non sperar più |
| di poter mai più spiegar | *dalla bella servitù* | dalla bella servitù |
| fuor de' lacci, o core, il volo. | *di poter spiegar il volo.* | di poter spiegar il volo. |
| Consolarti ben potrai | *Consolar bensì tu puoi* | Consolar bensì tu puoi |
| ché a provar i lacci suoi | ché a provar i lacci suoi | ché a *provare* i lacci suoi |
| non sei primo e non sei solo. | non sei primo e non sei solo. | non sei primo e non sei solo. |

It is noticeable that the original poem contains a certain amount of phrase-repetition for rhetorical effect (*alla caccia . . . alla caccia*; *all'erta, all'erta*; *e già, e già*). Such repetition lays a trap – like the huntress Clori of the poem – for the unwary purloiner of the text who copies from the underlaid words, since it risks confusion with the repetitions that composers introduce on their own initiative, sometimes even in recitatives. When Porpora came to use the text, probably in the mid-1720s, whoever revised it for him (or he may have made the adaptation himself) seems to have made heavy weather of these repetitions programmed into the literary text.[19] Lines 1–2 of the first aria are conflated into a single, ungainly *decasillabo* that makes little metrical sense in isolation; the word-order of the first line of the recitative is transposed; and its last two lines are reduced, none too happily, to a single *endecasillabo*. Two internal lines are

---

[19] London, Royal College of Music, MS 824, ff. 113–16. Concordances, variously for soprano and alto, exist in Bologna (Civico Museo Bibliografico Musicale), Hamburg (Staats- und Universitätsbibliothek 'Carl von Ossietzky'), Munich (Bayerische Staatsbibliothek), Naples (Conservatorio di Musica 'S. Pietro a Majella') and Washington (Library of Congress).

clipped from the recitative, and an extra line is inserted in a different place – an act of surgery that triggers much change in the surrounding lines. The recitative ends up slightly condensed, with eight lines. The first tercet of the second aria is comprehensively modified, the original second line (*di poter mai più spiegar*) contributing most of the material to the new third line (*di poter spiegar il volo*). The adapter links the new opening line of this aria to the last line of the recitative by opening with a chiasmic repetition of its last two words, *sei preso*, as *Preso sei*. Otherwise, there are incidental changes of words, such as the replacement of *passo* by *varco*.

Vivaldi accepts the text for the first aria more or less as bequeathed to him by Porpora, changing only the opening words of the last line. He replaces the central recitative by as minimal a text as it would have been possible to devise – one very probably of his own composition. Quadrio, the partisan of recitative, would have shaken his head knowingly. The recitative's third and last line omits the word *preso*, thereby sacrificing Porpora's textual link to the second aria. However, Vivaldi makes a link of a different kind by repeating the '-ato' rhyme in the first line of the aria. He wreaks havoc on its first tercet by inserting two extra half-lines (. . . *mio cor piagato,* | *non sperar* . . .) that turn it into a quatrain destructive of the stanza's symmetry. His evident purpose was to provide a rhyming companion for the second line, *dalla bella servitù*, since at the end of the first line he had replaced *più* by *piagato*. Vivaldi's intervention is both clever and amateurish: clever, because it knocks the text efficiently into the shape he wishes it to have; amateurish, because it is so poetically inept. Comparing Vivaldi's text with the one set by Heinichen, we witness a poetic degradation that has to be deplored, even if, in modern conditions, we are more exercised by the music than by the words.

Vivaldi's *Qual per ignoto calle*, RV 677, has a single known literary concordance, the text of an anonymous cantata included in a volume at the British Library containing cantatas by Arrigoni, D'Astorga, Bigaglia, Giovanni Bononcini, Gasparini, Hasse, Lotti, Mancini, and Alessandro Scarlatti.[20] An attempt to establish the composer's identity will be made in Chapter 6. For the present, all that needs to be said is that its text is practically identical with Vivaldi's, the differences being the presence of an apostrophizing 'o' before *Irene* in the first aria, *tanta doglia* instead of *tante pene* in the second recitative, and *folgori* instead of *turbini* in the second aria. The filiation of the two texts and the chronology of the two settings remain obscure.

Another cantata for Dresden, *All'ombra di sospetto*, exists in a setting attributed to Bigaglia in Naples.[21] Diogenio Bigaglia (c.1676–c.1745), a Benedictine who rose to become prior of the Venetian monastery of S. Giorgio Maggiore (today home to the Istituto Italiano Antonio Vivaldi), was a prolific composer of rather anaemic music, both sacred and secular. The continuo cantata was a genre in which he was especially active, and it can be assumed that he frequented some

---

[20]  London, British Library, Add. Ms. 14213, ff. 63–70.
[21]  Naples, Conservatorio di Musica 'S. Pietro a Majella', 33.4.88, ff. 17–24. I am grateful to Enrico Careri for having inspected and reported on this source.

of the same Venetian salons as Vivaldi. His text differs at several points from our composer's. Variant lines are listed below.

| line | Bigaglia | Vivaldi |
|---|---|---|
| 7 | ch'addolcisca *l'amar* con finti vezzi. | ch'addolcisca *il penar* con finti *vezzi*. |
| 12 | *che son fidi* e costanti, | *che fedeli* e costanti |
| 13 | *sono ingannati* da lusinghe accorte | *vengon delusi* da lusinghe accorte |
| 15 | Più *d'uno* così langue, | Più *d'ognun* così langue, |
| 19 | di *bellezza vezzosa* | di *vezzosa bellezza* |
| 22 | mai spera *egli d'aver*, sin ch'ingannato | mai *spera di goder*, sin ch'ingannato |
| 23 | viene amante schernito *e abbandonato*. | viene amante schernito *et ingannato*. |

As Francesco Degrada remarks in his edition of Vivaldi's cantata, the repetition of *ingannato* at the end of line 23 (the closing line of the second recitative) is certainly a mistake. This does not prove that Bigaglia's text, or one closely cognate with it, served Vivaldi as raw material. Vivaldi's copy text, minus that error, could in theory have been a primitive version of Bigaglia's poem. But the probability, taking into account the general picture, is that the deviations of Vivaldi's text are the result of his usual tinkering.

For the sake of completeness, it should be mentioned that a different setting exists of the spurious cantata *Ingrata Lidia, ha vinto il tuo rigor* (RV 673), attributed to Giovanni Bononcini.[22] There is also a second setting, by Francesco Bartolomeo Conti, of the text of *Prendea con man di latte*, RV 753, a similarly dubious work.[23]

Vivaldi's methods of obtaining or fashioning cantata texts also included the importation, collage style, of fragments taken from other sources. In two known instances, the cantatas RV 663 and RV 651/683 (these are two settings of the same text), the borrowed words come not from other cantatas but from opera librettos.

RV 651 and 683 introduce as the third and fourth lines of the first recitative the first half of the opening quatrain of Cosroe's aria 'Gelido in ogni vena' in Metastasio's *Siroe, re di Persia* (III.5), given its first outing in the setting by Vinci performed at Venice's premier theatre, the Teatro S. Giovanni Grisostomo, in early 1726.[24] Vivaldi's interest in this aria text, which invites the musical depiction of shivering, is shown by his appropriation of it for his own *Siroe*, performed in the following year in Reggio Emilia. In *Siroe* the 'iciness' arises not from freezing temperatures but from the situation of the character who sings the aria: Cosroe, king of Persia. He is in a state of horrified shock, having (so he believes) delivered his own son Siroe to execution for treason just before learning, in the previous scene, of his innocence:

---

[22] Copies in Berlin, Staatsbibliothek 'Preußischer Kulturbesitz', Mus. ms. 30074, pp. 270–77, and London, Guildhall Library, G. Mus. 449, no. 2.

[23] Sondershausen, Stadt- und Kreisbibliothek 'J. K. Wezel', Mus. B4:1.

[24] *Siroe* was the second opera of the season performed at that theatre. Approval for the granting of a licence to publish the libretto, an essential prerequisite for its staging, was given by the civil and ecclesiastical censors on 27 January 1726.

| Gelido in ogni vena | Icily in every vein |
|---|---|
| scorrer mi sento il sangue; | I feel my blood flowing; |
| l'ombra del figlio esangue | the shade of my dead son |
| m'ingombra di terror. | fills me with terror. |

Since their metre is *settenario*, these lines are compatible also with recitative. Needless to say, the situation depicted by Vivaldi in the cantata deals with a less serious matter: the rejection by Clori of her unnamed lover:

| Amor, hai vinto, hai vinto. Ecco il mio seno | Love, you have won. Behold my breast |
|---|---|
| da' tuoi strali trafitto. Or chi sostiene | pierced by your arrows. Now who will sustain |
| l'alma mia dal dolore abbandonata? | my soul, given up to grief? |
| *Gelido in ogni vena* | *Icily in every vein* |
| *scorrer mi sento il sangue,* | *I feel my blood flowing,* |
| e sol mi serba in vita affanno e pena. | and only sorrow and dread keep me alive. |
| Mi palpita nel petto | My heart beats in my chest |
| con nuove scosse il core. | with new thumps. |
| Clori, crudel, e quanto | Cruel Clori, how long |
| ha da durar quest'aspro tuo rigor?[25] | does your bitter rejection have to last? |

The iciness is at a pinch consonant with the lover's dread (*affanno*). In its context, the borrowing arguably adds no significant new incongruity to what is already present. One wonders whether Vivaldi wished the grafted snippet of text to be apparent to his audience as a deliberate intertextual reference. The probability is that he did not. In his musical borrowings, at any rate, our composer was always furtive.

For the aria opening *Scherza di fronda in fronda*, RV 663, Vivaldi transported without alteration the text (by Domenico Lalli) of an aria that he had used in 1721 in the opera *Filippo, re di Macedonia* (III.3).[26] (He also adapted the original music, as Chapter 5 will show.) This is a typical 'comparison' (or 'simile') aria in which a feature of the natural world – in this case, a bird fearful of becoming ensnared in a trap – is evoked to illustrate the human condition:

| Scherza di fronda in fronda | The little bird hops gaily but warily |
|---|---|
| incerto l'augelletto; | from leaf to leaf; |
| or corre su la sponda | now it runs on the bank |
| del chiaro ruscelletto. | of the clear-running brooklet. |
| Ma palpitante il core | But its heart always flutters |
| ha sempre per timore | from fear |
| perché fra duri lacci | that its foot may be caught |
| non resti il pie' ristretto. | in a cruel snare. |

Ingeniously and aptly, Vivaldi applies this simile in the cantata to the *topos* of the timid lover, Eurillo, who is wary of falling victim to one of the many nymphs lying in wait for him. In general, aria texts in operas and cantatas differ in subject

---

[25] The transcription is from RV 683 (RV 651 has a few variant readings).

[26] This opera, with which the carnival season opened at the Teatro S. Angelo, was the joint composition of Giuseppe Boniventi, who wrote the first two acts, and Vivaldi, who provided the third act.

and tone. Here, however, there is a happy coincidence of situation for Vivaldi to exploit.

The authorship and provenance of the rest of this cantata's text are hard to establish. Perhaps the borrowed aria was a replacement for another text that originally stood in the same position, in which case the author was probably someone other than the composer. Perhaps the poet was Lalli himself, delving back into his own works for the first aria. I suspect, however, that Vivaldi cobbled everything together himself. Doubtless, his cantata texts contain many similar borrowings that have yet to come to light.

By far the most celebrated instance of Vivaldi's *bricolage* in any genre is his four attempts to get both the music and the words right in the opening recitative of *Nel partir da te, mio caro*, RV 661.[27] The fullest and most penetrating discussion appears in Degrada's essay on Vivaldi's cantatas,[28] but there are useful earlier accounts from Dunham and Ryom.[29] Both Dunham and Degrada provide complete transcriptions of the three aborted openings and one completed movement.

Since RV 661 belongs to the group of cantatas composed for the court in Mantua, one would assume that Vivaldi was supplied by someone else with a text to set. Degrada reconstructs its first three lines convincingly as:

| | |
|---|---|
| Parto, sì parto, [addio, | I am going, yes, I am going, farewell, |
| lungi da te, mio bene, | far away from you, my love, |
| ma in pegno del mio amor ti lascio | but I leave you my heart as a pledge of |
| il core.] | my love. |

The bracketed portion is conjectural, since the underlaid text of the first version proceeds no further than the third word, and that of the second version no further than the second word. Both versions continue the vocal part for a few phrases with untexted notes, and both have blank bass staves. Vivaldi must have had a preconceived idea of how the text would continue under the notes already written and what the bass harmonies would be, but, following his usual custom, he began by sketching out the notes of the principal melodic part.

Why did he give up and start again? Perhaps the reason for breaking off the first draft was simply that the stress pattern of the opening words was incompatible with the proposed notes. *Sì* falls on the second beat and bears a stronger accent than the 'par-' that follows as a quaver between the beats – an obvious solecism. Unfortunately, the second draft offered little improvement, since it began with a pair of dactyls (quaver plus two semiquavers), which are almost comic in their repetitive effect and moreover introduce an undesirable dialoepha between the third and fourth words.

The third version, five bars of which were notated completely, made some progress, continuing the three lines quoted above with two more:

---

27  Foà 28, ff. 26–9.
28  Degrada, 'Note filologiche in margine all'edizione critica', pp. 371–7.
29  Dunham, 'The Secular Cantatas of Antonio Vivaldi', pp. 63–5; Ryom, *Les manuscrits de Vivaldi*, pp. 23–4.

| | |
|---|---|
| Gradiscilo, ti priego, | Receive it, I beg you, |
| poiché un dì lo gradisti. | since once you received it. |

But Vivaldi committed an error. He omitted the word *addio* at the end of the first line, and so reduced an orthodox *settenario* to a *quinario*. Degrada's transcription accepts the *quinario* as the intended first line, and his attempted explanation for Vivaldi's abandonment of the third draft is more elaborate than the one I have given here. It is true that in ordinary Italian poetry *quinario* metre can be a partner to *settenario* and *endecasillabo*, but this association does not apply, in my experience, to eighteenth-century recitative verse.

At this point a crisis occurred. Rather than go back and work on the same jinxed text once again, Vivaldi set – this time with his customary fluency – a paraphrase of it. The definitive stanza runs:

| | |
|---|---|
| Parto, mio ben, da te, io parto, addio; | I am leaving you, my love, I am leaving, farewell; |
| ma il cor qui resta in ossequioso pegno. | but my heart is staying here as a humble pledge. |
| Di gradirlo ti priego, | I beg you to receive it, |
| e all'afflitto mio core | and to reward my wounded heart |
| donali in premio almeno un dolce amore. | with at least a sweet affection. |

Who wrote the second version of the text, which improves marginally on the abysmal literary quality of the first? Most commentators have assumed that it was Vivaldi himself. He certainly claimed authorship of the sonnets on *Le quattro stagioni*, and on that evidence would easily have been capable of such a task.[30] Degrada is sceptical, believing that the replacement text was provided by someone else.[31] Although Degrada does not actually claim this, the reviser could well have been the original poet. We sense from Goldoni's report of his encounter with Vivaldi in 1735 (in connection with the revision of Zeno's libretto for *Griselda*) that the composer was quite capable of throwing back in a poet's face anything with which he was dissatisfied. So, ironically, this may have been one instance where his meddling took the form not of direct intervention but of persuading a collaborator to have a second try.

Among cantata composers who were also poets Vivaldi occupies the humblest imaginable place. Quantz tells us that Alessandro Scarlatti penned the texts for a great number of his own cantatas,[32] and the shining example of Benedetto Marcello naturally leaps to mind. Vivaldi did not have the educational background or breadth of culture – nor, perhaps, the patience and inclination – to take his ventures into the realm of poetry beyond the point where their products were merely serviceable. For all his success at the peak of his career, his mentality never fundamentally outgrew that of a jobbing musician. However, he had the good sense to choose – or, when he could not choose, to adapt – texts that showed off his musical talents to their best advantage.

---

[30]  The copies in Manchester of these concertos, prepared in the composer's *atelier*, describe the sonnets as his *composizioni* (in the early eighteenth century *composizione* more often denotes a literary than a musical composition).

[31]  Degrada, 'Note filologiche in margine all'edizione critica', pp. 375–7.

[32]  'Herrn Johann Joachim Quantzens Lebenslauf, von ihm selbst entworfen', in Friedrich Wilhelm Marpurg, *Historisch-kritische Beyträge zur Aufnahme der Musik*, vol. 1, Berlin: Schütz, 1755, pp. 197–250, at p. 229.

## The Composer and the Singer

Composers and singers were natural partners. In the opera house either party could ride to fame – or slide into infamy – on the back of the other. Singers had the upper hand in this relationship. In any human chain of transmission, such as that running from the librettist via the composer to the singer, the last 'link' holds the greatest power, since he or she is at the interface with the public, where the process ends. It was therefore not the composer's job to 'push' a singer into unfamiliar regions for the sake of art or his own reputation. His task was to assess the singer's qualities (in terms of strength, compass, timbre, dramatic expression, etc.) and write music that gratified him or her, at the same time avoiding anything that might reveal weaknesses.

For a composer working for a single institution or in a single milieu, a perfectly customized music was the ideal. However, for composers whose 'client base' was diverse and sometimes unknowable in advance, excessive customization was a drawback, since it placed obstacles in the way of subsequent use by different performers in other locales. Vivaldi is the supreme example of a composer who liked to spread risk and acquire wider fame by serving simultaneously a multitude of patrons and clients all over Europe. How proudly he boasted, in his famous letter of 16 November 1737 to Guido Bentivoglio d'Aragona, of maintaining a correspondence with nine 'high princes' (*principi d'altezza*), all of whom, one presumes, were his customers. For the mature Vivaldi, therefore, customization was nearly always tempered by the anticipation of recycling.[33] For this reason, the choral parts written for female 'basses' at the Pietà, normally to be sung an octave above their notated pitch, were made to work equally well when sung without transposition by male voices, allowing the works containing them to pass successfully into the repertory of all-male church choirs and, much later on, of mixed choirs. Although relatively few of Vivaldi's cantatas survive in more than a single source, there is ample evidence from annotations in the manuscripts stored in his personal archive (e.g., instructions for transposition, small revisions to notes or words, the allocation of a serial number) that the composer reissued them on many occasions.

One could use the slightly oxymoronic phrase 'generic customization' to describe the degree to which the vocal parts in Vivaldi's chamber cantatas are tailored to the singer. They have an objectively determinable compass, but one also capable of instant expansion or contraction with a few strokes of the composer's pen (such minor amendments abound in the scores). They take no apparent account of the difference in timbre between female (soprano, contralto) and high male (soprano castrato, alto castrato, counter-tenor) voices. Any part headed by a C clef on the lowest stave-line is for 'soprano', whatever its peculiarities; any with a C clef on the middle line is for 'alto'. Their written-in ornamental detail is fairly standard for the given level of difficulty. Obviously, singers had the

---

[33] An exception should be made for a few violin concertos exploiting the ultra-high register that Vivaldi seemingly reserved for himself as showpieces.

opportunity to introduce their 'trademark' embellishments as part of their impro-visational practice both in the *da capo* repeat of the 'A' section of an aria and – with even more freedom – in cadenzas.

Who were the singers of Vivaldi's cantatas? At Mantua, where Vivaldi received his first opportunity to compose cantatas in quantity, they came in at least four categories. First, there were the amateurs: members of the ruling house and their companions. As Chapter 4 will show, the family of the governor, Prince Philip, had members capable of sustaining a solo part not merely in a cantata but even in a full-length serenata. Next, there were the salaried household musicians. In seasons when opera was running, this would be the main platform for their talents, but in the greater part of the year, when the theatres fell silent, a diet of cantatas made up their daily bread. Third, there was the penumbra of singers not attached to the court but resident locally and therefore available for engagement on an occasional basis. In Mantua the singers attached to the local cathedral, S. Pietro, and to the ducal church of S. Barbara formed such a nucleus.

Last but not least, there were the numerous itinerant singers, many of interna-tional stature, who were permitted by patent to style themselves 'virtuosi' or 'servi' of Prince Philip and doubtless paid occasional visits to Mantua.[34] Their ranks included such luminaries as the soprano Cecilia Belisani, the alto Giovanni Battista Carboni, the tenor Annibale Pio Fabri, the soprano Margherita Gualandi, the alto Giovanni Battista Minelli, the soprano Pietro Morigi, the soprano Giuseppa Pircher, and the bass Angelo Maria Zanoni.[35] The contracts governing such patents were very varied in nature. Some brought membership of the ducal household (*famigliarità*) or a passport, some not. They normally entailed, in addi-tion to the title, a monetary payment to the singer, who might in return have to perform occasional duties at court. In effect, the system was a form of cross-advertising whose billboards were the cast-lists in opera librettos: singers gained the prestige of recognition by a ruler; rulers gained the prestige of supporting celebrated artists.

In the case of the Mantuan cantatas, it is a hopeless task to assign individual compositions, even speculatively, to named singers on the basis of their musical features, since the number of possible candidates in each vocal category is so vast. At best, one can suggest which cantatas were conceived for professional, and which for amateur, singers. The cantatas sent to Dresden in 1733 (see Chapter 6) were composed for a small nucleus of highly skilled court singers, all of whom had served at least part of their apprenticeship in Venice and must have been known personally to Vivaldi. Here, some guesses are possible.

In the intervening years, cantatas by Vivaldi must have been performed in Venice at private 'academies' of the kind held by Angioletta Bianchi. There is a

---

[34] On the practice of granting such patents, see Paola Besutti, *La corte musicale di Ferdinando Carlo Gonzaga ultimo duca di Mantova. Musici, cantanti e teatro d'opera tra il 1665 e il 1707*, Mantua: Arcari, 1989. Mantua's change from independent duchy (under Ferdinando Carlo) to dependent province (under Prince Philip) made no difference to the practice, although Philip's 'virtuosi' were, naturally, different from those of his predecessor.

[35] It was Zanoni, also a player of the viola da gamba, who took the rôle of the crotchety tutor Nicena in Vivaldi's opera *L'incoronazione di Dario*.

hint in Vivaldi's correspondence that he attended musical gatherings at the house in Venice of the famous singer Faustina Bordoni, who was to marry the composer Hasse in 1730 and had earlier been associated with (and in one English source identified as the lover of) the violinist-composer Mauro D'Alay, a member of Vivaldi's circle in the mid-1720s.[36]

These diverse destinations explain the great diversity of compass, style, and level of difficulty among Vivaldi's cantatas. To give a flavour of this range, extracts from the soprano part of two cantatas are quoted as Example 3.1. In each case, the extract comprises the first and second vocal periods of the final aria. Since final arias are commonly set to texts that propose a resolution to the problem (of separation, rejection, timidity, etc.) addressed in the earlier part of the cantata, they tend to be lighter in spirit and style than the preceding ones. They prefer brisk tempos and 'short' metres such as 3/8 or 2/4.

Example 3.1a represents the Mantuan cantatas at their simplest and most straightforward. Indeed, it retains something of the *faux-naif* quality of Vivaldi's arias for minor characters in his early operas. The vocal line displays a note-worthy thematic economy: the three-note stepwise descent, the first note often anticipated by an upbeat, comes back repeatedly in various guises and is present equally in the ritornellos, interludes, and accompaniment provided by the bass. The 'B' section, despite its new text, is based on exactly the same material. This aria should be described as 'monomotivic' rather than 'monothematic', since it is the building block itself, not any larger structure formed from it, that stays constant. One sees well why Karl Wörner was able to view Vivaldi as the inventor of the *thematische Arbeit* that became the glory of Viennese Classicism.[37]

Extended melisma is reserved for the syllable 'sa-' of *sani* ('assuage'). Here, the illustration of the text is perfect, since on all three occasions the vocal line performs a smoothing, stroking motion suggestive of a hand applying balm. The whole section has an emphatically vocal character: most motion is conjunct, and the wider intervals employed now and again are easy for the voice to negotiate. To recall Mattheson's description, there are no 'violin leaps' here. Copious rests allow the voice to recover between phrases.

The two periods are modelled on the two sections of simple binary form. The three-bar cadential phrase ending the second period (bars 67–9) echoes the one ending the first period in the dominant (bars 27–9), with some rhythmic variation. Such matching of section endings is normal in binary-form instrumental movements of the time. The tonal and thematic design of the opening of the second period likewise follows a routine familiar from binary form. First, we have a statement in the dominant of the opening phrase (bars 34–9); then a statement in the tonic replicating the opening of the first period (bars 41–46); and finally a modified restatement of the same material that introduces a subdominant inflection via a tonic seventh (the E flat in bars 48–9) and thereby keeps the tonal momentum going.

Its phrase structure is perhaps the most sophisticated aspect of this otherwise

---

[36] See pp. 123–4.
[37] Karl H. Wörner, *Das Zeitalter der thematischen Prozesse in der Geschichte der Musik*, Regensburg: Gustav Bosse Verlag, 1969, pp. 67–73.

Ex. 3.1a  Vivaldi, *All' ombra d'un bel faggio*, RV 649: 'Vorrei, mio ben, da te',
vocal periods 1–2

unpretentious 'A' section. As Table 3.1a reveals, three-bar units dominate,
although there are enough two-bar and four-bar units to set up interesting asym-
metries. Add to this the complications introduced by the insertion of uniformly
one-bar instrumental interludes between the subunits (shown within square
brackets in the table), and we have a section full of fascinating ambiguities of
phrasing, where endings may be heard equally well as openings.

Table 3.1a  Structure of the first and second vocal periods (with tailpiece) in
'Vorrei, mio ben, da te', from *All'ombra d'un bel faggio*, RV 649 (c.1720)

| Bars | Section | Phrase structure |
| --- | --- | --- |
| 14–29 | 1st vocal section | 3 + 3 + [1]  + (2 + 2 + 2) + 3 |
| 34–62 | 2nd vocal section | 3 + 3 + [1] + 3 + 3 + [1] + 3 + 3 + [1] + (1 + 1 + 1+ 1) + 3 [+ 1] |
| 63–69 | tailpiece | (1 + 1 + 1 + 1) + 3 |

*Note: quaver upbeats are discounted in the calculation.*

The vocal compass employed in this section (*f'*–*a''*), which the 'B' section does not modify except to add *e'*, is very compact. Note that instead of reserving the highest note, *a''*, for a single climax, Vivaldi returns to it periodically. The idea of having a single climactic note was not foreign to the musical thought of the period – the *d'''* to which Vivaldi soars eight bars before the end of his *Laudate pueri Dominum* RV 601 is a striking case in point – but it was at least as common to 'stake out the boundary' by reaching the highest note repeatedly, as Vivaldi does here.

All in all, this aria, from *All'ombra d'un bel faggio*, RV 649, exemplifies to perfection the tradition of the *cantata da camera*. Without being undeveloped in any way, it exercises due moderation in such matters as length and technical difficulty. What may on the surface appear artlessness is in reality the product of a great artistry that probably owes more to instinct and experience than to conscious calculation. It represents the ideal 'social' music – accessible to competent amateur singers and suitable, if need be, for self-accompanied performance.

Example 3.1b shows the composer in his post-*galant* phase. It breaks the bounds of the pure chamber style to become, so to speak, 'opera by other means' – the ideal material with which an accomplished professional singer can regale his or her patron in private surroundings. The cantata, *Par che tardo oltre il costume*, RV 662, exists in an autograph score datable to c.1731. In every respect, this aria is more expansive than the one we have just considered. Its vocal compass is wider (the voice rises to the note *c'''*, which, characteristically, it 'hits' on three separate occasions); its phrases are spun out further; its melismas are more extravagant; it includes more decoration in the shape of trills, appoggiaturas, etc.; its rhythms are more varied; its thematic material is more diverse.

Once again, the model of instrumental binary form lurks in the background. But here, it is a progressive version of binary form, the so-called 'rounded' binary form, that asserts itself. In bar 53 we find a varied reprise, textual and musical, of the opening of the first vocal section. This feature, which entails an unusual second return to the opening word of the text ('Allor'), is not standard in the *da capo* aria. Its inclusion, besides revealing Vivaldi's background in instrumental music, demonstrates his admirable preoccupation with musical unity. The reprise is far from mechanical: two bars (53–4) that repeat the opening without alteration are followed by five (55–9) that reproduce it in paraphrase, whereupon the music moves to entirely new material.

Vivaldi's approach is no longer strictly monomotivic. The section is based on three primitive melodic archetypes: the scale, the broken-thirds progression (which may be regarded as an elaborated scale), and the repeated note. All three elements are rhythmicized in different ways, and the first two appear in both descending and (less often) ascending form. The 'stutter' figure first introduced in bar 70 (this is a favourite building-block of Vivaldi in his late period, best known from its appearance in the Sinfonia to *L'Olimpiade*) may seem entirely new, but is in reality only a different way of presenting the repeated-note idea.

As usual, Vivaldi pays attention to the possibilities for word-painting. The descending scale in semiquavers marking the arrival of the word *Notte* in fact refers – very effectively – to the veil (*velo*) that Night draws over the earth. On

Ex. 3.1b  Vivaldi, *Par che tardo oltre il costume*, RV 662: 'Allor che in cielo', vocal periods 1–2

Ex. 3.1b Vivaldi, *Par che tardo oltre il costume*, RV 662: *cont.*

this occasion, Vivaldi initially ignores the temptation to illustrate the word *dolori* ('sorrows'): good composers know that word-painting has to be rationed in order to stand out and avoid impeding the musical flow. However, he is able to illustrate this word economically and subtly in bars 61 and 63, where the diminished third produced by chromatically altered ornamental resolutions of a suspension hints at discomfort. The most prominent instances of coloratura writing occur, however, on syllables of neutral words (*avrò* and *ristoro*). Here, Vivaldi could be accused of insensitivity – one recalls how scandalized Berlioz became at Mozart's extravagant melisma on the '-rà' of *sentirà* in Donna Anna's aria 'Non mi dir, bell'idol mio' in *Don Giovanni*, which is an exactly parallel case. In his defence, Vivaldi would doubtless have pleaded that melisma was mandatory for structural and stylistic reasons, and that it was the poet's task, not his, to supply suitably expressive words at pre-cadential points. (He might have appended the remark that all other Italian composers did likewise.)

As in the other aria, melodic contour, modulation, and phrase structure are handled consummately. There is the same beautiful balance between the expected (literal repetition or symmetry) and the unexpected (modified repetition or asymmetry). Table 3.1b reveals a phrase-structure even more complex than that of 'Vorrei, mio ben, da te'. Modulatory inflections, such as the hint of D minor in bars 42–6 and the turn to B flat major in bars 60–61, occur just at the right point to save the music from stasis. It is arguable, however, that 'Allor che in cielo' lacks personality in comparison with 'Vorrei, mio ben, da te'. By choosing (for perfectly understandable reasons) to keep abreast of the stylistic changes spearheaded by the Neapolitans, Vivaldi may have sacrificed a little of what made him distinctive. Put more succinctly, he traded originality for fashionability. There is no clear-cut answer to this charge. The same problem affected all Italian composers of Vivaldi's generation (Albinoni and E. F. Dall'Abaco spring first to mind) who attempted to continue their successful careers after the mid-1720s under the new stylistic conditions brought about by Neapolitan dominance. But if Vivaldi succumbed, he certainly did so to a lesser degree than many around him.

One would expect there to be less distinctiveness about Vivaldi's recitatives, given the limited room for manoeuvre within the conventions that governed it. On the whole, this is true, but there are signs everywhere of effort to achieve intensity

Table 3.1b  Structure of the first and second vocal periods (with tailpiece) in 'Allor che in cielo', from *Par che tardo oltre il costume*, RV 662 (c.1731)

| Bars | Section | Phrase structure |
|------|---------|------------------|
| 13–29 | 1st vocal period | 2 + 3 + 2 + 4 + 6 |
| 33–52 | 2nd vocal period (1) | 3 + 4 + 2 + 4 + (2 + 2) + 3 |
| 53–80 | 2nd vocal period (2) | 2 + 3 + 2 + (2 + 2 + 2) + 4 + (2 + 2 + 2) + 3 + 2 |
| 81–85 | tailpiece | 2 + 3 |

*Note: quaver upbeats are discounted in the calculation.*

and originality of effect: in short, to be expressive. The composer's letter of 2 January 1739 to Guido Bentivoglio d'Aragona, in which he takes satisfaction from the applause gained by certain scenes consisting wholly of recitative in his opera *Farnace* as produced at Ancona, shows how seriously he regarded recitative composition.

About the melodic design of his recitatives there is little to say except that Vivaldi deploys the full range of effects (leaps, stepwise motion, note-repetition, chromatically altered intervals) that one would expect from a resourceful composer of his time. One interesting detail is that on two occasions, in RV 656 and 657, he ends the vocal line of a recitative on a monotone that acts, in harmonic terms, as an 'inverted' pedal: a pitch that grates against some of the harmonies below it. Example 3.2 shows the last five bars of the central recitative in *Geme l'onda che parte dal fonte*, RV 657. Such a cadence, commonly associated with languishing (as here) or dying, has a decidedly seventeenth-century ring about it. By Vivaldi's maturity, it was no longer current, and its resuscitation here, and in RV 656, is an unexpected archaism.[38]

The more personal quality in Vivaldi's cantata recitatives comes from their bold, sometimes frankly outlandish, chord juxtapositions, which in turn generate unusual vocal inflections. A central concept for the analysis of his harmony is that of ellipsis. Progressions that would normally take three chords to achieve are effected in only two, since the linking chord is merely understood, not literally present. The progression between the third and fourth bars of Example 3.2 offers an excellent illustration. Ordinarily, one would expect a chord of D minor or D major to link the dominant seventh chord on A in bar 14 to the diminished triad on D sharp in bar 15. Vivaldi short-circuits the process, producing a much more arresting effect. Occasionally, he exploits real (as opposed to merely notated) enharmonic change. Example 3.3, taken from *Par che tardo oltre il costume*, shows him first, in bars 6–7, introducing an elliptical progression (from D sharp to G sharp in the bass, omitting an intervening chord of E), and then, in bars 7–8, reinterpreting the G sharp as A flat, which allows him to continue by treating this note as the submediant of C minor.

---

[38]  Schmitz draws attention to this cadence (*Geschichte der weltlichen Solokantate*, p. 151), using it to demonstrate his observation that Vivaldi is superior in inventiveness to Albinoni as a composer of recitatives. He does not, however, point out its ancestry in seventeenth-century music (or, for that matter, Albinoni's own use of the very same cadence).

Ex. 3.2 Vivaldi, *Geme l'onda che parte dal fonte*, RV 657: recitative, bars 12–16

Ex. 3.3 Vivaldi, *Par che tardo oltre il costume*, RV 677: recitative, bars 1–8

Arioso is a device rarely used in Vivaldi's recitatives, although it is handled expertly when it appears. Timms identifies only two passages of arioso in them, occurring in RV 677 and RV 680, respectively.[39] To these one may add certain bars in the first recitative of the recently discovered *Tremori al braccio e lagrime sul ciglio*, RV 799, and a short phrase in the middle of the second recitative of *Elvira, anima mia*, RV 654. The motivation for an arioso is always to be found in the words. In RV 654 the cue is *tormento* (causing the singer to flail about in chromatic broken chords); in RV 677 it is *terribile tempesta* (a scale in the voice and undulating broken chords in the bass); in RV 680, *corro* (an ascending scale) and, separately, *Deh per pietade, Amore* (a brief prayer to Cupid over a solemn bass of repeated quavers); in RV 799, *Amor sen' ride* (Cupid's mockery is expressed through a repeated 'laughing' phrase).

In the cantatas with full instrumental accompaniment, where *recitativo accompagnato* and *recitativo obbligato* become available, Vivaldi deploys the full arsenal of devices. In ascending order of complexity, these are:

1. Simple recitative, as in continuo cantatas.
2. Simple recitative reinforced by unison strings (violins and violas play in the upper octave).
3. Harmonized recitative (upper strings share the rhythm of the bass).
4. Patterned recitative, with independent note-values in the accompanying parts. In this kind of recitative the vocal part has to be sung in strict time.
5. Dialoguing recitative, where vocal and instrumental phrases alternate, usually with overlapping.

How these different types combine to make up a composite recitative movement will be discussed later in connection with individual cantatas.

## The Composer and the Accompaniment

The accompaniment for Vivaldi's continuo cantatas would almost always have been harpsichord (or spinet) plus cello, or either separately. There is no intrinsic reason why lute, theorbo, or guitar could not also have served, either alone or in combination with the named instruments, but there is no specific evidence, internal or external, that this was ever so. In fact, the bass parts of Vivaldi's continuo cantatas are without exception conceived imaginatively for cello, within whose normal compass they remain. This is not quite the same as saying that they are 'for' cello *tout court*. Doubtless, they were often played in performance, and even more often in rehearsal, on the keyboard. But they fit the cellist's hand better than the harpsichordist's, and their occasional marks of phrasing seem designed for a stringed instrument. Take, for example, the ritornello with which the first aria of *All'ombra d'un bel faggio*, RV 649, opens (Example 3.4). A harpsichord can hardly compete with the cello in lending eloquence to the slurred semiquavers or in giving weight to the individual notes of the broken chords in quavers. Then

---

[39] Timms, 'The Dramatic in Vivaldi's Cantatas', p. 115.

Ex. 3.4 Vivaldi, *All'ombra d' un bel faggio*, RV 649: 'Senti che ti risponde', opening

there are those rapid repeated notes and compound intervals that the cello executes easily but which become a struggle for any keyboard instrument, as Example 3.5, the accompaniment to the start of the first vocal period in the first aria of *Perfidissimo cor! Iniquo fato!*, illustrates.

Ex. 3.5 Vivaldi, *Perfidissimo cor! Iniquo fato!*, RV 674: 'Nel torbido mio petto', bars 5–8 (bass)

The merits of the harpsichord emerge more fully in recitatives, since it is able to provide a continuous chordal accompaniment, whereas a cello, even applying ingenuity, can produce chords only intermittently. However, intermittent chords are probably all that most recitatives require. Gasparini, whose advice has to be taken seriously, since he was Vivaldi's colleague and must have been referring as much to vocal chamber music as to opera, tells the harpsichordist to sustain bass notes and their chords until they decay naturally. Other authorities and observers, however, are unanimous in identifying short 'attacks' as the normal mode of performance for Italian recitative. Take, for example, the eye-witness account of Joachim Christoph Nemeitz, a Saxon court official who visited Venice in 1721. Nemeitz precedes his discussion of the accompaniment with some interesting remarks on the performance of recitative that, although they concern opera, have relevance also for the cantata:

> So far as vocal music is concerned, their language [Italian] itself seems to have a special advantage over others in that its vowels sound very good when they wish to execute florid passages. Indeed, even when they converse among themselves, the tone of their voices rises and falls as if they were singing. Hence the recitatives in their opera are made to conform to ordinary speech, becoming something neither wholly sung nor wholly spoken, and the actors observe neither the metre nor the length of the prescribed notes, but deliver the words slowly or quickly as they deem appropriate, and as the action demands. The

accompaniment, consisting of harpsichord, theorbo, and great bass, always follows the lead of the singer or actor. It does no more than to punctuate the music occasionally, thereby assisting the singer to maintain pitch.[40]

Rousseau's *Dictionnaire de musique* confirms this 'dry' mode of performance. 'In Italian recitative', he writes, 'whatever the length of a bass note, it must be struck only once: firmly and with a full chord; one strikes the chord again only it changes over the same note'.[41] From certain rare performance directions in Vivaldi's scores, such as 'arcate lunghe' ('long bows'), one receives further confirmation that short attacks were the 'default' mode in his recitatives.

In the previous chapter Vivaldi's failure to give the harpsichord any obbligato passages was mentioned. In fact, he seems to have had a near aversion to the harpsichord that strikes one as curious in a composer who otherwise was so ready to explore the full instrumental gamut. Claims have been made that he played the harpsichord himself, but none of the evidence stands up to close scrutiny. A transcription by Giazotto of a secret agent's report that mentions Vivaldi's playing of the harpsichord at a function held in Venice at the Spanish ambassador's house in 1739 must be discounted, since no one has managed to locate the document independently.[42] A reference to him as 'Maestro di spineta' in a Pietà document of 1736 is an obvious error: even if he was (of sorts) a harpsichord-player, he should have been identified there by his official title, which was *Maestro de' concerti*.[43]

Obbligato parts for harpsichord are meagre in Vivaldi's music, both in quantity and in substance. The aria 'Io sono quel gelsomino' in *Arsilda, regina di Ponto* (I.15) makes the two harpsichords in unison play broken chords in the right hand to create a shimmering background. The work once identified and even published as the harpsichord concerto RV 780 is now agreed to be nothing of the sort (the choice of harpsichord as solo instrument resulted from a misunderstanding of the significance of the word 'cembalo' in the title), and the number has been withdrawn. Otherwise, there are merely instructions for the harpsichord or harpsichords to arpeggiate an improvised accompaniment; these are found in at least two concertos (RV 249 and RV 293) and three operas (*Orlando finto pazzo*, *Giustino*, and *Orlando furioso*). By comparison, the organ is lavishly treated, on

---

40 Joachim Christoph Nemeitz, *Nachlese besonderer Nachrichten aus Italien*, Leipzig: Gleditsch, 1726, p. 425: 'Es scheinet auch, was die *Vocal-Music* betrifft, ihre Sprache an sich selbsten eine sonderbahre *avantage* vor andern darinn zu haben, daß ihre *vocales* sehr wohl lauten, wann sie einige Läuffe machen wollen. Ja, wann sie auch in gemeinen Umgang mit einander sprechen, erheben sie den Thon der Stimme, und lassen ihn auch wieder fallen, so daß es scheinet, als wann sie die Worte her sängen. Daher geschichts, daß ihre *recitative* in den *Opern* zu einer gewöhnlichen Rede dergestalt *accommodiret* sind, daß es eigentlich kein Singen und auch keine Rede ist, und die *Acteurs* weder *mesure* noch *valeur* in denen ihnen vorgeschriebenen *noten* halten, sondern nach ihren Gutdüncken die Worte langsahm oder geschwind hervorbringen, nachdem es die *action* erfodert; da dann das *accompagnement* vom *Clavecin*, *Thuorbe* und grossen *Bass* sich allemahl nach dem Sänger oder *Acteur regliren* muß; jenes aber nicht mehr thut, al zuweilen nur um den andern *Tact* einmahl anzuschlagen, damit der Sänger im *Ton* erhalten werde.'

41 Rousseau, *Dictionnaire de musique*, art. 'Accompagnement', pp. 6–15, at p. 13.

42 Giazotto, *Antonio Vivaldi*, pp. 309–10.

43 Venice, Archivio di Stato, Ospedali e luoghi pii diversi, Busta 703, Scontro, f. 59.

Ex. 3.6  G. B. Pescetti, *Di sì bel faggio all' ombra*: 'Come va l'ape nel prato', opening

one occasion receiving an idiomatic part that features interplay between the two hands (in the second slow movement of the early sonata RV 779). All things considered, the primacy of the cello in the cantatas, where instrumental display is concerned, comes as no surprise.

It will be interesting to illustrate at this point the possibilities that Vivaldi gave up by pushing the harpsichord so firmly into the background. Giovanni Battista Pescetti's setting of *Di sì bel faggio all'ombra*, contained in the Hamburg manuscript mentioned earlier in connection with settings of Metastasio's *T'intendo, sì, mio cor*, employs a treble line for the harpsichordist throughout the ritornellos of both arias.[44] The opening ritornello of the first aria is shown as Example 3.6. Pescetti was a noted harpsichordist and the composer of numerous harpsichord sonatas, whose quality is praised by Newman.[45] As in the typical 'accompanied' aria, the ritornello is recognized by its treble line (which here pre-echoes that of the voice); its bass is strictly functional and would make little musical sense if

44  Hamburg, Staats- und Universitätsbibliothek 'Carl von Ossietzky', Musiksammlung, M A/833:2, pp. 390–6.
45  William S. Newman, *The Sonata in the Classic Era*, 2nd edn, New York: Norton, 1972, pp. 684–6.

simply harmonized in the normal manner with chords above. Vivaldi certainly knew Pescetti's music, incidentally, since the composer's father, Giacinto Pescetti, served the Pietà as organ technician and harpsichord tuner from 1697 onwards; and in 1728, when Vivaldi directed the music at the Teatro S. Angelo, Pescetti was one of the two up-and-coming composers (the other was Galuppi) to whom the second carnival opera, *Gl'odii delusi dal sangue*, was entrusted.

In the seven cantatas with a full string accompaniment – RV 679, 681, 682, 683, 684/684a, 685, and 686 (the last with a pair of horns added) – Vivaldi employs the same resources that he would use in most operatic arias. There is little to distinguish the cantata arias from their operatic counterparts, although the fact that no inter-genre borrowings have so far been discovered suggests that the composer kept the two areas apart in his mind. In a 'blind' test one would perhaps identify the first aria of RV 683, 'Passo di pena in pena', as coming from a cantata: the severity of its counterpoint and the complexity of its thematic development mark it out as a piece for connoisseurs that would probably have fared badly in the opera house. There is perhaps a tendency for cantata arias not to stray too far from a *mezzo carattere*, avoiding the absolute extremes of expression. This is in keeping with the civilized, temperate atmosphere of a *conversazione*, where, however cruelly Cupid's darts pierced Silvio or however miserably Aminta pined for Filli, the company would all take refreshment and depart for home contentedly.

Finally, we must consider the obbligato parts for flute and violin in *All'ombra di sospetto*, RV 678, and *Lungi dal vago volto*, RV 680, respectively. Their rôle is not accompanimental in the strict sense. In ritornellos and linking passages they supply treble lines similar to that for keyboard shown in Example 3.6. In the vocal sections, however, they become true partners for the voice: the texture is effectively that of a chamber duet in which one 'voice' remains mute. Vivaldi seeks ways of making the obbligato instrument a protagonist in the story recounted by the text. In both arias of RV 678 the transverse flute, the perfect embodiment of the *galant* style, represents the flattering (*lusinghiero*) but deceptive charms (*finti vezzi*) of love; it relentlessly ensnares the lover in imitative play or in chains of parallel sixths and thirds. In the first aria of RV 680 the violin represents picturesquely the forest birds, to whom the singer confides the anguish of his separation from the beloved; when he sings, in the second aria, of being reunited with her, the violin is transformed into the beloved herself, double stops conveying the hefty abandon of the lovers' embraces. As their popularity in modern performance attests, these cantatas are so successful at integrating the obbligato instrument, conveying the principal *affetto*, and summoning up interesting textures and imitative play that one can only regret how few they are.

# CHAPTER FOUR

# The Mantuan Cantatas

## *Vivaldi's Mantuan Episode*

The period spanning little more than two years that Vivaldi spent at the court of the governor of Mantua, Prince Philip of Hesse-Darmstadt, is one of the most clearly defined, and most singular, of his career. His experiences in Venice, his instincts and his strategic sense must all have told him that the life of a *maestro di cappella* at a court would reduce his freedom of action beyond tolerable limits, yet he took the bait. The experiment was ultimately unsuccessful, even if Vivaldi was able to extricate himself neatly and remain on good terms with a patron whose name he could continue to parade on title-pages and in librettos, and who occasionally commissioned music from him. Moreover, the contact with members of the nobility of the Habsburg domains that residence in Mantua brought him proved fruitful in later years. Service at Mantua was the first stepping stone towards his meeting with Emperor Charles VI in 1728, his visit to central Europe in 1729 – and perhaps, ultimately, to his ill-fated journey to Vienna in 1740.[1]

Ever since Vivaldi's operas made their mark on the Venetian stage in the mid-1710s, their composer became 'hot property'. When the elector of Bavaria, Maximilian II Emanuel, newly restored to his capital city of Munich after the conclusion of the War of the Spanish Succession, asked his wife, Electress Therese Kunigunde, who had not yet returned from her exile in Venice, for advice on musicians to recruit for his *Hofkapelle*, she mentioned the name of Vivaldi, presumably in connection with the post of *Kapellmeister*. Her letter has not survived, but we can guess much of its content from Maximilian Emanuel's slightly dismissive reply:

---

[1] Secondary literature on Vivaldi's connections with Mantua, with an understandable emphasis on opera, is abundant. The most significant items, in order of publication, are: Claudio Gallico, 'Vivaldi dagli archivi di Mantova', in Francesco Degrada (ed.), *Vivaldi veneziano europeo*, pp. 77–88; Luigi Cataldi, 'Il teatro musicale a Mantova (1708–1732): studi sulle fonti documentarie', unpublished dissertation, Parma, 1983–4; idem, 'I rapporti di Vivaldi con il "Teatro detto il Comico" di Mantova', *Informazioni e studi vivaldiani*, vi (1985), 88–109; idem, 'Alcuni documenti relativi alla permanenza di Vivaldi a Mantova', ibid., viii (1987), 13–22; idem, 'La rappresentazione mantovana del "Tito Manlio" di Antonio Vivaldi', ibid., 52–88; idem, 'L'attività operistica di Vivaldi a Mantova', in Antonio Fanna and Giovanni Morelli (eds), *Nuovi studi vivaldiani*, pp. 131–45. I am grateful to Luigi Cataldi for additional information and opinion communicated through private correspondence.

Concerning the composer called Vivaldi, I have not seen any of his compositions but can well believe that they are excellent, since I trust your judgement. We are not in a very good position to hand out more pensions than necessary, but if the sum were small, you could come to an agreement with him. Torri [the *Kapellmeister* designate] is very good at composition and has an exquisite feel for opera.[2]

Perhaps the sum demanded by Vivaldi was not small enough for the Bavarian court. Or perhaps his *amour propre* would not allow him to occupy a position subordinate to Torri. At any rate, we hear nothing more about this pension.

The genesis of Vivaldi's engagement at Mantua appears to have been the production of his new opera *Armida al campo d'Egitto*, his sixth for Venice, at the Teatro S. Moisè. This opera opened on 15 February 1718. Perhaps Prince Philip, visiting Venice for carnival, as so many among the higher European nobility did, attended this production. The sequel was a new production in Mantua at the Teatro Arciducale (also called the Teatro Comico), a civic theatre under patronage of the ruler, for which two members of the cast remained the same (Antonia Merighi as Armida and Rosa Venturini as Osmira). At around the same time Vivaldi was appointed *Maestro di cappella di camera* to the court at a handsome monthly salary of 680 Mantuan *lire*. The title's termination, 'di camera', identified his responsibilities as those pertaining only to secular music; a separate *maestro di cappella*, Pietro Crescimbeni, attended to sacred music at the ducal church. Vivaldi was also permitted – perhaps required – to take a hand in the management of the theatre, a task for which his similar activity in Venice had prepared him well. His new post in Mantua did not prevent him from supervising the production in Florence of a new opera, *Scanderbeg* (for which he had presumably entered into a contract prior to his appointment), in June 1718, and Philip even provided him with a letter of recommendation to Anna Maria de' Medici, dowager electress of the Palatinate, who had returned to her native city. Nor was Vivaldi inhibited from fulfilling commissions received from other patrons: a receipt dated 19 April 1719 for 'un pachetto con carte musicali' supplied to the Bohemian count Wenzel von Morzin (among which *Le quattro stagioni* probably figured) points to this parallel activity.[3]

Giovanni Battista Vivaldi stayed with his son in Mantua for long periods. We know this because he was sometimes not present in Venice to collect in person his salary, paid every two months, from the ducal church. Presumably, he did not reside continuously in Mantua during the whole of the period, because otherwise he would have sought formal leave of absence from S. Marco – as he was to do in 1729, when he accompanied his son on his transalpine travels.

---

[2]  Letter of 21 October 1714 (Munich, Bayerisches Hauptstaatsarchiv, Geheimes Hausarchiv, Korrespondenzakten 753/9), transcribed in the original French in Berthold Over, 'Antonio Vivaldi und Therese Kunigunde von Bayern', *Studi vivaldiani*, iv (2004), 3–7, at 4.

[3]  On Vivaldi's relationship to Morzin, see Michael Talbot, 'Wenzel von Morzin as a Patron of Antonio Vivaldi', in Konstanze Musketa and others (eds), *Johann Friedrich Fasch und der italienische Stil: Bericht über die Internationale Wissenschaftliche Konferenz am 4. und 5. April 2003 im Rahmen der 8. Internationalen Fasch-Festtage in Zerbst*, Dessau: Anhalt-Edition, 2004, pp. 67–76.

Vivaldi's fortunes rose to a climax in the carnival season of 1718–19, when his operas *Teuzzone* and *Tito Manlio* were produced at the Teatro Arciducale. He seemed set to achieve similar success in the following season, when his *La Candace o siano Li veri amici* was due to be staged as the second opera, following the pasticcio *Alessandro cognominato Severo*. Then disaster struck. On 19 January 1720 the dowager empress Eleonora Magdalena Theresa von Neuburg, mother of Charles VI, suddenly died, plunging the empire into compulsory mourning and causing the immediate cessation of public entertainments. The season was aborted, and Vivaldi found himself unexpectedly in a position where, if he remained in Mantua, he would have time on his hands, so far as opera was concerned, for at least another year. (In fact, the Teatro Arciducale did not reopen for opera until 1 June 1722, when Boniventi's *Il Climene* took the stage.) Vivaldi therefore petitioned Philip for release from his post, collected the last instalment of his salary on 26 February 1720 and was back in Venice probably by the end of the following month, armed with a letter of recommendation from Philip to Johann Baptist Colloredo-Waldsee, the imperial ambassador to Venice.

Was Vivaldi glad to go? In fact, the death of the dowager empress and its consequences probably came as a windfall, since they provided a plausible pretext for leaving. During his two years in Mantua he had extracted whatever benefits were at hand, including a title infinitely grander than that of sometime violin master at the Pietà, and Philip's continued patronage was to serve him well. In 1725 his opera *L'Artabano* (only the third since the theatre's reopening) played at the Teatro Arciducale, and in carnival 1732, the last season in which it was to host opera, Vivaldi took control of its management and musical direction, treating the Mantuan public to revivals of his *Semiramide* and *Farnace*. In 1726 he wrote a serenata (in the libretto given only the generic description of 'Serenata a quattro voci') that was performed on 31 July to mark Philip's birthday eleven days earlier. This composition is lost, but from its libretto we can glean valuable clues of the highest relevance for Vivaldi's cantatas composed in Mantua.

## The Mantuan Court

Philip was no ordinary patron. His commitment at Mantua to music and spectacle was hardly less intense than that of his notoriously prodigal predecessor, Ferdinando Carlo, the last Gonzaga duke. He was born in Darmstadt on 20 July 1671 as a younger brother to Ernst Ludwig (1667–1739), who became reigning landgrave (initially under a regency) in 1678.[4] Interestingly enough, Ernst Ludwig possessed musical talents: his *Douze suites et symphonies*, engraved in score at Darmstadt in 1718, are of a quality to merit modern revival. Philip, who had a similar practical involvement with music (as we shall learn from a cantata text), pursued a military career. In 1691–92 he served in the English army fighting

---

4 Biographical details concerning Philip and his family are taken mainly from Carl Knetsch, *Das Haus Brabant. Genealogie der Herzoge von Brabant und der Landgrafen von Hessen*, Darmstadt: Historisches Verein für das Großherzogtum Hessen, 19[18]–31, pp. 310–11, 314, and 436.

against France in the Netherlands at the head of a regiment bearing his name. In 1693, while in Brussels, he took the unprecedented step for anyone in his family of converting to Catholicism. For a brief period in the summer of 1695 he relapsed into Lutheranism, but this was the only dent in an otherwise rock-hard commitment to his new faith. In 1693, the day after his official conversion, he married Princess Maria Theresia von Croy und Havre.

Philip steadily ascended the military ladder of the Habsburg empire. Meanwhile, his first surviving son, Joseph, was born in 1699. As a token of his conversion, Philip forced Joseph, who might reasonably have expected, as the eldest living son, to enjoy the privileges of primogeniture, into the church. Joseph received his tonsure in Mantua in 1728 and rose in the ecclesiastical hierarchy to become bishop of Augsburg in 1740. A first daughter, Maria Friederica, was born in 1705. One year later, a second daughter, Maria Theodora arrived. She was to leave the court to marry Antonio Ferdinando Gonzaga, duke of Guastalla, in 1727.

In 1707 Philip once again saw military action as imperial and French-Mantuan forces battled in northern Italy. On 13 March 1707 imperial troops led by Philip entered Mantua. He was made governor of its fortress and supreme commander of the imperial forces left behind in Lombardy as the campaign continued. In June 1707 he departed to wage war on the Spanish in Naples. In April 1708, during his absence, a further son, Leopold, was born in Mantua. It was Leopold who was to carry on the family's military tradition in place of Joseph. In July 1708 Philip was put in command of the victorious imperial troops in Naples, where he remained for six years. In Italy he was always known as 'landgrave', for whereas in Germany, as in England, only eldest sons succeeded to the family title, in Italy, following age-old custom, all sons shared the title without distinction. So 'Prinz Philipp' became 'langravio Filippo'.

Meanwhile, in 1710, Mantua had been declared a hereditary possession of Austria. To mark its new status, it needed a governor to replace the temporary administrator, Count Giovanni Battista di Castelbarco, who had acted since 1707. On 21 September 1714 Philip was appointed to the post, which he took up on 29 December.

Shortly before this climax to his career, the prince had been visited by tragedy. His wife Maria Theresia died in May 1714. From that point until his death Philip remained an eligible widower, whose 'availability' is subtly alluded to in certain cantata texts. He made one determined effort to break his widowerhood, becoming engaged on 30 December 1718 to Eleonora Luisa, princess of Guastalla – and widow of Francesco Maria de' Medici (1642–1711), to whom she had conspicuously failed to give a son to carry on the Medici name. Vivaldi's *Tito Manlio*, a much grander affair than the preceding *Teuzzone*, was intended to celebrate the wedding; but, unexpectedly and abruptly, it was called off in the middle of the bride's progress to Mantua. Some blamed her notoriously flighty character, others the obduracy of the Guastalla court. *Tito Manlio* apparently went ahead as programmed, and it is interesting to note that Eleonora continued to be named as protectress of the Teatro Arciducale in the librettos for the operas of the following season. Philip's engagement was formally annulled only on 7 December 1721.

His courtly ambitions eventually proved Philip's undoing. From the local historian Federigo Amadei (1684–1755) we learn that Charles VI recalled him in 1735 in order to replace him with someone with fewer princely airs ('qualche personaggio che meno odorasse del sublime carattere del sangue principesco').[5] Retiring to Vienna, Philip died there on 11 August 1736.

We do not learn of any interest in music or drama on the part of princess Maria Friederica, but her three younger siblings all participated actively in court entertainments. Between 1716 and 1726 they took leading rôles in four plays with music and two works of serenata type that were performed before the court.

The first of the plays was *L'Alessandro*, with Joseph in the title-rôle, which was given on 8 June 1716 in the Sala di Troia (the reception room in the ducal palace decorated with frescoes by Giulio Romano depicting scenes from the *Aeneid*). Setting a pattern followed in the later plays, members of the court participated as actors, as orchestral players in the prologue and as dancers in the *intermedi*. The format was thus that of the French *tragédie-ballet*. *L'Alessandro* was performed to mark the birth of the archduke Leopold of Austria – a highly significant political event, since the arrival of a male heir to Charles VI promised (in the event, vainly, since Leopold died young) to secure the imperial succession without invoking the Pragmatic Sanction of 1713 and prickly questions of female precedence.[6]

The later plays involved all three of Philip's children as performers. The first was *L'Antioco* (after Thomas Corneille), given on 21 April 1721. This production was described as just a *divertimento* for the three children, but its real purpose may have been to signal the end of the year-long period of mourning at court. There followed *L'Arminio* (after Jean Galbert de Capistron), performed in the little court theatre during the carnival of 1722 in honour of Philip's brother Henry, a distinguished military commander, and *Rodoguna, principessa de' Parti* (after Pierre Corneille), performed in the same theatre on 3 June 1722 before the visiting prince and princess of Modena.[7]

The first of the entirely musical works was *Amore sul monte overo Gli amori di Diana e d'Endimione nel monte Lamo di Paria*, a 'pastorale in musica' for four voices performed privately ('in camera'), likewise on the occasion of Henry's visit in early 1722. In this small-scale composition (the libretto has only 19 pages) Theodora took the role of Diana; Joseph, that of Endimione; countess Margherita 'Facipecora' Pavesi Furlani, that of Serpilla; the prince of Squinciano, that of Aminta.[8]

The high point of the princely pair's musical outings came on 31 July 1726, when they took the rôles of Elpino and Eurilla in the previously mentioned *Serenata a quattro voci*, a substantial work (with ten closed numbers in each of its

---

5  Quoted after Cataldi, 'L'attività operistica di Vivaldi a Mantova', 132 (n. 4).

6  The performance was reported in a news sheet (*Gazzetta di Mantova*) for 12 June 1716. See Cataldi, 'La rappresentazione mantovana del "Tito Manlio" di Antonio Vivaldi', 58–9.

7  A libretto for *L'Arminio* survives: see Claudio Sartori, *I libretti italiani a stampa dalle origini fino al 1800*, 7 vols, Cuneo: Bertola & Locatelli, 1990–94, no. 2793. The prince and princess of Modena were regaled in addition with Boniventi's opera *Il Climene*.

8  The absence of Leopold from the cast is revealing: evidently, he was no singer. 'Facipecora' is placed within quotation marks, since it appears to be a nickname rather than a given name or surname.

two parts) paying fulsome homage to Philip on his birthday.[9] The libretto set by Vivaldi was written by Vittore Vettori, a prominent local poet who was possibly in court service.[10] The locale was the palace known as 'La Favorita'. On this occasion, Joseph and Theodora were partnered once again by Margherita Pavesi Furlani (taking the male role of Tirsi), and also by countess Maria Caterina Capilupi Biondi (as Fillide). This is the last known production to include members of the Mantuan court as performers. That there were, apparently, no sequels is hardly surprising, given that the star couple, Joseph and Theodora, were very soon to move on to the priesthood and to matrimony, respectively.

What is remarkable about this serenata (although there are parallels in some smaller-scale serenatas performed slightly later in Vienna by junior members of the imperial court) is that the singers, under the flimsy disguise of nymphs and shepherds of Arcadia, play themselves. Joseph and Theodora (Elpino and Eurilla) recount the vicissitudes of their unsettled upbringing during the War of the Spanish Succession, while the two countesses (Fillide and Tirsi) reveal to them the identity of the benign ruler of the country to which they have travelled: Philip, going under the Arcadian name of Daliso.

In this serenata there are thus five Arcadian names attached to five identifiable members of the court. The interesting question is this: are these names picked at random from the general Arcadian stockpile, or do they represent established identities equivalent to the 'academic' names, Arcadian or otherwise, adopted by members of academies (for example, the librettist Vittore Vettori was known as 'Lo Schizzinoso' – 'The Fastidious' – within Mantua's Accademia dei Timidi)? The evidence provided by the texts of the cantatas that Vivaldi wrote during his three years in Mantua suggests that some of the names were fixed, and consequently that these cantatas were performed at gatherings of a more or less stable group of people capable of recognizing and appreciating the allusions contained in them. In other words, the cantatas were composed for a kind of informal academy comprising members of the court, their guests and visitors, and musicians, resident or itinerant, in their service.

## A Mirror of Court Life

A good way to begin a general survey of Vivaldi's twelve surviving 'Mantuan' cantatas is by considering the data collected in Table 4.1.[11] Its first column gives the RV numbers. Those from RV 649 (where the cantatas begin in the catalogue) to RV 665 are continuo cantatas for soprano, which are listed alphabetically by

---

9   This work, RV 692, is discussed briefly in Talbot, 'Vivaldi's Serenatas', p. 92. In Vivaldian literature it is sometimes known as 'Queste, Eurilla gentil', following the first line of text.

10  Vettori (1697–1763), born in Ostiglia but domiciled in Mantua, was a medical doctor by profession. A publication of 1739 (*Discorso e poesie recitate pubblicamente nel solito loro teatro* [. . .] *dagli Accademici Timidi di Mantova* [. . .]) identifies him as the 'primo consigliere e primo censore' of this literary academy. If it were certain that he was already in Mantua by the end of the second decade of the century, he would be reckoned a likely candidate as author of some of the cantata texts set by Vivaldi.

11  Many of the ideas in this section, and some short portions of text, were given a first outing in

Table 4.1 Vivaldi's Mantuan cantatas

| RV | Location | Paper | Rastrography | Hand | Voice | Compass | Number | Other marks | Transposition | Subject | Object |
|---|---|---|---|---|---|---|---|---|---|---|---|
| 649 | Foà 28, 33–6 | B30 | 10/184.8(1) | autograph | Soprano | $e^{b'}$–$a''$ | Cantata 4:ᵃ | p. 10 | alla 3:ᵃ b. | Tirsi | Eurilla |
| 652 | Foà 27, 18–21 | B27 | 10/184.25(1) | Scribe 4* | Soprano | $d'$–$g''$ | | S. 8; 2i | | Daliso | Climene |
| 653 | Foà 28, 30–1 + 24–5 | B27 | 10/184.25(1) | Scribe 4* | Soprano | $e^{b'}$–$a''$ | | S. 4̲ | | – | Lidia |
| 654 | Foà 28, 15–18 | B27 | 10/184.25(1) | Scribe 4* | Soprano | $d'$–$a''$ | 2da | p: 8 | | Fileno | Elvira |
| 658 | Foà 28, 23 + 32 | 30 | 10/184.8(1) | Scribe 4* | Soprano | $e^{b'}$–$a''$ | Cantata 7:ᵃ | 2̲: Pa: | 4:ᵃ alla 3:ᵃ alta; alla 5:ᵃ Alta in Alto | – | – |
| 659 | Foà 28, 13–14 | 30 | 10/184.8(1) | Scribe 4 | Soprano | $b^b$–$b^{b''}$ | Cantata 5:ᵃ | | | – | Tirsi |
| 661 | Foà 28, 26–9 | 30 | 10/184.8(1) | autograph | Soprano | $d'$–$a^{b''}$ | Cantata Xii:ᵐᵃ | | | – | – |
| 665 | Foà 28, 19–22 | B27 | 10/184.25(1) | Scribe 4 | Soprano | $c'$–$a''$ | | | | Clori | Daliso |
| 680 | Foà 27, 33–40 | B30 | 10/184.8(1) | Scribe 4 | Soprano | $e^{b'}$–$a''$ | | | | – | Elvira |
| 685 | Foà 27, 27–32 | B30 | 10/184.8(1) | autograph | Alto | $b$–$d''$ | | | | Clori | Mons. di Bagno |
| 686 | Foà 27, 41–52 | B30 + B6 | 10/184.8(1) + 10/184.7(1) | autograph | Alto | $g$–$c''$ | Cantata Prima | | | – | Filippo |
| 799 | Vienna, Ges. der Musikfreunde, VI 61340 | | ? | Scribe 4* | Soprano | $d^{b'}$–$a^{b''}$ | | | | – | Elvira |

text incipit. RV 680 is the sole example within this group of a cantata for soprano and instruments, while RV 685 and 686 are cantatas for alto and instruments. RV 799 owes its high number to its recent discovery (all RV numbers from RV 751 onwards are accessions to the original catalogue and therefore do not follow the usual ordering criteria).

Column 2 gives the location. 'Foà' stands for 'raccolta Mauro Foà' (at the Biblioteca Nazionale Universitaria, Turin). It can be seen that the seven Mantuan cantatas in Foà 28 occupy a continuous bloc running from f. 13 to f. 36.[12] Paul Everett has suggested that in some cases the Turin volumes, into which Vivaldi's mostly loose manuscripts were bound after the composer's death, preserve an original ordering in his archive.[13] Where the Mantuan cantatas are concerned, I would be inclined to keep an open mind. Similarity of page-dimensions is likely to have been an equally important and often independent factor in determining the location of the manuscripts. Note that each of the twelve cantatas survives in only a single manuscript. Had the Turin manuscripts not come to light, at most the lone cantata in Vienna would be known today.

Column 3 identifies the paper type, following a system of classification devised and developed by Everett. There is as yet no complete published cata-logue of the paper types encountered in Vivaldi's manuscripts, but Everett and others have quoted them individually as the need has arisen.[14] With one exception (RV 686), each manuscript uses only one paper type. The papers are all of 'royal' dimensions (*foglio reale*) and in oblong quarto format, measuring around 23cm (vertical) by 31cm (horizontal), with small variations between the different types.[15]

Column 4 identifies the rastrography – Everett's term for the characteristics of the pattern made by the pre-ruled staves. In Italy, music dealers, and sometimes the paper manufacturers themselves, used a multi-nibbed instrument called a *pettine* (literally, a 'comb') to draw staves across each page. Particularly in music paper prepared in the Veneto, such instruments could rule ten, twelve, or even more staves in a single action, thereby requiring only one 'pass' to complete the page. The number of staves per page is consistently ten in the Mantuan cantatas,

Michael Talbot, 'Vivaldi's "Academic" Cantatas for Mantua', in Ivan Klemenčič (ed.), *300 Years Academia Philharmonicorum Labacensium 1701–2001: Proceedings of the International Symposium held in Ljubljana on October 25th and 26th 2001*, Ljubljana: Založba ZRC, 2004, pp. 157–70.

12  The peculiar 'nested' arrangement of the manuscripts of RV 653, RV 661, and RV 658, reflected in their irregular foliation, results from an error of binding.

13  Paul Everett, 'Vivaldi's Marginal Markings: Clues to Sets of Instrumental Works and Their Chronology', in Gerard Gillen and Harry White (eds), *Irish Musicological Studies, I: Musicology in Ireland*, Dublin: Irish Academic Press, 1990, pp. 248–63, at p. 254.

14  Everett has been extraordinarily generous in allowing scholars access to his database of paper types and rastrographies in advance of their complete publication in a catalogue, and I would like to record my thanks to him for providing extra information from it via private correspondence.

15  The papers are normally left untrimmed on their fore-edge and their lower edge; the upper edge, where a knife has cut the paper along the first fold to separate the folios, is straighter. The page dimensions given in catalogues and in prefaces to editions frequently give conflicting informa-tion: it is admittedly very hard to measure paper size accurately when manuscripts are tightly bound in very large volumes, and when fraying at the exposed edges introduces irregularity.

as can be seen by the '10/' opening each entry in this column. This was an ideal number for continuo cantatas, allowing five two-stave systems per page. It was equally suited to arias and accompanied recitatives with four-part strings, where two five-stave systems would be employed. The number following the oblique is the combined vertical span, expressed in millimetres, of the staves – the distance from the highest to the lowest stave-line. Final bracketed numbers serve to distinguish two otherwise identical rastrographies. It is important to remember that, whereas more than one rastrography can appear in conjunction with a single paper type in commercially produced Venetian music paper, no rastrographies ever partner more than one paper type. Rastrography is therefore a closer means of identification than paper type as defined by watermarks and other characteristics.

There are two major groups, as defined by paper and rastrography, among the Mantuan cantata manuscripts. The first comprises RV 652, 653, 654, and 665. The same paper and rastrography appear in some pages of the manuscript of the violin concerto RV 229 in Turin, and the same paper with a different rastrography is used, alongside other papers, for the scores of *Teuzzone* and *Tito Manlio*. Batches of music paper featuring the same paper type and rastrography were usually 'consumed' by the composer and members of his *atelier* quite quickly, especially if belonging to this common variety. We can therefore place the B27 manuscripts in late 1718 and/or early 1719.

The second, larger group comprises RV 649, 658, 659, 661, 680, 685, and 686. Its B30 paper appears with identical rastrography in the concertos RV 160, 210 (Turin manuscript), 250, and 536, and in the loose aria of uncertain provenance 'La pastorella sul primo albore', RV 749.7.[16] Since RV 686, as we shall see, can have been composed no earlier than April 1719, it appears that the B30 group as a whole is of slightly later date than the B27 group. The B6 paper used for part of the RV 686 manuscript establishes a link to further coeval works: the concertos RV 121, 151 (the autograph manuscript), 229, 231, 332, and 534, and the *introduzione* RV 639a.

Column 5 identifies the hands. There are only two: those of Vivaldi himself (in all cases, these are composition manuscripts, not autograph copies) and of Scribe 4, his father. The asterisks following the '4' denote the presence in five cantatas of autograph corrections, alterations or annotations. It is interesting that no further copyists participated in this activity. The implication is that the preparation of cantatas, unlike that of operas, was a private affair that did not concern professional copyists.

Column 6 gives the voices employed. With two exceptions, RV 685 and 686, the singer is a soprano. In late Baroque cantatas generally, the soprano voice predominates, accounting for about three quarters of the preserved total. It enjoyed greatest public favour and prestige, was cultivated both by male (castrato) and female singers, and boasted numerical supremacy among the

---

[16] 'RV 749' is the general number under which Ryom groups loose arias that at present cannot be assigned to other works. A full list is given in Peter Ryom, 'RV 749', *Informazioni e studi vivaldiani*, xiv (1993), 5–49.

professional singers most likely to sing cantatas: those employed by courts. Most of the remainder were written for the alto voice. Tenors existed, naturally, but they had no separate repertory in the continuo cantata, merely singing soprano parts an octave lower.[17] Bass voices, which required a different style of treatment (entailing the frequent doubling or paraphrasing of the instrumental bass), had a small 'niche' repertory. So far as we know, Vivaldi wrote no bass cantatas, although his expertise at writing *arie all'unisono* for bass voice in his operas suggests that he would have made a success of it.

Column 7 gives the vocal compass. No fewer than four cantatas employ the compass $e^{b'}-a''$, and most of the others for soprano exceed it by no more than one note at either end. The great exception is RV 659, which, on account of its much wider compass ($b^b-b^{b''}$), must have been written for a different singer.

Column 8 records a series of annotations taking the form of ordinal numbers preceded (except in the case of RV 654) by the word 'Cantata'. It appears that, while still at Mantua, Vivaldi was asked to have a set of cantatas for soprano (twelve in number?) copied. The series led off, appropriately, with the accompanied cantata in praise of Prince Philip, RV 686, and continued with continuo cantatas. The annotations are an *aide-mémoire* to the copyist regarding the chosen sequence of the works, which may, of course, have been quite different from the order of their composition and first performance. Only six out of the twelve extant cantatas are so numbered. Unless the ordinal number was on occasion allocated tacitly, one has to assume that the third, sixth, and eighth to eleventh cantatas were works that are today lost (with the possible exception of RV 799). Extrapolating, one might calculate that the total number of cantatas written by Vivaldi in Mantua was about twice as many as we possess today, or around twenty-four – and this calculation assumes that the set was assembled towards the end of his period of residence.

Column 9 lists various other short annotations, mostly autograph, found in the manuscripts. Their significance is enigmatic. The 'S' preceding a number in RV 652 and 653 could stand for 'Soprano'. The 'p' preceding a numeral in RV 649 and 654 is possibly a reference to a page of the copied manuscript (in which new cantatas would not necessarily begin on a fresh page), but a gap of only two pages seems puzzlingly small if a 'third' cantata has to be inserted between them. These annotations establish, at any rate, that the cantatas were copied on more than one occasion.

Column 10 lists instructions for transposition. As we shall see concretely in the case of RV 796, it was common practice to transpose the pitch of cantatas by up to a fifth in order to bring them within the range of other voices or voice-types. This task was in principle simple enough for a copyist to undertake unaided. The first instruction listed for RV 658 means: 'fourth [cantata] taken up a third' (whether a major or a minor third would be clear from the context); the second instruction means: 'taken up a fifth and notated in the alto clef'. In fact, the latter is not a

---

17   This practice is referred to in Legrenzi's *Cantate and canzonette*, Op. 12, of 1676, G. B. Brevi's *I deliri d'amor divino*, Op. 5, and Bernardo Gaffi's *Cantate da camera* of 1700. There are some 'accompanied' cantatas expressly for tenor: here, the presence of the violin and viola parts makes the choice of octave (soprano or tenor) critical.

direction for transposition at all: it prescribes only a change of clef, from soprano to alto, as a result of which Middle C moves two lines higher.[18]

In columns 11 and 12 we arrive at the main point for discussion: the Arcadian names present in the texts and their significance. By 'subject' is meant the shepherd or nymph in whose voice the poet speaks, or whose voice he quotes. The 'object' is the object of his or her desire.

Four names appear more than once. Daliso appears as subject in RV 652, as object in RV 665; Tirsi appears twice, as subject and object, respectively (RV 649 and 659); Clori appears twice as subject (RV 665 and 685); Elvira appears three times as object (RV 654, 680, and 799). Moreover, we remember Daliso as the disguise for Philip in the *Serenata a quattro voci*, and Tirsi as that for Margherita Pavesi Furlani. Eurilla (present as object in RV 649) is the name adopted by Philip's daughter Theodora in the same serenata. It seems beyond coincidence that three names should appear in both contexts.

Recent writing on the cantata and serenata has drawn attention to the use, sometimes consistent and repeated, of Arcadian names in reference to real persons. For instance, Ellen Harris shows how the 'Olinto' in Handel's serenata *Oh, come chiare e belle*, HWV 143, is to be identified with Prince Francesco Maria Ruspoli, who in Arcadia was styled 'Olinto Arsenio'.[19] Even more numerous are the cantatas written for the Ruspoli household or for Arcadian gatherings hosted by it in which the name 'Daliso' appears. The etymology of the name is uncertain – it is not taken from classical mythology – but it seems to have some connection with Delos, Apollo's birthplace.[20] Prince Ruspoli's son Bartolomeo bore the Arcadian name of 'Dalgiso Asteronio', and it is more than likely that the very large number of 'Daliso' cantatas produced within the Roman orbit from no later than 1708 (the date of Handel's *Amarilli vezzosa*, HWV 82) to at least 1717 (that of Gasparini's *Qui di natura a scorno*) were written in homage to him.[21] The substitution of 'Daliso' for 'Dalgiso' could have arisen for the sake of euphony.

It is not too far-fetched to imagine that Philip and his court, newly established in Mantua, paid the Roman Arcadians the sincerest form of flattery. Both 'Daliso' cantatas appear to allude to events in the life of the prince. In *Si levi dal pensier*, RV 665, Clori attempts to erase from her mind her wandering lover, Daliso, who won her heart through the playing of a 'concave instrument' (the kithara, commonly cited in poetry to denote the violin and other stringed instruments). Addressing the company of shepherds, who represent her suitors, she chides them for their lack of constancy and warns them that on his return from 'Adria' (the ancient city on the Adriatic, a common poetic synonym for Venice), Daliso will

---

[18] See, however, Francesco Degrada's different view in his Critical Notes to the Ricordi edition (1993) of RV 658.

[19] Harris, *Handel as Orpheus*, p. 117.

[20] Carlo Vitali, in private correspondence, wonders whether it might mean 'follower of Apollo'.

[21] This idea was first mooted in Fourés and Talbot, 'A New Vivaldi Cantata in Vienna', 104–5. Composers who wrote 'Daliso' cantatas in Rome include Bononcini, Caldara, Fregiotti, Gasparini, Handel, Mancini, Benedetto Marcello, Alessandro and Domenico Scarlatti, and Zipoli.

know how to act like Ulysses and take a cruel revenge on them. Finally, addressing Daliso himself, she rounds on him for his desertion of her and reminds him that others are not immune to her charms. Who Clori is remains obscure. She may have been an actual person, perhaps a lady of the court, who harboured, or was rumoured to harbour, amorous feelings for Philip. Or she may be an allegory for the court itself. Philip's crime is to have paid a pleasure-visit to Venice, as he doubtless did at least once every year.

In *Aure, voi più non siete*, RV 652, Daliso, now the subject, laments the absence of his beloved, Climene. The breezes and the shade of beeches have lost their attraction for him, and he asks the stream to convey his lamentations to her. Wandering alone in the wood, he finds everywhere reminders of Climene – her name carved on a tree-trunk; a narcissus eclipsed in whiteness by her breast; a meadow in which he opened his heart to her. He ends by acknowledging that although the stream kisses and brings benefit to its banks, he remains tormented by thoughts of Climene.

The elegiac tone of the stanzas suggests that Climene's departure is a euphemism for her death. Could she be Philip's late wife Maria Theresia? If so, this cantata could be the secular counterpart to the ecclesiastical commemoration that he no doubt performed annually.

At this point, we might also consider an isolated 'Daliso' cantata almost certainly written for Mantua (its manuscript survives in Darmstadt, in the Hessische Landes- und Hochschulbibliothek) by Mauro D'Alay (c.1690–1757), a younger contemporary of Vivaldi whose path frequently crossed his in the 1720s and whom we will discuss more fully in the next chapter. The cantata *Amo Daliso, è ver*, set for soprano and continuo, possibly dates from the mid-1720s, since it displays a number of *galant* mannerisms.[22] The content of its text is singular. In an opening aria the obviously female singer laments that she has lost her heart to Daliso but has been unable to tell him that she is of royal birth (and therefore a potential bride for him). Her situation is described poignantly in the first aria:

| | |
|---|---|
| Nacqui al regno e nacqui al trono, | I was born into a throne and a kingdom |
| e pur sono sventurata pastorella. | and yet I am an unfortunate shepherdess. |
| Cominciò la mia fortuna | My fortune showed itself |
| dalla cuna a mostrarsi a me rubella. | to be adverse right from my birth.[23] |

In a second recitative, the royal shepherdess prays to God to let her identity be made known to Daliso, and the final comparison aria likens her firstly to a boat that needs a star by which to navigate and then to a young turtle dove that needs to be taught by some older bird how to fly.

The intended reading of this text is perhaps that Philip, remaining eligible after

---

22   Shelfmark: Mus. ms, 1046. This cantata was singled out by Schmitz (*Geschichte der weltlichen Solokantate*, p. 156), who writes of its 'original harmonic turns' ('originellen harmonischen Wendungen').

23   I learned recently from Lowell Lindgren that the text of this aria is plagiarized from Silvio Stampiglia's libretto for *Il trionfo di Camilla* (first set by Giovanni Bononcini for Naples in 1696). The fact of its plagiarism does not diminish, of course, its possible relevance to its new context.

the fiasco with Eleonora de' Medici, is in the sights of some young lady attached to, or visiting, his court, who is of higher birth than her ostensible status suggests but needs advice from others on how to pursue her suit. Who this lady might be eludes our knowledge. Certainly, dynastic wars in Europe, especially the War of the Spanish Succession, had left the continent awash with stranded royalty.

Clori returns in *O mie porpore più belle*, RV 685, to congratulate Monsignor Antonio dei Conti Guidi di Bagno (1683–1761) on his consecration as bishop of Mantua.[24] Antonio was appointed on 15 April 1719 and consecrated on 1 May, although he did not take possession of the see until 21 October.[25] Once again, Clori possibly stands for Philip's court. There is a truly awful pun in the opening aria stanza, where 'Manto' (the traditional personification of Mantua) is made to rhyme with 'manto', the prelate's purple mantle.

In *All'ombra d'un bel faggio*, RV 649, Tirsi (Countess Margherita Pavesi Furlani) is the subject, Eurilla (Princess Theodora) the object. Tirsi is, of course, a male shepherd, so the love that he/she expresses could be taken as sexually ambiguous. In fact, erotic love is probably being used here as an innocent analogue of the due devotion shown by a lady-in-waiting to her mistress. Tirsi stands in the shade of a beech tree. Enamoured of Eurilla but inhibited by shyness, he tells her that the stream is saying that it would like to run down to the sea but is obstructed by rocks. Eurilla sits down on the grassy bank beside the stream and asks Tirsi to explain himself more clearly. Tirsi then asks her to reciprocate his love.

In *Indarno cerca la tortorella*, RV 659, Tirsi becomes the object. The unnamed subject is very likely Eurilla. Here, the opening aria stanza voices the thought that the turtle dove – a traditional emblem of fidelity in both classical literature and biblical lore – always laments its separation from its mate. The subject, identified 'poetically' as masculine through the use of the adjectival form 'vicino' at the very end of the recitative stanza, laments that he has to remain separated from Tirsi but hopes to return. He describes how hope lessens the pain of separation. The same-sex relationship of mutual devotion between Tirsi and the subject forms a perfect counterpart to that between the heroine Judith and her handmaiden Abra in Giacomo Cassetti's libretto for Vivaldi's *Juditha triumphans*, expressed through the aria 'Veni, veni me sequere fide', where a soprano chalumeau acts the part of a turtle dove.

In *Del suo natio rigore*, RV 653, the unnamed subject confesses how, although hardened against love, he became enamoured of Lidia after seeing her weep. Her tears provided the point of entry for Cupid's dart. In this instance, one must be cautious about presuming that Lidia represents a real individual rather than a fictitious, off-the-peg character, although one suspects the presence of a concrete allusion.

The three cantatas in which Elvira appears, each time as object, form – or at

---

24 Vivaldi refers to him in the title as 'Monsignor da Bagni': accuracy in rendering surnames was not one of his strengths.

25 See the fuller account in Francesco Degrada's Critical Notes to the Ricordi edition. Degrada wonders whether 'Clori' represents the city (as opposed to the court) of Mantua, but I consider this unlikely, given the presence of Manto in that rôle.

least can be formed into – a little story. The name itself is interesting. It does not come from the classical or Renaissance repertory of names, and it has Spanish associations (as we know from Mozart's *Don Giovanni*) that might be relevant to the identity of the person.[26]

In *Tremori al braccio e lagrime sul ciglio*, RV 799, the unnamed lover breaks out in sweat and trembles at his inability to confess his love to Elvira. He describes how Elvira is unaware of his love, which he resolves to disclose. In the final aria stanza he does this, although not without qualms.

We learn from *Elvira, anima mia*, RV 654, that the lover's name is Fileno. He bears the sad tidings to Elvira that he has to leave and declares that his absence from her will make him miserable. He asks her for one last kiss before his departure.

In *Lungi del vago volto*, RV 680, the homeward-bound lover – presumably the same Fileno – expresses the agonies of separation that he has suffered. He sees Elvira approaching in the distance, and his excitement unsettles him. He asks the birds of the wood to attract her hither with their song. Elvira duly arrives to a rapturous reunion.

Could this be the court's playful re-enactment of a romance that its members witnessed? The notion is not improbable, for we know that certain cantata cycles by Caldara and Marcello were designed, like the madrigal comedies of old, to plot a narrative.[27]

There is no clinching argument to confirm this interpretation of the Mantuan cantatas as a chronicle or mirror of court life. However, the separate small pieces of evidence supporting the hypothesis are so numerous that it deserves serious consideration.

### Individual Works

In the discussion of individual cantatas in this section, and in its counterparts in the following two chapters, the order in which works appear will be strictly in accordance with their RV number (i.e., moving down the first column of Table 4.1). This procedure inevitably ignores the chronology of their composition and juxtaposes stronger and weaker works randomly, but it has the important advantage of aiding the reader's orientation.

---

26  It is pertinent to add that a *damigella* named Elvira, presumably the same person, is mentioned in passing in the libretto of Boniventi's *Il Climene* (II.4) of 1722. I am grateful to Luigi Cataldi for pointing this out to me.

27  Caldara's cantatas are the six written in Milan in August 1711 that all begin 'Caro Daliso mio' (information from Brian Pritchard); Marcello's cantatas are the two cycles, each of twelve works, written between January and March 1713, and October and December 1713, respectively. On the latter, see Marco Bizzarini, *Benedetto Marcello. Le cantate profane. I testi poetici*, Venice: Edizioni Fondazione Levi, 2003, pp. xvii–xix.

## RV 649: *All'ombra d'un bel faggio* (RARA)

We have already quoted the opening ritornello of this cantata's first aria (Example 3.4) and the vocal part of the 'A' section of its second aria (Example 3.1a). Its recitatives are a little unmemorable, but nicely fashioned; particularly attractive is the swift turn to G minor from E minor in bars 13–15 of the first recitative. This is another instance of ellipsis: the 'missing' chord is that of G major, which bridges the two mutually remote keys. In the same recitative there is one bar with only two crotchet beats. Since most movements in common time in the music of Vivaldi and many of his contemporaries make a practice of using the half-bar rather than the full bar as the effective metrical unit, the anomaly is more visual than aural. Some of Vivaldi's 'odd' 2/4 bars seem to have been created purely by accident, as when the composer moved to a new system or turned a page but overlooked that he needed to complete an existing bar before proceeding to the next.

The first aria shows the strengths of Vivaldi's modular method of constructing a movement. Having introduced, in the first bar of the ritornello, an apt figure to illustrate the murmur of a brook (see Example 3.4), he takes it into the vocal line, where it generates both imitative play with the bass and, via sequential repetition, extended melismas on the 'cor-' of *correr* ('run'). The basic premise of this monomotivic approach is that the germinal motive has enough plasticity to fit a great variety of harmonic contexts. Vivaldi has the talent and imagination to devise such motives, and the result, at its best, is a movement in which the demands of unity and variety are both satisfied in full. At the same time, he has a sure sense of when to inject new material so as to preserve a movement from monotony. As Example 3.1a shows, the new impetus provided by the syncopations of the melismatic passages (see bars 21 and 55) arrives just in time to prevent the music from chasing its own tail.

Neither aria contains a fermata for the insertion of a vocal cadenza. Indeed, this feature is wholly absent from the Mantuan cantatas, and its solitary appearance in a Vivaldi cantata aria (in RV 679) predictably postdates 1720.

Unusually, but certainly not uniquely, Vivaldi's composition score of RV 649 is not headed with the composer's name. There was, of course, no overriding reason for any manuscript that remained in his personal archive to bear his name, since this could always be added to the copies made from it before they passed into circulation.

To illustrate the tendency of Arcadian poetry to restrict itself to a very narrow range of words and images, some examples can be quoted of other cantatas or duets of which the first line combines the two keywords *faggio* ('beech') and *ombra* ('shade'): *Di sì bel faggio all'ombra* (Pescetti); *Sotto l'ombra d'un faggio, sul margine d'un rivo* (A. Scarlatti, Mancini); *Sotto l'ombra d'un faggio Aminta il pastorello* (de Majo); *Vieni all'ombra di quel faggio* (anon.); *Sotto l'ombra d'un faggio, piangente e sospirante* (A. Scarlatti); *D'un faggio a l'ombra assiso* (Steffani). A similar constellation of closely related first lines clusters around the titles of most of Vivaldi's cantatas.

RV 652: *Aure, voi più non siete* (RARA)

The first aria of this eloquently elegiac cantata, 'Ti confido il pianto mio', is remarkable for keeping the thematic material of the voice and bass distinct from start to finish. The continuo has continuous *ondeggiando* semiquavers expressing the motion of the stream, while the soprano sings mostly in conjunct quavers that represent Daliso's sighs for his lost Climene. After Scribe 4 had copied out this cantata, Vivaldi revisited it – one cannot tell whether immediately after copying or on a later occasion – and made some very deep cuts. On the composer's general propensity to apply cuts when revising his music, Degrada has made a very astute observation:

> The remarkable fact is that Vivaldi's revisions tend almost invariably towards a tightening of the structure vis-à-vis its original, usually more expansive, form; the impression they give is that of a composer who writes impulsively (who can forget the 'furie de composition' that flabbergasted Président [Charles] de Brosses?) and only later passes a critical eye over his work, striving to purge it of redundancy or at any rate to express himself more effectively and succinctly.[28]

The opening of the same aria, quoted as Example 4.1, shows this pruning in action. The example gives the introductory ritornello, first vocal period, and linking ritornello. Originally eighteen bars long, this passage was reduced to thirteen and a half bars simply by deleting the portions rendered in small notes. These portions could all be sacrificed, since they repeated, literally or in paraphrase, material adjacent to them. For most other composers, such ruthless cutting would have played havoc with the phrase structure. For Vivaldi, this is less of a problem, since his 'bottom up' method of composition, where symmetry and asymmetry jostle promiscuously, remains resilient in the face of such surgery. In the case under consideration, the outcome is certainly an improvement: the harmonic rhythm of the ritornello becomes tauter, and the unfortunate bar 10, which needlessly holds up the descent of the melodic line, disappears.

The second recitative, beginning 'Infelice Daliso', is an object lesson in tonal planning. The word 'planning' may be a misnomer, since Vivaldi could have arrived at the result merely via instinct and experience – but the effect is the same. This movement is based on modulation chains ascending and descending by fifths. The first chain (bars 1–6) starts in B minor and moves flatwards through E and A minor to D minor. It then moves over to the major side and descends from B flat to E flat major (bars 7–8). Returning to the minor side, it embarks on another, longer modulation chain (bars 9–17) that moves up sharpwards from C minor via

---

28  Degrada, 'Note filologiche in margine all'edizione critica', p. 377: 'Il dato singolare è che le correzioni vivaldiane tendono quasi uniformamente alla ricerca di un dettato più sintetico rispetto a una prima formulazione generalmente più espansa; l'immagine che esse forniscono è quella di un musicista che compone di getto (come non pensare alla 'furia inventiva' che lasciò sbigottito il Presidente De Brosses?) e che successivamente passa al vaglio critico il proprio lavoro, studiandosi di eliminare il superfluo, o comunque di esprimersi in maniera più efficace e stringata.'

Ex. 4.1 Vivaldi, *Aure, voi più non siete*, RV 652: 'Ti confido il pianto mio', opening

Ex. 4.1  Vivaldi, *Aure, voi più non siete*, RV 652: *cont.*

G, D, A, and E minor to B minor. To finish, it slips over once more to the major side and passes from G major to C major (bars 18–20). What lends added meaning to the tonal design is its close correlation with the mood of the text. The first shift to the major occurs just at the point where Daliso sees the first of his reminders of Climene (her name carved on a tree-trunk), and the second shift comes, poignantly, at the start of the final couplet of the stanza, where Daliso bids his memories be silent so as not to overwhelm him.

In the second aria ('Le fiorite e belle sponde'), which is light and breezy in style, Vivaldi integrates voice and bass more closely. The opening ritornello, prefiguring the vocal line, introduces a delightful figure (an ascending six–three triad rhythmicized as quaver, quaver, crotchet) that depicts the lapping of its banks by the stream. Scalar movement in a variety of guises informs most of the thematic material of this aria, contributing to the sense of continual movement.

There are two interesting structural details to be mentioned. The second vocal period begins with an exact reprise of the first seven bars of the first vocal section. This is a progressive feature that makes the 'A' section resemble the simple version of sonata form sometimes called 'sonatina' form, where, once the second key has been confirmed at the end of the exposition, an immediate return is made to the home key, in which the music remains thereafter (this form is standard in Rossini overtures). An immediate reversion to the tonic following the central modulation is encountered similarly in several of Vivaldi's bipartite concerto slow movements – for example, that of *La primavera*, RV 269.

The surprise about the form of the 'B' section of this aria is that both of its 'structural' cadences are in the same key – A minor. This identity of key is very rare in the Baroque *da capo* aria. In Vivaldi, it occurs only in a small minority of arias – but the fact that it occurs at all is noteworthy. Vivaldi's aim seems to be to broaden and simplify the formal outline, giving the 'B' section a more uniform character.

### RV 653: *Del suo natio rigore* (RARA)

Vivaldi made later corrections to this cantata in similar fashion to RV 652. Its first aria summons up the disconsolate Lidia, on whom the unidentified subject of the cantata takes compassion. Vivaldi employs powerful, if traditional, ways of conveying the idea of weeping. Already on the third beat of the first bar there is a Neapolitan Second to colour the minor tonality. The downward flow of tears is expressed by a descending scale in bar 2, and in bar 3 a longer descent introduces the device sometimes known as the 'iambic prime', whose repetitive stutter has been employed by composers from the Baroque *Seufzer* right up to modern times to represent sighing or sobbing.[29] Example 4.2 gives the opening up to the first vocal cadence. Later on (in bar 19), the inversion of the 'stutter' phrase creates a melodic augmented second. Vivaldi's liberal use of this interval within a melodic phrase is a hallmark of his style. One hesitates to say that he invented its melodic use in Western art music; but one can safely claim that he was the first great composer to exploit its melodic potential conspicuously and frequently.

In contrast, the second aria ('Sempre invano il Dio d'amore'), which describes the subject's love for Lidia, is almost skittish in character. Here, the keyword is 'vezzi' – the charms with which Cupid delights the heart. In a texture that at certain points becomes as elaborately contrapuntal as two-part writing permits, Vivaldi allows an exhilarating game of 'tag' to develop between treble and bass. There is a complex interplay of conflicting accents, phrases starting variously on the first and the second beat of the bar. Example 4.3 shows the first fourteen bars of the 'B' section. The mood, and the musical means of achieving it, are very similar to those of the aria 'Chi seguir vuol la costanza', given its first outing in *Ottone in villa* (I.5) and much used subsequently. This is vintage early-period Vivaldi.

### RV 654: *Elvira, anima mia* (RARA)

This is another heavily 'corrected' cantata. Its first aria, 'Partirò, ma vedrai quanto', is only one of several that we shall encounter in the Mantuan group to use the *passus duriusculus*, a downward movement by chromatic steps from tonic to dominant, the traditional emblem of lament (here, signifying departure from

---

[29] The term 'iambic prime' was coined by Joachim Braun, who refers to it in 'The Double Meaning of Jewish Elements in Dmitri Shostakovich's Music', *Musical Quarterly*, lxxi (1985), 68–80.

Ex. 4.2  Vivaldi, *Del suo natio rigore*, RV 653: 'Quei begl'occhi io pianger vidi', opening

Elvira). In the opening ritornello, shown as Example 4.4a, the *passus duriusculus* appears in the course of the lower 'part' of a self-accompanied line.[30] Both this and the upper 'part' that responds to it employ syncopated slurring, a Vivaldian speciality. The affective significance of the slurs becomes clearer later on when, in halved note-values, they appear during a melisma on the '-lor' of *dolor* (Example 4.4b). Schmitz, who knew none of the Mantuan cantatas, wrote of Albinoni's superiority to Vivaldi as a melodist in arias written in slow tempo.[31] This movement proves him over-hasty, for it has shapely contours, expressive intervals, and a sense of balance equal to the best of Albinoni.

In the second recitative ('Passo al rogo fatal, e son già cinto') the *passus duriusculus* turns up again (shorn of its first note) in the soprano part of a brief arioso passage highlighting the word *tormento* (Example 4.5). Sadly, the final aria, 'Pupille vaghe', fails to maintain the quality of the earlier movements. It is thematically diffuse and has a notably perfunctory 'B' section – always a symptom of low creative energy.

---

30  A 'self-accompanied' line is one in which, by constant movement between registers, the impression of two or more contrapuntally interacting lines is produced.
31  Schmitz, *Geschichte der weltlichen Solokantate*, pp. 150–1. Schmitz's real quarrel was with the extravagant *fioritura* of the Dresden cantatas, which he knew well.

Ex. 4.3  Vivaldi, *Del suo natio rigore*, RV 653: 'Sempre invano il Dio d'amore',
bars 57–73

Ex. 4.4  Vivaldi, *Elvira, anima mia*, RV 654: 'Partirò, ma vedrai quanto', extracts

Ex. 4.5  Vivaldi, *Elvira, anima mia*, RV 654: 'Passo al rogo fatal, e son già cinto', bars 7–10

Vivaldi penned an enigmatic inscription – 'Lasciar le Semicrome' – at the head of the last movement. Degrada, in the Critical Notes to the Ricordi edition, wonders whether it means that the harpsichordist, as opposed to the cellist, should refrain from playing the semiquavers of the bass. I doubt that this interpretation is correct, since the informality of the phrase is uncharacteristic of Vivaldi's directions to performers. Perhaps 'lasciar' should be understood in the sense of 'retain' ('lasciar stare') rather than 'omit' ('lasciar fuori'), in which case the purpose of the phrase might be to rescind an earlier oral instruction to the copyist.

### RV 658: *Il povero mio cor* (ARA)

The imposing first aria of this cantata is dominated, once again, by the chromatic *lamento* bass. Its opening ritornello is a self-accompanied line that cleverly prefigures the opening of the first vocal section by making the upper 'part' a good approximation to the soprano melody and the lower 'part' a simplified version of its bass. Incredibly, the 'B' section has both of its cadences in B flat minor, the lowered seventh degree of the tonic, C minor. This key lies right outside the *ambitus*, and the return to the 'A' section for the reprise inevitably gives a jolt. This movement expresses as clearly as any other in Vivaldi's oeuvre his readiness to explore unusual tonal designs within structures that in all other respects are conventional.

After a short but expressive recitative, we arrive at the second aria, 'Disperato, confuso, agitato'. Vivaldi conveys the unbalanced state of mind described by the text effectively enough, using hammered repeated quavers in the bass and a syncopated 'sawing' rhythm (quaver, crotchet, quaver) in the soprano part. The vocal line is splendidly mobile, rising to great heights and falling to great depths. All the same, this aria errs by being too repetitive for its own good: the syncopations are so unrelenting that their effect becomes inappropriately comic in certain places.

### RV 659: *Indarno cerca la tortorella* (ARA)

The first aria of this cantata, which introduces once again the *lamento* bass and the device of a self-accompanied ritornello theme, is pleasingly varied in rhythm and melodic design. Scalar movement dominates, but this is expressed variously as two-note 'sighing' figures, three-note 'slide' figures and long sweeps of semiquavers. The 'B' section comes to a glorious finish with a descending scale running the full length of the movement's unusually wide compass (*b" flat* to *b flat*) in illustration of the word *sparge* ('spreads'). An interesting formal detail is that the second vocal period includes, half-way through, a reprise of the material of the first vocal period in the manner of 'rounded' binary form, which c.1720 was beginning to supersede simple binary form in longer instrumental movements. But instead of returning to the text and word-setting of the opening two lines, Vivaldi presents a jumbled and partly garbled version:

bars 11–21   Indarno cerca la tortorella, la tortorella al suo compagno di far ritorno.
bars 54–62   Di far ritorno invano cerca al suo compagno la tortorella.

This unforced alteration, which perhaps puzzled Vivaldi's singers, is harmless enough. It does, however, betray the fact of the composer's background in instrumental music. For him, the melody has an intrinsic status independent of the words, which are, so to speak, its necessary but not always identical clothing.

The second aria, 'La sola spene', mirrors the first in its slow tempo, its use of a *lamento* bass, and its inclusion of a reprise to different words (this time, those of the fourth and fifth lines). To give the outer movements of a work common structural, technical, and expressive characteristics (in addition to the obvious identity of key) is a characteristic found over and over again in Vivaldi's instrumental music, so one is not surprised to encounter it also here, where the reigning *affetto* in the two arias (the grief of separation) is identical. There is, however, an interesting additional element in the second aria: a repetitive use of the harsh melodic interval of a diminished third, which occurs ten times in the movement (ignoring the *da capo* repeat).

## RV 661: *Nel partir da te, mio caro* (ARA)

The first aria of this attractive cantata has a breathless quality arising from its segmentation into two-bar units. Vivaldi uses rhythmic variety and strong contrasts between syllabic and melismatic delivery of the words to counterbalance this regularity. The movement gets off to a very good start with a ritornello theme of real character (Example 4.6): the tonicization of the dominant note in bar 2 imparts a spin to the music that lends it a powerful forward momentum. The rippling arpeggios in bar 7 and subsequently are used very effectively in alternation with vocal *fioritura* during the melismatic passages. The first vocal period cadences in the relative key, C minor – another unconventional but, for Vivaldi, scarcely unexpected choice.

From the smooth efficiency of the recitative one would never guess what travails, described in Chapter 3, Vivaldi went through to complete it. Gaiety returns in the second aria, 'Di quel volto sempre amato'. This is a compact aria of more conventional cast than the first. The movement contains three delicious melismas comprising four 'dotted' groups (dotted semiquaver plus demisemiquaver) plus a longer concluding note. On the first two occasions the figure aptly illustrates the word *invola* ('steals'), alluding to the meaning of its root, *vola* (meaning 'flies'). On the third occasion, in the 'B' section, it accompanies the '-lor' of *dolor* – not quite as fittingly, but at least without incongruity. Vivaldi

Ex. 4.6  Vivaldi, *Nel partir da te, mio caro*: opening ritornello

does not quite have Handel's flair for introducing dotted rhythms in order to lend vitality and memorability to a phrase, but his touch is very sure on this occasion.

### RV 665: *Si levi dal pensier* (ARA)

This bittersweet cantata is more sophisticated than it looks. Its opening aria deals with Clori's unsuccessful attempts to banish Daliso from her mind. Vivaldi captures the idea of obsession brilliantly by treating in constant imitation the lively phrase that opens both the initial ritornello and the first vocal period. The word *lusinghier* ('flattering', 'attractive') is the cue for some extravagant melismas that reveal the depths of Clori's infatuation.

In contrast, the bass in the second aria, 'Vanne sull'Adria, infido', is very simple and characterized by much note-repetition. The repeated notes may be widely spaced (in which case they may be separated by rests) or continuous. Vivaldi was in the vanguard of the composers who, in the 1720s, adopted the 'drum bass' (called *Trommelbaß* by German writers) as a simple but effective means of securing rhythmic animation without harmonic complexity. Like many good devices, it suffered from over-generous application. Quantz castigated its near-universal use in the Italian music of his time. His view of typical Italian basses was that they were 'neither imposing nor melodic, nor having any especial connection with the principal part'.[32] He went on: 'Even in their solo sonatas they cannot tolerate a bass that now and again moves in a melodic manner. They prefer it if the bass is treated very drily, sounding only intermittently or drumming constantly on a single note'. C. P. E. Bach was no more sympathetic to the device. And yet: the *Trommelbaß* proved its worth all through the rest of the century and beyond. Who would dare to argue that the repeated bass quavers in the finale of Haydn's Symphony no. 49 (*La Passione*) or in the first movement of Beethoven's String Quartet in C minor, Op. 18 no. 4, were out of place?

The depth of Vivaldi's addiction to drum basses is seen in the revisions he made in the 1720s to some of his violin sonatas composed in the previous decade (a comparison of the 'Dresden' and 'Manchester' versions of the C minor sonata, RV 6, will exemplify this) and in the substituted movements in the 1739 version (RV 611) of his *Magnificat*. His fondness for them stemmed not only from their intrinsic convenience but also from his lifelong penchant for pedal-notes and his wish to direct the listener's attention unreservedly towards the principal part. The

---

32  Johann Joachim Quantz, *Versuch einer Anweisung die Flöte Traversiere zu spielen*, p. 313.

Ex. 4.7 Vivaldi, *Si levi dal pensier*, RV 665: 'Vanne sull'Adria, infido', bars 10–35

first vocal period of 'Vanne sull'Adria, infido', shown as Example 4.7, illustrates the device in operation. Could the bass have been handled in a more complex manner without detracting from the raciness of the vocal part? Does the immobility of the 'drumming' passages (bars 15–22 and 26–30) not make an attractive contrast with the more dynamic material surrounding it? In short, Vivaldi's drum basses always have to be assessed in their context, not damned in advance.

## RV 680: *Lungi dal vago volto* (RARA)

This cantata with violin obbligato is the jewel of the Mantuan group. It is not pre-eminent merely because of the added contrapuntal part, but Vivaldi's creative flame may have received extra inspiration from the challenge this posed.

No concept in the whole cantata repertory is more certain to elicit graphic word-painting than that of distance (*lungi, lontano, lontananza*, etc.). Schmitz provides music examples of three instances: by Antonino Biffi, Lodovico Busca, and Alessandro Scarlatti, respectively.[33] Vivaldi conforms to tradition in a rather

---

[33] Schmitz, *Geschichte der weltlichen Solokantate*, pp. 102, 119, and 129.

Ex. 4.8  Vivaldi, *Lungi dal vago volto*, RV 680: opening

eccentric way, for the wide interval duly appears – but only after the illustrated word (*lungi*) has been and gone (Example 4.8). There is no mistaking, however, the eloquence and power of this recitative, which repeats certain phrases for added emphasis. Just before the end, where Elvira's lover makes a short prayer to Cupid, Vivaldi inserts four bars of what Rousseau called 'récitatif mesuré'.[34] This is not true arioso, since the voice continues to sing syllabically, but it is not ordinary recitative either, since the bass moves in even quavers (with a 'drumming' pattern, in fact), thereby forcing the singer to adhere to a strict tempo.

As remarked at the end of Chapter 3, the arias of this cantata have much of the substance of chamber duets (leaving aside the violin's task of punctuating them with quasi-orchestral ritornellos). Vivaldi works systematically towards the climaxes, his method being the time-honoured one of proceeding in clearly defined stages. As Table 4.2 shows, passages in parallel motion are the chief instruments of climax. They symbolize joyful union or synchronized feelings. Vivaldi makes these passages more interesting by introducing birdsong effects (bars 17–18, 23–4, and 35–6) or enlivening them with syncopation (bars 37–8 and 57–8).

The final aria, 'Mi stringerai, sì, sì', follows a similar course. Its muscular ritornello, full of double stopping, already depicts the embrace of the reunited lovers. Particularly impressive is the tailpiece to the second vocal period (shown as Example 4.9), where the violin returns to its ritornello material, and the voice supplies a new counterpoint to it opening with percussive repetitions of the two words *sì* (to the love between the two) and *no* (to the prospect of future separation). The repetition of these particular words – which, in addition to its possible inanity, plays havoc with prosody – has been ridiculed by commentators ever since the eighteenth century. Here, however, the effect is gloriously uplifting.

---

[34] Rousseau, *Dictionnaire de musique*, art. 'Récitatif', p. 404.

Table 4.2 Structure of the first aria, 'Augelletti, voi col canto', from *Lungi dal vago volto*, RV 680

| Bars | Section | Voice/Violin | Texture |
|------|---------|--------------|---------|
| 1–8 | ritornello (g→g) | violin | solo |
| 9–13 | first vocal period | voice | solo |
| 14–16 | ritornello (c→c) | violin | solo |
| 17–20 | second vocal period (1) | voice and violin | parallel motion |
| 21–2 | linking phrase (c→g) | violin | solo |
| 23–32 | second vocal period (2) | voice and violin | parallel motion, then dialogue (bar 36), then imitation (bar 30) |
| 33–9 | tailpiece | voice and violin | dialogue, then parallel motion (bar 36) |
| 40–5 | ritornello (g→g) | violin | solo |
| 46–50 | third vocal period | voice | solo |
| 51–3 | ritornello (B♭→B♭) | violin | solo |
| 54–61 | tailpiece | voice and violin | voice solo, then parallel motion (bar 56), then voice solo (bar 59) |

Ex. 4.9 Vivaldi, *Lungi dal vago volto*, RV 680: 'Mi stringerai, sì, sì', bars 81–7

Although the main key of this work is E flat major, G minor has a special salience. It is the key of the first aria and also the final destination of the 'B' section of the second aria. Elsewhere, I have written about key relationships in Vivaldi's works that I describe as 'privileged'.[35] These are two-way relationships that are not reducible to generic relationships based on harmonic function (e.g., between a major key and its mediant minor) and in consequence occur both more frequently and in less predictable contexts than is the case with other, similarly related keys. Two such pairs can be identified in Vivaldi's music: E flat major/G minor and C major/E minor. It really does seem that Vivaldi assigned intrinsic

---

[35] Talbot, 'How Recitatives End', p. 187. The cantatas emphasizing the E flat major/G minor relationship are RV 659, 663, and 667; those emphasizing the C major/E minor relationship are RV 652, 667, and 668.

expressive value to certain keys over and above their functional rôle. Perhaps his background as a violinist influenced him in this, or perhaps a trace of modal 'ethos' inherited via the *tuoni* of the seventeenth century survived in his thought.

## RV 685: *O mie porpore più belle* (ARA)

Vivaldi's two Mantuan cantatas with instrumental accompaniment do not compare in quality and musical interest with the superb accompanied cantatas of the next period (RV 683 and 684, in particular). They were both 'occasional' works, perhaps composed in a hurry and not engaging the composer's imagination very strongly. Maybe their blandness and relative brevity were 'designed' features, in the sense that the cantatas were intended to form a small part of a complex ceremony in which it would have been a mistake to obtrude unnecessarily.

RV 685 opens with an aria in minuet rhythm announcing Guidi's coronation as bishop. Minuets, especially quicker ones in 3/8 metre, were commonly used at the time to express rejoicing (this is how Johann Kuhnau celebrates Hezekiah's recovery and the victories of David and Gideon in his *Biblische Historien* of 1700). Vivaldi's aria is almost vulgarly triumphalist in mood, recalling Ozias's aria 'Gaude felix' in *Juditha triumphans* (Example 4.10). In the vocal sections Vivaldi employs a sparse *bassetto* accompaniment on unison upper strings, except at the climactic points, where the vocal line is superimposed on ritornello material in the manner already described for RV 680.[36]

The recitative, 'simple' in type, occupies a mere five bars. Unexpectedly, the second aria, 'No, non vidi il più gentile', does not employ the full string ensemble but contents itself with a solo violin. It is very unusual in Baroque multi-movement works for the two framing movements not to have identical scoring and not to call on all the performers. There are, however, precedents in Vivaldi's other works for such asymmetry. For instance, his *Salve Regina* in F major, RV 617, opens with a movement in which the only accompanist (apart from the continuo player) is a solo violin; the orchestra is used only in subsequent movements. It is probably no coincidence that here, too, the solo violin causes the deviation from the expected pattern. In certain circumstances, it seems, Vivaldi wished at all costs to bring himself, as a virtuoso of the violin, to the fore. In RV 685 the violinist-composer pays a personal, visible homage to the prelate. Was he angling for an extra-large *regalo* (gratuity)? Perhaps so – and quite blamelessly, according to the custom of the time. This second aria is fluent and totally unmemorable – 'Vivaldi-lite', one might jocularly say.

## RV 686: *Qual in pioggia dorata i dolci rai* (RARA)

Since the text of this cantata speaks of 'un giorno sì sereno' ('so serene a day'), one imagines that it was composed for Philip's birthday or name-day. To the

---

36  A *bassetto* (literally, a 'little bass') is a bass line similar to that of a continuo part but placed in a higher octave, where it is typically played by violins and/or viola. Such *bassetti* are apt to cross the vocal line but continue even then to function as true bass parts by virtue of their distinct timbre and characteristic shape.

Ex. 4.10  Vivaldi, *O mie porpore più belle*, RV 685: opening

string ensemble a pair of horns is added. These not only augment the grandeur of the orchestral sound but also contribute what one could term a symbolical element. Brass instruments were associated above all with the courtly lifestyle. Trumpets evoked the world of military endeavour and, more generally, of pageantry and court ritual, while horns accompanied the favourite pastime of hunting and represented the leisurely pursuits of a nobleman. To include horns in an orchestral composition dedicated to a nobleman (as Bach did so conspicuously in his *First Brandenburg Concerto*) was in itself an act of tribute.

Whereas German composers – among them, Bach, Telemann, and Fasch – on occasion worked actual horn calls into their parts for the instrument, Italian composers were content with more generic effects, making full use of such features as the 'horn fifth' (the interval between the sixth and ninth harmonics of the natural instrument, used, in two-part writing for horns, as a point of transition between a third and a sixth) and rapid repeated notes. Except in one instance (the use of horns in F in the tonal context of C minor in *Farnace*), Vivaldi's use of horns – invariably in pairs – is by his exacting standards rather conventional and unadventurous, although perfectly idiomatic.

There is some uncertainty about where the horn players used in the performance of RV 686 came from. Cataldi has pointed out that no horn players are present in contemporary lists of the members of the court orchestra, the 'Regia Ducal Cappella'.[37] His opinion is that they were recruited specially for the occasion. However, the orchestra did have three trumpeters, who may well have doubled on the lower instrument. It is perhaps significant that in eighteenth-century Italy the horn was often viewed as a second species of trumpet: a *tromba da caccia*, as opposed to a *tromba lunga*.

Nothing need be said about the two recitatives of RV 686 except that the first is introduced by the direction 'arcate lunghe'. This is an unusual direction for the

---

37  Cataldi, 'I rapporti di Vivaldi', 90–92.

bass in simple recitative (it makes obvious sense in accompanied recitative, where the upper strings sustain their sounds). Perhaps it signifies the participation of a larger than normal number of instruments. Another possibility is that, if the performance was held outdoors, Vivaldi wished to ensure that the sound carried effectively. In all other respects, this recitative and its sequel are perfectly conventional.

The two arias are given over, somewhat wearisomely, to the tonic and dominant harmonies that come naturally to the horn idiom. The entire 'B' section of the first aria is *all'unisono* (the horns are silent). Marcello is particularly scathing about this expedient, writing:

> In addition, the modern *maestro di cappella* will have to write *canzonette*, especially for contraltos and mezzo-sopranos, where the bass instruments accompany or play the same thing in the lower octave, while the violins play it in the upper octave, with all the parts written in the score, so that the piece can be described as 'in three parts' even though this aria in reality consists of a sole part diversified only by virtue of being reproduced in higher and lower octaves.[38]

In fact, Vivaldi does not trouble to create even the visual illusion of three-part writing, for he writes the 'B' section on only two staves: one for the alto and one for all the instruments.

### RV 799: *Tremori al braccio e lagrime sul ciglio* (RARA)

Many of the Vivaldi works unearthed in recent years have been either incomplete or unremarkable in quality (which is not to say lacking in historical interest), but this work ranks high on all counts, being easily the best of the Mantuan continuo cantatas of more serious cast. How its manuscript arrived separately in Vienna is impossible to say. It may have been a member of a set, copied from an autograph manuscript once in Vivaldi's own collection but today lost, that subsequently became detached from its companions. At one stage, RV 799 was bound into a volume together with cantatas by Attilio Ariosti and Emanuele D'Astorga, but there is no evidence of any original connection with those works.[39]

The opening of RV 799 is arresting: four bars of 'measured' recitative starting with three trilled notes expressive of trembling (Example 4.11). The first aria, 'Quando chiami dolce e cara', introduces the *lamento* figure very discreetly (it is broken up by *notes échappées*) in the middle of the opening ritornello. With great ingenuity, Vivaldi works the same phrase into the vocal line during the second and third vocal periods, stamping a strong sense of unity on the movement. The second aria, 'Quello che senti, o bella', is styled as a siciliana in 12/8 metre. In

---

38  Marcello, *Il teatro alla moda*, p. 21: 'Dovrà il maestro di cappella *moderno* ancora compor *canzonette* particolarmente in *contralto* o *mezzo soprano*, che i *bassi accompagnino o suonino* la medesima cosa all'*ottava bassa* e li violini all'*ottava alta*, scrivendo sulla *partitura* tutte le *parti*, e così s'intenderà di *comporre a tre*, benché l'*arietta* in sostanza sia d'una *parte* sola diversificata solamente per *ottava in grave* e in *acuto*.'

39  Details are given in Fourés and Talbot, 'A New Vivaldi Cantata in Vienna', p. 102.

Ex. 4.11  Vivaldi, *Tremori al braccio e lagrime sul ciglio*, RV 799: opening

Vivaldi's music, *alla siciliana* stylization is very common (think of the main slow movement of the D minor concerto RV 565 or of the 'Domine Deus, Rex caelestis' movement in the *Gloria* RV 589), so it is perhaps surprising that this is our first encounter with it in the cantatas. Cleverly, Vivaldi allows some relief from the prevalent stereotyped rhythms. A rising phrase broken up by quaver rests is used to illustrate the word *scherzare* ('play'), while a complementary descending phrase is employed for *sospiro* ('sigh'). In both arias the continuo bass participates effectively in contrapuntal imitation and dialogue with the voice. Although both arias are in slow tempo and the minor mode, their mood is subtly different. In the first aria the singer, representing Elvira's bashful lover, is lachrymose and self-absorbed; in the second, he has not lost his natural timidity but has at least resolved to try his fortune and to that extent is thinking positively. If Elvira's suitor, or would-be suitor, was present in the audience before whom RV 799 was performed, he might even have considered the portrait quite flattering.

# CHAPTER FIVE

# Cantatas of the Middle Years

## *Vivaldi's* Blütezeit

The 1720s were Vivaldi's glory years. On his return from Mantua, he slipped back effortlessly into his former pattern of activity. In October 1720 his new opera *La verità in cimento* signalled, just in time for Marcello's satire, his return to the world of Venetian opera. Very soon, he became an operatic composer in demand outside Venice. In 1721 he received a *scrittura* (commission) for Milan. Commissions for Rome (1723, 1724), Mantua (1725), Florence (1727), and Reggio Emilia (1727) followed. Many of these external commissions required him to take personal charge of the performance *in situ*, obliging him, despite his precarious health (his *strettezza di petto* has been identified with near certainty as bronchial asthma), to venture abroad. Within Venice, his career as a composer of opera was reinforced in many seasons by his direction of the music at the S. Angelo theatre, which allowed him, so to speak, to offer himself commissions, while choosing as partner composers younger men who as yet posed no threat to his dominance.[1]

Like several other Venetian opera composers (Lotti and Albinoni spring to mind), Vivaldi established a close partnership with a leading female singer. Since he was a priest, there was no question of pursuing this relationship as far as marriage – tongues wagged furiously enough at the mere suggestion of a close professional association. The singer was Anna Tessieri (better known as Anna Girò), who, together with her half-sister and chaperone Paola, formed part of Vivaldi's entourage from the mid-1720s onwards. Born in Mantua around 1710, Girò sang in opera for the first time in Vicenza in 1723 and made her Venetian début in 1724. Vivaldi first employed her in *Farnace* (1727, carnival) and thereafter rarely dispensed with her services. She was in Vienna with him when he died in 1741. His dependence on her probably exceeded her dependence on him: significantly, she did not follow him to central Europe in 1729 and secured good operatic parts during his absence. Her stage career continued for some years after his death, ending only when she married a count from Piacenza in 1748. Although she doubtless learned much from Vivaldi and remained loyal to his interests, it

---

[1]  For a survey and evaluation of Vivaldi's operatic activity in the 1720s, see Reinhard Strohm, *Essays on Handel and Italian Opera*, Cambridge: Cambridge University Press, 1985, pp. 122–63, and Michael Talbot, 'A Venetian Operatic Contract of 1714', in Michael Talbot (ed.), *The Business of Music*, Liverpool: Liverpool University Press, 2002, pp. 10–61.

would be a mistake to regard her, as some commentators have seemed to do, as simply his 'creature'. Her voice was not strong, and her contralto (really, mezzo-soprano) register was of only average compass – from about *a* to *e''*, judging from surviving parts – but her stage presence and acting ability were universally admired. Certainly, she should be regarded as the possible original singer of any Vivaldi cantatas for mezzo-soprano notated in the alto clef dating from after c.1726.[2] At a deeper level, she may even have influenced decisively Vivaldi's taste and imagination.

Vivaldi's production of instrumental music proceeded apace. In July 1723 the Pietà, whose *Maestro di coro* was now the castrato singer and composer Carlo Luigi Pietragrua, drew up a contract with Vivaldi according to which he would supply its *coro* with two concertos per month at the price of one sequin each and take three or four rehearsals of the new compositions if residing in Venice at the time. Effectively, this was a form of re-engagement as *Maestro de' concerti* that spared him the drudgery of giving lessons or committing him to weekly atten-dance. The agreement remained in force until Vivaldi's expedition to central Europe in 1729, by which time over 140 concertos had been supplied.

Nor was Vivaldi inactive in the domain of sacred vocal music, even though he no longer had an institution to keep regularly supplied with psalms, Mass settings, and motets. Roman patrons commissioned sacred works from him, and it was during the 1720s that he inaugurated his impressive series of works for double choir and orchestra (*in due cori*), which provide a shop-window for his contra-puntal skills and ability to handle large forces.

During this decade Vivaldi cultivated assiduously his international connec-tions. He wrote music for foreign embassies in Venice: the imperial ambassador commissioned his serenata *La gara della Giustizia e della Pace*, RV 689 (date unknown, but not long after 1720), and the French ambassador his serenata for the wedding of Louis XV (RV 687) in 1725 and the impressive *La Senna festeggiante*, RV 693, of 1726. It is revealing that whereas the dedicatees of the two major collections of concertos (Opp. 3 and 4) that he had published in the previous decade were Italians – Grand Prince Ferdinando of Tuscany and the Venetian nobleman (and violin pupil) Vettor Dolfin – those of their counterparts in the 1720s (Opp. 8 and 9) came from German-speaking Europe: Count Wenzel von Morzin and Emperor Charles VI himself. Increasingly, Vivaldi's dealings with foreign patrons and customers occurred outside the ambit of their visits to Venice.

Undoubtedly, Vivaldi's international reputation stood at its highest during this decade. This can be seen not only indirectly, from the volume of music copied or external commissions obtained, but also from direct testimony. Reporting on the performance of the Wedding Serenata on 12 September 1725, a writer in the *Mercure de France* for October described Vivaldi (p. 2418) as 'le plus habile compositeur qui soit à Venise' – 'the most able composer in Venice'. This placed him above Lotti, the *Primo maestro* of S. Marco, and above Albinoni, the most

---

[2] On Girò's career and vocal qualities, see John Walter Hill, 'Vivaldi's Griselda', *Journal of the American Musicological Society*, xxxi (1978), 53–82.

productive composer of operas in the city.[3] In fact, Vivaldi had become more esteemed abroad than at home. It was Venetians, not foreigners, who picked holes in his harmony and mocked his *parvenu* aspirations.

Like any successful composer in his later forties and fifties, Vivaldi acquired his share of acolytes. From what we know of his biography, he was more interested in passing on his craft to well-heeled nobles than to impecunious musicians, and one cannot point to a close musical or personal relationship with any leading figure in Venice. He was more generous, however, towards composers who were too young or too modest in talent to upstage him, and theirs are the names that appear most often in association with his. Two composers in particular deserve mention, since they have a likely connection with his cantatas: Giovanni Francesco Brusa (c.1700–1768) and Mauro D'Alay (c.1690–1757).

Brusa came from a Venetian citizen family and originally cultivated music, as a singer and composer, on an amateur basis.[4] He burst on the scene with his opera *Il trionfo della virtù*, which was staged at S. Giovanni Grisostomo, with Faustina Bordoni as Cornelia, in the autumn of 1724.[5] This was followed by *L'amore eroico* at S. Samuele in the Ascension season of 1725 and *Medea e Giasone* at S. Angelo in the carnival of 1727 (the latter inserted between the autumn opera, *Dorilla in Tempe*, and the second carnival opera, *Farnace* – both by Vivaldi).[6] A German correspondent reported enthusiastically on *L'amore eroico* to Johann Mattheson, praising it for its musical adventurousness (which included the use of melodic augmented seconds) and singling out for brief analytical commentary two arias that had especially captivated the public.[7] We find a violin concerto by Brusa near the end of a surviving partbook for Anna Maria, principal violinist at the Pietà, which contains the additions to her repertory during a period running from 1723 to 1726; its presence there suggests Vivaldi's advocacy.[8] Of Brusa's cantatas more will be said later.

After 1727 Brusa's active interest in music seems to have undergone a steep decline. In 1726 he had been elected 'fourth' organist at S. Marco (i.e., he played the second small portable organ), a low-paying and rather undemanding post compatible with his *dilettante* status, but by 1740, when a successor, Antonio Cortona, was appointed, he had evidently given it up. His operas come to an

---

3   Benedetto Marcello, who held aloof from opera, disqualified himself from consideration by that fact.

4   'Citizen' (*cittadino*) is used here in a technical sense to denote the social stratum intermediate between the patriciate and the populace (*popolo*). *Dilettanti* remained defined by their social rank: Albinoni belonged to the *popolo*, Marcello to the nobility.

5   I am grateful to Berthold Over, author of the new article on Brusa for *Die Musik in Geschichte und Gegenwart*, for sharing information on this composer with me.

6   Brusa composed a further opera, *Arsace*, for the Teatro Ducale, Milan (August 1725). A recitative and two arias for *Medea e Giasone* composed by Vivaldi, apparently at an earlier date than Brusa's music, survive as RV 749.11, 13, and 16.

7   Johann Mattheson, *Critica musica*, 2 vols, Hamburg: author and heirs of T. von Wiering, 1722–5, vol. 2, pp. 286–7. Strohm's description of Brusa as 'insignificant' (*Essays on Handel and Italian Opera*, p. 155) is too unkind. Certainly, he was young and relatively untested, but in 1727 he appeared a rising star.

8   See Michael Talbot, 'Anna Maria's Partbook', in Helen Geyer and Wolfgang Osthoff (eds), *Musik an den venezianischen Ospedali/Konservatorien vom 17. bis zum frühen 19. Jahrhundert*.

abrupt halt after *Medea e Giasone*. He became a civil servant, and by 1757 had risen to the position of *Sovrintendente al dazio dell'oglio*, or Superintendent of the Tax on Oil.

In 1756 his musical activity unexpectedly revived, and this time Brusa built himself a flourishing career on the strength of it. Together with his wife and children, he formed a little operatic troupe. His compositions included serious and comic operas, serenatas, and sinfonias. In 1765, when Galuppi left Venice for St Petersburg, Brusa replaced him as *Maestro di coro* at the Incurabili, a post that he filled very competently and diligently until his death in 1768.

Mauro D'Alay, whom we have already met in connection with his cantata *Amo Daliso, è ver*, was, like Vivaldi, a violinist-composer. Up to about 1724, his career was undistinguished and centred on his home town of Parma. Following Faustina Bordoni's début there, the two appear to have struck up a partnership that may have lasted until Faustina transferred her affections to Hasse. It was Faustina who insisted to the directors of the Royal Academy of Music that D'Alay (popularly known as 'Mauro' or 'Maurino') accompany her to London in her first season (1726).[9] D'Alay returned there on her second (1727) and third (1728) visits. He played solos in the opera orchestra on the second visit; a satirical pamphlet from that year, *The Contre Temps, or Rival Queens: A Small Farce*, inspired by the famous 'spat' between Faustina and Cuzzoni, hints that he and Faustina were lovers. In 1728 he published in London the set of six cantatas and six violin sonatas (the last actually plagiarized from Tartini) listed in Tables 1.2 and 1.3. These were dedicated to Charles Lennox, duke of Richmond, who had been the prime mover in bringing Faustina and D'Alay to England.

D'Alay was also the composer of several violin concertos, twelve of which were published by Le Cène in 1727. Two appear alongside those of Brusa, Tartini, and (predominantly) Vivaldi himself in Anna Maria's Partbook.[10] They seem to have been added to her repertory in 1725 and 1726. Faustina sang in Venice in the carnival season of 1725, and very probably returned to her Venetian house, free of engagements, following her appearances in Vienna in the autumn and carnival of 1725–26, so it seems likely that, as her inseparable companion, D'Alay was also frequently in Venice in the middle years of the 1720s.[11] The style of his concertos reveals a definite Vivaldian influence, although D'Alay's music has an annoying propensity to meander aimlessly in a way quite foreign to its model.

It may be a little misleading to speak of a Vivaldi 'circle' including Brusa and D'Alay that was active in Venice in the mid-1720s, since this would imply that Vivaldi consciously strove to form a group of acolytes around him – something against which his temperament probably rebelled. More likely, the three men

*Symposion vom 4. bis 7. April 2001 Venedig*, Rome: Edizioni di Storia e Letteratura, 2004, pp. 23–79, at pp. 52–4.

9   For information on D'Alay's presence in London, see Elizabeth Gibson, *The Royal Academy of Music 1719–1728: The Institution and its Directors*, New York and London: Garland, 1989, pp. 348–82 passim.

10  Venice, Conservatorio di Musica 'Benedetto Marcello', fondo Correr, B. 55 n.133.

11  Faustina's house was by the Rio di S. Polo, almost opposite the Teatro S. Angelo on the far side of the Grand Canal.

were brought together by having, at specific junctures, a common patronage or place of activity.

## Cantatas for all Occasions

More than two-thirds of Vivaldi's cantatas have no known connection with Mantua. Nearly all of them fall chronologically between 1720, the year of his return to Venice, and c.1733, when he sent a group of eight cantatas to the court of Dresden. Just two cantatas lie outside this time-frame: RV 681 probably predates the Mantuan group, while RV 682 postdates the Dresden compilation. Significantly, both are 'accompanied' cantatas – therefore more likely to have been commissioned for one special occasion than to belong to a group of works associated with the regular meetings of an *accademia*. RV 796, too, could be a work composed before 1718, although this is far from certain.

Once again, a table is as good a way as any to launch the discussion. In Table 5.1 the non-Mantuan cantatas, with the omission of four cantatas found only in the Dresden compilation (RV 674, 676, 677, and 678), are listed. A bracketed (1) or (2) appended to the RV number in the first column means 'first manuscript' or 'second manuscript'. The sixth column makes a distinction among autograph manuscripts between 'composition manuscript', 'composition copy', and 'fair copy'. The first is an original draft, which in Vivaldi's case is likely to be untidy in appearance and to contain numerous corrections and deletions; the second is copied from an exemplar but makes deliberate modifications, premeditated or spontaneous, to it; the third is a simple copy made by the composer himself. The dates of composition proposed in the last column can be arranged chronologically as follows:

| | |
|---|---|
| Definitely before 1718 | RV 681 |
| Possibly before 1718 | RV 796 |
| 1721 or later | RV 663 |
| c.1725 | RV 679 |
| Between 1726 and c.1731 | RV 651 and 683 |
| 1727–28 | RV 667, 669, 684, and 684a |
| Before c.1731 | RV 650, 655(1), 656(1), 657(1), 662(1), and 666 |
| c.1731 or earlier | RV 660, 664, 670, and 671 |
| c.1731 | RV 668 |
| 1734 or later | RV 682 |

Note that in every case these are dates inferred from internal evidence (the manuscript) or external evidence (the music), and usually from both. A degree of fuzziness is inevitable, given the lack of precise information in the sources.

The oldest work, RV 681, is also the only Vivaldi cantata (leaving aside the spurious RV 753) of which an original source survives in Great Britain. This is a copy made in northern Europe: the paper is Dutch, and the hand appears to be English.[12] The manuscript formerly belonged to Dr Thomas Bever (1725–91), a

---

[12]  See Francesco Degrada's Critical Notes to the volume in *NEC*.

Table 5.1 Vivaldi's cantatas outside the Mantuan and Dresden groups

| RV | Location | Paper | Rastrography | Hand | Manuscript type | Voice | Compass | Accompaniment | Estimated date of composition |
|---|---|---|---|---|---|---|---|---|---|
| 650 | Foà 27, ff. 18–21 | B48 | 10/190.8(3) | autograph | fair copy | Soprano | $e\flat'$–$a''$ | continuo. | before c.1731 |
| 651 | Foà 27, ff. 10–13 | B48 | 10/186.2(2) | Scribe 4 | fair copy | Soprano | $e\flat'$–$a''$ | continuo | between 1726 and c.1731 |
| 655(1) | Foà 28, ff. 193–6 | B48 | 10/190.8(3) | autograph | fair copy | Soprano | $d'$–$g''$ | continuo | before c.1731 |
| 656(1) | Foà 28, ff. 181–4 | B48 | 10/190.8(3) | autograph | fair copy | Soprano | $f'$–$a''$ | continuo | before c.1731 |
| 657(1) | Foà 27, ff. 6–9 | B48 | 10/186.9(1) | autograph | fair copy | Soprano | $c'$–$c'''$ | continuo | before c.1731 |
| 660 | Foà 27, ff. 22–25 | B48 | 10/192.1(4) | autograph | composition copy? | Soprano | $c\#'$–$a''$ | continuo | c.1731 or earlier |
| 662(1) | Foà 27, ff. 2–5 | B48 | 10/186.9(1) | autograph | fair copy | Soprano | $c'$–$c'''$ | continuo | before c.1731 |
| 663 | SLUB, Mus. 1-J-7, pp. 57–63 | ? | 10/? | J. G. Grundig (= 'Hofnotist A') | fair copy | Soprano | $b\flat'$–$g''$ | continuo | 1721 or later |
| 664 | Foà 28, ff. 185–8 | B5 + B? | 10/190.1(4) + 10/188.3(1) | autograph | composition copy? | Soprano | $c\#'$–$a''$ | continuo | c.1731 or earlier |
| 666 | Foà 28, ff. 189–92 | B5 | 10/185.3(2) | Scribe 4 | fair copy | Soprano | $e'$–$a''$ | continuo | before c.1731 |
| 667(1) | Foà 28, ff. 177–80 | #5 | 10/192.8(2) | autograph | fair copy | Soprano | $g'$–$b''$ | continuo | 1727–28 |
| 668 | Foà 28, 197–200 | B5 | 10/190.1(4) | autograph | composition manuscript | Soprano | $e'$–$a''$ | continuo | c.1731 |
| 669 | Foà 27, ff. 14–17 | #5 | 10/192.8(2) | Scribe 4 | fair copy | Soprano | $d'$–$a''$ | continuo | 1727–28 |
| 670 | Foà 28, ff. 201–4 | B48 | 10/190.8(3) | autograph | composition copy? | Alto | $c\#'$–$e''$ | continuo | c. 1731 or earlier |
| 671 | Foà 28, ff. 205–8 | B48 | 10/186.2(2) | autograph | composition copy? | Alto | $b$–$d''$ | continuo | c. 1731 or earlier |
| 679 | Meiningen, Staatl. Museen, Max-Reger-Archiv, Ed 82ᵇ, no. 12, ff. 107–16 | ? | 10/? | Viennese copyist? | fair copy | Soprano | $c\#'$–$g''$ | strings | c.1725 |

Table 5.1 Vivaldi's cantatas outside the Mantuan and Dresden groups (*cont.*)

| RV | Location | Paper | Rastrography | Hand | Manuscript type | Voice | Compass | Accompaniment | Estimated date of composition |
|----|----------|-------|--------------|------|-----------------|-------|---------|---------------|-------------------------------|
| 681 | Oxford, Bodleian Library, Ms. Tenbury 1131, ff. 5–10 | ? | 8/? | unknown copyist | fair copy | Soprano | $c'$–$g''$ | strings | before 1718? |
| 682 | Foà 27, ff. 262–7 | B5 + B47 | 10/186.9(2) + 10/196.2(1) | unknown copyist | supervised copy | Soprano | $e'$–$a''$ | strings | 1734 or later |
| 683 | Foà 27, ff. 53–61 | B30 + B48 | 14/195.9(1) + 10/186.9 | autograph + unknown copyist (alto part) | fair copy | Alto | $b$–$d''$ | strings | between 1726 and c.1731 |
| 684 | Foà 28, ff. 2–3 and 6–12 | B47 | 10/198(3) + 10/192.2(2) | autograph | fair copy | Alto | $g$–$f''$ | strings | 1727–28 |
| 684a | Foà 28, ff. 4–5 | B9 | 10.185.1(1) | autograph | composition manuscript | Alto | ? | strings | 1727–28 |
| 796(1) | SLUB, Mus. 1-J-7, pp. 50–56 | German | 10/? | J. G. Grundig (= 'Hofnotist A') | fair copy | Soprano | $e'$–$a''$ | continuo | before 1720? |
| 796(2) | SLUB, Mus. 2389-I-500 | B? | 10/? | Scribe 4 | fair copy | Soprano | $b^{b'}$–$f''$ | continuo | before 1720? |

notable English collector of music. The volume in which it is included as the second item is a binder's collection containing works by Purcell, Pepusch, and other musicians domiciled in England. It passed from the library of St Michael's College, Tenbury, to the Bodleian library in 1985 but has retained its former shelfmark.

Ostensibly, this is a cantata for soprano, two violins, and continuo. It is evident, however, that a part for viola, which has to play a *bassetto* in several vocal periods where the bass is silent, is missing. This is not such a strange occurrence, since if the cantata reached England as a set of parts rather than a score, and if the viola part then became lost, any score based on the extant parts would inevitably be defective – without necessarily seeming so at first glance. An exactly parallel case is seen in the motet *Carae rosae, respirate*, RV 625.[13] This, too, has survived only in England, and lacks its viola part. It could well be that RV 681 and RV 625 belonged to the same consignment of music by Vivaldi, which was brought over in separate parts to England c.1715. Since RV 681 cannot be given a satisfactory performance without a viola part, the volume in *NEC* contains one, reconstructed by the present writer, in an appendix.

The cantata's early date is revealed most clearly by the *faux-naïf* style of the second aria, and by the repetition (shown via a repeat sign) of its first vocal period. These are features that in Vivaldi's vocal music occur only in the arias (including the 'church' arias of motets) of the second decade of the eighteenth century. The pastorale-like quality of the first aria (with its long chains of thirds over pedal basses in 12/8 metre) and the self-consciously inventive string accompaniment for the recitative – which includes a fairly outlandish enharmonic change in the move from bar 23 to bar 24 – support the same conclusion.

Nothing in the conventionally Arcadian text of the poem suggests a place of performance. Given the period, Vivaldi could easily have composed the cantata for one of Angioletta Bianchi's soirées.

As the cantata's high RV number implies, the authorship of RV 796, *Usignoletto bello*, has not always been clear. The volume Mus. 1-J-7 in Dresden, which is the principal subject of the next chapter, opens with three works that do not form part of Vivaldi's 'Dresden compilation' of c.1733. These are:

Antonio Tozzi, *Dunque il perfido Enea* (soprano and instruments)    pp. 1–49
[Vivaldi], *Usignoletto bello*, RV 796 (soprano and continuo)    pp. 50–56
Vivaldi, *Scherza di fronda in fronda*, RV 663 (soprano and continuo)  pp. 57–63

Since the manuscript of the second work does not bear the name of a composer, it has not always been regarded as authentic. Ortrun Landmann presciently chose to include it as '*RV deest*' in her 1981 catalogue of Vivaldi works in the SLUB, arguing that since its paper and handwriting were exactly the same as those of the work that followed it (RV 663) in the same volume, its composer could reasonably be expected to be the same.[14] In 1991 Karl Heller endorsed Landmann's conclusion, adding that the cantata's style was perfectly Vivaldian.[15] The reward

13  See the discussion of RV 625 in Talbot, *The Sacred Vocal Music*, pp. 199–203.
14  Landmann, 'Katalog', p. 157.
15  Heller, 'Zu einigen Incerta', pp. 52–7.

for their persistence arrived in 1992, when a second manuscript of the same cantata, attributed to Vivaldi and written in the hand of Scribe 4, was auctioned in London at Sotheby's. By good fortune, it was the SLUB that acquired it. In this second manuscript the cantata, still for soprano, is in E flat rather than G major. Internal evidence – the presence of otherwise unaccountable copying errors in the E flat version – shows that this is not the original key, which leaves G major as the likely original key.[16]

A few years earlier, Manfred Fechner had provided enlightenment on the copyist.[17] He identified the person responsible for making the copies of RV 796 and RV 663, previously known among students of the Dresden repertory merely by the name of 'Scribe A' ('*Schreiber* A'), as Johann Gottfried Grundig (1706–73), who was employed by the *Hofkapelle* specifically as a copyist. Grundig probably initiated this activity no earlier than the mid-1720s and possibly as late as 1728, when the death of Jean-Baptiste Volumier allowed Johann Georg Pisendel to assume leadership of the orchestra.

Just because Grundig copied both RV 796 and RV 663, one cannot assume *a priori* that the two works were originally associated. In fact, each may have arrived in Dresden at a separate time and by a different route. As we saw in Chapter 3, RV 663 can date from no earlier than 1721, because of its borrowing from *Filippo, re di Macedonia*. But RV 796 certainly seems earlier. It is rhythmically, tonally, and structurally very simple – exactly the sort of cantata that would have struck Burney as 'very common and quiet'. Could it not have been taken back to Dresden from Venice in 1717 by Pisendel and his companions, about whose activities we will learn more in Chapter 6?

It was Francesco Degrada who discovered that *Scherza di fronda in fronda*, RV 663, was related by text and music to the homonymous aria, scored for soprano, two violins, and bass, attributed to Giuseppe Maria Orlandini in a vast anthology of operatic arias preserved at Paris in the Bibliothèque Nationale.[18] The text of the aria is indeed found in the third act of *Filippo, re di Macedonia*, which, on the evidence of the libretto, was set by Vivaldi (Giuseppe Boniventi composed the two preceding acts). Could this aria have been specially written by Orlandini for inclusion in Vivaldi's otherwise lost portion of the score, or could Vivaldi himself, no stranger to plagiarism, have surreptitiously appropriated it from an existing work by Orlandini? The style of the aria, which Degrada transcribes in full in an appendix to his edition in *NEC*, looks perfectly Vivaldian. The problem, however, is that Orlandini's normal style resembles 'Vivaldi without eccentricities': the aria contains only faint hints of Vivaldi's idiolect (the features of his style shared with no other composer). Understandably, Degrada is reluctant to come down firmly on one side or the other.

---

[16] For this reason, Karl Heller's edition of RV 796 for *NEC* is based on the G major version.

[17] Manfred Fechner, 'Bemerkungen zu einigen Dresdner Vivaldi-Manuskripten: Fragen der Vivaldi-Pflege unter Pisendel, zur Datierung und Schreiberproblematik', in Antonio Fanna and Giovanni Morelli (eds), *Nuovi studi vivaldiani*, pp. 775–84, at pp. 779–82.

[18] Paris, Bibliothèque Nationale, Vm.[7] 7964, vol. 2, pp. 221–3. See Degrada's Critical Notes to the *NEC* volume (1994).

There is, however, one extra factor to bring into the equation that tips the balance in favour of Vivaldi's authorship. This is, simply, that of the sixteen arias besides 'Scherza di fronda in fronda' in the group attributed to Orlandini, no fewer than six are revealed to come from operas by other composers.[19] 'Prende ardire e si conforta' is from Vinci's *Didone abbandonata* (Rome, Teatro Alibert, 1726); 'Torrente cresciuto', from Porpora's *Siroe, re di Persia* (Rome, Teatro Alibert, 1727); 'Ombra cara, ombra adorata', from Leo's *Catone in Utica* (Venice, S. Giovanni Grisostomo, 1729); 'Se al mormorio dell'onde', from Sarri's *Didone abbandonata* (Turin, Teatro Carignano, 1727); 'Dirle puoi', from Gasparini's *Nino* (Reggio Emilia, Teatro delle Commedie, 1729); 'Non disperar, cor mio', from Mancini's *Trajano* (Naples, S. Bartolomeo, 1723). This means that no credence whatever should be placed in the heading 'Aria del signor Orlandini' prefaced to the movement. By default, the presence of the aria's text in the *Filippo* libretto and the subsequent availability of both text and music to Vivaldi become the strongest evidence for its authorship.

To convert an aria with orchestral accompaniment into a continuo aria is no easy task. One cannot simply retain the bass in its original form and jettison the strings. The reason is that the rhythmic activity that propels the music forward, to say nothing of the thematic interest, is concentrated in the upper part or parts. A functional bass part in an orchestral texture has neither the inner vitality nor the shapeliness to survive without alteration in a continuo cantata. In particular, the bass of cantata ritornellos needs to be able to stand alone. By a fortunate happenstance, we are able to see how Vivaldi approached the task of remodelling the bass. On the vacant last page of the score of an early chamber concerto (RV 103), a bass part for this movement has been messily sketched by an unknown scribe.[20] Perhaps this was a student of the composer, and perhaps the purpose of the exercise was to save Vivaldi time while giving this assistant practice in the art of such conversion. In Example 5.1 the violin parts (which are mostly in unison) and the bass of the operatic aria are shown for the first vocal period, and below them both the sketch and the 'finished' bass as transmitted by RV 663. The three sources are all in different keys (the operatic aria in F major, the sketch in B flat major, and the cantata aria in E flat major). To facilitate comparison, the sketch and the cantata bass have been transposed to F major. The sketch and the cantata bass have also been displaced by half a bar so as to line up with the model.

The original bass moved in crotchets, on occasion introduced by rising *tirata* figures prefiguring, and then echoing, the melisma, expressive of running (*corre*), in the vocal part. Vivaldi's assistant, followed by the composer himself, sacrificed this illustrative detail, preferring instead to have a continuous 'rocking'

---

19  The attributions have been checked with RISM on-line (accessible via www.nisc.com), and I was able also to receive valuable information from Reinhard Strohm.

20  Turin, Biblioteca Nazionale Universitaria, Giordano 31, f. 234v. Degrada both reproduces in facsimile and transcribes this sketch in his edition. On balance, he considers it more likely that it is a subsequent attempt to condense the cantata once written, seeing that its ritornellos are much shorter, and bearing in mind Vivaldi's propensity to cut rather than to expand. However, this does not explain the corrections to the sketch occurring in passages identical with those of the finished cantata.

Ex. 5.1  Vivaldi, *Scherza di fronda in fronda*, RV 663: first vocal period

quaver bass that adds a little extra harmonic content but whose most important function is to retain the continuous quaver movement that – of necessity – was introduced in the ritornello. Vivaldi accepted almost without change the bass sketched for the vocal periods. However, he expanded the ritornellos (which are substitutes for, rather than arrangements of, those in the operatic aria). The opening ritornello grows from a rather over-symmetrical four bars to six bars; the medial ritornello of the 'A' section, from one bar to three bars; the concluding ritornello, from five bars to six.

The changes to the vocal part are less far-reaching. Naturally, the imitation by the second violin, which keeps the movement going in the second half of the opening bar, is foregone (this particular 'tag' is a *topos* of the early eighteenth century – Albinoni uses it to open the first concerto of his Op. 5 concertos of 1707). Vivaldi turns the triplet semiquavers in the second and fourth bars of the first vocal period into duplets – not for any deep thematic purpose (triplets are retained in the seventh bar), but merely as a technical simplification. When

Ex. 5.1  Vivaldi, *Scherza di fronda in fronda*, RV 663: *cont.*

drafting the new bass, his assistant must have been told that the melody of the vocal sections would remain essentially the same.[21]

How soon after the opera's production Vivaldi had recourse to this aria is anyone's guess. In general, he borrowed when music was fresh in his mind, so one would expect a date not much later than 1721, or even 1721 itself. The style of the cantata is at any rate indistinguishable from that of the Mantuan group.

'Che giova il sospirar, povero core', RV 679, has an interesting German connection, since it survives only in a volume once belonging to a patron of the composer, Duke Anton Ulrich of Saxe-Meiningen (1687–1763).[22] As early as 1723 Anton Ulrich was collecting concertos by Vivaldi, sent to him by the

---

21  This would also explain why the corrections in the sketch are found predominantly in the freely invented ritornellos rather than in the closely derived vocal periods.

22  On Anton Ulrich and his musical collection (which contained over 170 cantatas), see Lawrence Bennett, 'A Little-Known Collection of Early-Eighteenth-Century Vocal Music at Schloss Elisabethenburg, Meiningen', *Fontes Artis Musicae*, xlviii (2001), 250–302.

Table 5.2  The cantatas contained in Meiningen, Max-Reger-Archiv, Ed 82$^b$

| Folios | First line | Composer | Scoring | Compass | Hand |
|--------|-----------|----------|---------|---------|------|
| 1–8 | Movo il pie', il sguardo giro | N. Porpora | Soprano, violin. | $e'-g''$ | A |
| 9–14 | Dimando al ruscelletto | F. Stiparoli | Soprano | $d'-g''$ | A |
| 15–24 | Quel basso vapore | F. Stiparoli | Alto, strings | $a-e''$ | A |
| 25–32 | Coll'amare e col servire | D. Nanini | Tenor, strings | $e-f\#'$ | B |
| 33–44 | Sotto l'ombra d'un faggio | G. de Majo | Alto, violins. | $b-e''$ | A |
| 45–56 | Parto, addio: il mio destino | G. de Majo | Alto, strings | $c\#'-d''$ | A |
| 57–66 | Io non so dir se per sentier nascoso | F. Brusa | Soprano, strings | $d'-g\#''$ | A |
| 67–78 | So che sospiro, e sento | F. Brusa | Soprano, strings | $d'-g''$ | A |
| 79–92 | Però che scende in petto | F. Brusa | Soprano, strings | $d'-g''$ | A |
| 93–106 | Vezzose pupillette, i vostri sguardi | F. Brusa | Soprano, strings | $d'-a''$ | A |
| 107–16 | Che giova il sospirar, povero core | A. Vivaldi | Soprano, strings | $c\#'-g''$ | A |
| 117–21 | Son pellegrino errante | M. D'Alay | Soprano | $d'-a''$ | C |

composer's patron in Prague, Wenzel von Morzin;[23] in 1741, on his ill-fated visit
to Vienna, Vivaldi attempted to secure an audience with the duke, but in vain.[24]
The volume in question belongs to a large group of such volumes containing
music procured during a period spent by Anton Ulrich in Vienna from the end of
1725 to 1728. These volumes all contain music acquired in 1726 and 1727 and
bound in the latter year. All are inscribed with the initials 'A.U.D.S.' (standing for
'Antonius Ulricus Dux Saxoniae') followed by '1727'. The content of the volume
that interests us (shelfmarked Max-Reger-Archiv, Ed 82$^b$) is listed in Table 5.2.

Not mentioned in the table is the fact that the twelfth and last cantata, the one
by Mauro D'Alay, is inscribed to Faustina ('per la Sig.$^a$ Faustina'). This legend
confirms, of course, the closeness of the pair. Equally usefully, it defines
Faustina's compass as it existed c.1725 ($d'-a''$).[25] Since the other soprano cantatas
in the volume have very similar compasses, one is led to speculate that they were
all composed for Faustina, who was in Vienna in the autumn of 1725 and the
carnival of 1726. It is noteworthy that these cantatas all contain very long
melismas in which breath control (Faustina's *forte*) is paramount, and avoid
extra-wide leaps, for which she had no liking. The orchestrally accompanied,
outwardly very similar cantatas by Vivaldi and Brusa could even have been
performed at Faustina's house in Venice, with which we know that Vivaldi was
acquainted.[26] Porpora's cantata, on the other hand, is unlikely to have been

---

23  Herta Oesterheld, 'Autographe, ja oder nein?', in *Wertvolle Objekte und Sammlungen in den
Museen des Bezirkes Suhl*, Meiningen: Staatliche Museen Meiningen, 1974, pp. 91–107, at 107.

24  Ibid., p. 94.

25  On Faustina's compass, see Michael Talbot, 'Francesco Conti's Setting of Pietro Pariati's
*Pimpinone*', in Alberto Colzani and others, *Il teatro musicale italiano nel Sacro Romano Impero
nei secoli XVII e XVIII. Atti del VII Convegno internazionale sulla musica italiana nei secoli
XVII–XVIII, Loveno di Menaggio (Como), 15–17 luglio 1997*, Como: A.M.I.S., 1999, pp.
149–66, at pp. 152–3.

26  In a letter written in January 1729 to Prince Carl Ludwig Friedrich of Mecklenburg-Strelitz,
Vivaldi speaks of rehearsing in Faustina's house. See Rudolf Eller, 'Vier Briefe Antonio
Vivaldis', *Informazioni e studi vivaldiani*, x (1989), 5–22, at pp. 10–11.

performed in Venice, which this composer probably visited for the first time in preparation for carnival 1726, when his first opera for the city, *Siface*, was staged. Faustina could still have been the intended singer, however, since she visited Porpora's home base of Naples in 1723.

The identity of the copyist responsible for ten items in the volume (his hand is termed 'A' in the table) is unknown. He may have been a professional Viennese copyist or, alternatively, a musician in the employ of Anton Ulrich who travelled with him to Vienna.

The cantatas RV 683 and RV 684 are best examined in conjunction. Although they are assigned to different chronological categories in the list on p. 124, their similarities are so strong that they may be companion works. They are Vivaldi's only cantatas for alto and strings, and their similarity of vocal compass (respectively, *b–d''* and *g–f'*) suggests that the singer was the same. Given the highly dramatic quality of their texts, one thinks immediately of Anna Girò, whose mezzo-soprano compass would have fitted the ranges.[27] It may be significant that RV 683 comes complete with a set of mostly autograph parts, a sign that Vivaldi organized its performance.

It recently came to light that RV 683 is included, together with thirteen other cantatas for alto and 'Stromenti', in an inventory of the portion of the musical collection of Friedrich Carl von Schönborn that passed on his death to the court of Bamberg.[28] This elder brother of the more celebrated Rudolf Franz Erwein von Schönborn (an assiduous collector of Vivaldi's music) became in 1729 both Prince-Bishop of Würzburg, in succession to his uncle Lothar Franz, and Prince-Bishop of Bamberg, in succession to his elder brother Johann Philipp Franz. Since, on his death in 1746, it became necessary to divide the music that he had collected during his reign between the two principalities, to which two different persons had succeeded, a formula was agreed whereby Würzburg received two thirds, Bamberg one third.[29] Unfortunately, all the music listed in the Bamberg inventory is lost.

The likelihood is that Friedrich Carl acquired these cantatas for a specific singer in his service (there is no corresponding collection for soprano voice). Since he visited Venice in the carnival season of 1725–26 (Domenico Lalli dedicated to him the libretto for Antonio Pollarolo's *Turia Lucrezia*, performed as the first carnival opera at the S. Angelo theatre), he may have obtained the cantata

---

[27] The compass in RV 684 is perhaps a little wider than one would expect for Girò, so the idea is advanced very cautiously.

[28] The other named composers are Bencini, Broschi, Caldara, Canuti, Cassotti, Hasse, Porta, Romaldi, and Wassmuth. The fourteen cantatas are collectively listed as item 19, which implies that they were collected into a single volume. The inventory abbreviates the title of the cantata to 'Amor hai vinto'. In fact, its complete first line runs: 'Amor, hai vinto, hai vinto: ecco il mio seno', the repetition of 'hai vinto' being essential for the metre.

[29] For a transcription of the inventory with an introductory essay, see Dieter Kirsch, 'Das Bamberger Drittel: Zum Repertoire der Würzburger und Bamberger Hofmusik unter Fürstbischof Friedrich Carl von Schönborn (1729–1746)', in Paul Mai (ed.), *Im Dienst der Quellen zur Musik: Festschrift Gertraut Haberkamp zum 65. Geburtstag*, Tutzing: Hans Schneider, 2002, pp. 39–55. I am grateful to Federico Maria Sardelli for alerting me to this publication. The location of the inventory is Staatsarchiv Bamberg, Sterbeakte B 84 Nr. 24.

from Vivaldi during his stay.[30] This was a season when Vivaldi directed the music at S. Angelo, and it may be no coincidence that, as we saw, the text of *Amor, hai vinto, hai vinto: ecco il mio seno* includes a couplet borrowed from Metastasio's drama *Siroe, re di Persia*, which was performed in Vinci's setting at the S. Giovanni Grisostomo theatre during the same carnival.

Whether RV 651, Vivaldi's cantata for soprano and continuo on the same text (with some variants), preceded or followed RV 683 is hard to say with confidence. It would be naïve to assume that the more elaborate setting was necessarily the later. The character of the textual variants, which were doubtless due to Vivaldi's usual tinkering, sheds no light on the question.

In the case of RV 684, the situation is more complicated.[31] Embedded in the nine folios (Foà 28, ff. 2–3 and 6–12) transmitting the completed cantata are two (ff. 4–5) that contain the opening two sides of a first aria whose text appears identical with that of the first aria of the completed version, although its music is quite different, and an abandoned sketch, without text or bass, for the opening of the following recitative.[32] The definitive version of the cantata not only has an entirely different first aria but adds an elaborate prefatory recitative to it, transforming the original ARA structure into RARA, matching that of RV 683.[33]

Paul Everett's researches into the chronology of Vivaldi's works locate the aborted version of the cantata, RV 684a, in the period 1727–28, contemporary with the operas *Orlando furioso* and *L'Atenaide*.[34] The definitive version was presumably composed very soon afterwards.

As Luigi Cataldi has commented, the poetic text of the cantata had a clear narrative shape in its original ARA version that was confused, though arguably also enriched, by the added recitative.[35] The original 'scenario' of the cantata was as follows:

Aria 1       The singer despairs of Dorilla's non-reciprocation of his love and vows to kill himself.

Recitative   He calls on the Shades of Night to receive him more graciously than Dorilla did.

---

[30] The title-page of the libretto names him merely as 'il Sig. conte di Schëmborn' [*sic*], but we can be quite certain that the reference is to Friedrich Carl, since his title of 'vicecancelliero [*sic*] del S. R. I.' also is given.

[31] For a detailed description of the cantata, see Luigi Cataldi, 'Da "Ah, ch'infelice sempre" a "Cessate, omai cessate". Riflessioni sulle varianti della cantata vivaldiana RV 684', *Studi vivaldiani*, i (2001), 137–52.

[32] Facsimile reproductions of these pages are included in Francesco Degrada's edition of RV 684 for *NEC*. The apparent non-completion of the aria is presumably due to the loss of a nested bifolio containing the rest of it.

[33] Eleanor Selfridge-Field claims (*The Works of Benedetto and Alessandro Marcello: A Thematic Catalogue with Commentary on the Composers, Repertory, and Sources*, Oxford: Clarendon Press, 1990, p. 75) that the cantata by Benedetto Marcello (listed as A53) that likewise opens 'Cessate, omai cessate' is a setting of the same text. This is rightly disputed by Marco Bizzarini (*Benedetto Marcello*, p. xv), who observes that the similarity does not continue beyond the first line. Deceptive common openings of this kind abound in the repertory of the Baroque cantata.

[34] Paul Everett, 'Towards a Vivaldi Chronology', in Antonio Fanna and Giovanni Morelli (eds), *Nuovi studi vivaldiani*, pp. 729–57, at 746–9.

[35] Cataldi, 'Da "Ah, ch'infelice sempre" a "Cessate, omai cessate" ', 138–40.

Aria 2     He imagines himself in Hades as an avenging Bacchante.

The text of the added introductory recitative goes as follows:

| | |
|---|---|
| Cessate, omai cessate, | Cease, henceforth cease, |
| rimembranze crudeli | cruel memories |
| d'un affetto tiranno; | of a despotic love; |
| già barbare e spietate | heartless and pitiless, |
| mi cangiasti i contenti | you have already turned my happiness |
| in un immenso affanno. | into immense sorrow. |
| Cessate, omai cessate, | Cease, henceforth cease |
| di lacerarmi il petto, | to tear my breast, |
| di trafiggermi l'alma, | to pierce my soul, |
| di toglier al mio cor riposo e calma. | to rob my heart of peace and calm. |
| Povero cor afflitto e abbandonato, | Wretched, injured and forsaken [you are], my heart, |
| se ti toglie la pace | if a tyrannical passion |
| un affetto tiranno, | can rob you of peace and tranquillity, |
| perché un volto spietato, un'alma infida, | because a pitiless face, a faithless soul, |
| la sola crudeltà pasce e annida. | harbours and nurtures nothing but cruelty. |

The first six lines of this stanza appear to be taken from the text of an aria, since they observe a rhyme-scheme (ABC I ABC) typical of arias but abnormal in recitatives, which, as Chapter 2 has already commented, prefer to reserve end-rhyme as a sign of closure. Equally unusual is the repetition of the first line as line 7. Stranger still is the poetic content. Without knowing the three stanzas that follow, one would imagine that this was the opening of a cantata in which the subject, though badly bruised in love, would vow to have one last try, or to forswear love altogether, or even to seek another object for his affections. There is as yet no hint that the *crudeltà* of the beloved is to be turned back on her, and by implication on the whole world. But that is perhaps the whole point. Instead of winning, forgetting, or replacing Dorilla, as the conventional dramaturgy of cantatas requires, the subject becomes a second, more terrible Dorilla: the *alma infida* of the first stanza transmutes into the *ombra baccante* of the last stanza.

Both here and, to some extent, in RV 683 the character of an operatic *scena* emerges. This quasi-operatic quality operates at all levels: textual, textural, and stylistic. Such music is for the gods and goddesses of the stage to sing to their admirers in the intervals between their stage appearances.

Also from 1727–28, according to Everett's findings, are the two continuo cantatas RV 667 and RV 669. Their manuscripts have a rare paper-type (called '#5' by Everett) and rastrography in common. There is even a textual connection: RV 667 speaks of Sylvia's unresponsiveness to her lover, while RV 669 celebrates the final victory over her resistance. The clear difference in vocal compass between the two cantatas makes it unlikely that they were written for the same singer, but they may share a reference to topical events in the manner of some of the Mantuan cantatas.

These two cantatas are clearly 'Neapolitan' (which is almost to say 'post-1725') in style. In both, the vocal line zigzags exultantly in wide arcs and is awash with trills, slides, and similar confections. Reinhard Strohm distinguishes between singers of 'modern' training and 'conservative' training.[36] Whereas the Mantuan cantatas suit a conservative vocal style, narrower in compass, and less angular in movement, from now on Vivaldi's cantatas for soprano will predominantly cultivate the modern style. This was an idiom for which Schmitz had little sympathy, as evidenced by his scornful dismissal of the first few bars for the singer in *Fonti del pianto*, RV 656, as a 'caricature' (*Zerrbild*).[37]

We come next to the twelve (thirteen if we include the separate alto part for RV 683) works making up what I term the '1731 compilation'. These are the cantatas for which the expression 'c.1731' appears in the final column of Table 5.1. The date is established in the usual way by concordances of paper and rastrography, which link them to the Turin score of *Farnace*, representing the new version performed at Pavia in May 1731. What are less clear are the purpose of the compilation and the closeness of the respective dates of composition to 1731. This was a year in which Vivaldi was busy re-establishing his position in Venice after his perhaps not wholly successful visit to Bohemia (and probably other parts of central Europe) in 1729–30.

From the types of manuscript with which we are dealing, dominated by fair copies, it is possible that several of the cantatas in the group – for example, RV 651 – had been in existence for a number of years. Two of the three copies are of cantatas for alto voice, which raises the possibility that these were arrangements of works originally for soprano. Only one cantata, RV 668, is preserved in the form of a composition manuscript.

There is also considerable heterogeneity of specification. Two cantatas, RV 657(1) and 662(1), have an identical compass of exceptional range (*c'–c'''*) and are obviously companion pieces. The compass of RV 656(1) is exceptionally narrow (*f'–a''*), while that of RV 667 (*g–b''*) embraces the combined alto and soprano registers. These cantatas may have been sent to their destination, as those of the Dresden compilation undoubtedly were, as an anthology that deliberately 'mixed and matched' different vocal specifications. Naturally, it was not the manuscripts today in Turin that left the composer's *atelier* but copies of them, or even, in some cases, the texts from which they were themselves copied (provided that these were sufficiently neat). From 1731 onwards, Vivaldi styles himself in opera librettos the *Maestro di cappella* of Francis Stephen, duke of Lorraine (later to become Francis I, the consort of Empress Maria Theresia). This was an essentially honorific title, but may have entailed the dispatch of some music. Could the 1731 compilation perhaps be connected with the new appointment?

However, the isolated alto (cum bass) part for RV 683 copied on paper of the same type (B48) as most of the rest of the compilation would be puzzling in that light. Its purpose seems to be to replace a missing or damaged part that shared the bibliographical characteristics of its companion parts rather than to prepare RV 683 for dispatch elsewhere.[38] It is just credible that the purpose of making fresh copies of so many works at a single time was not to fulfil an immediate

---

36  Lists of singers in both categories are presented in *Essays on Handel and Italian Opera*, pp. 135–40.

37  Schmitz, *Geschichte der weltlichen Solokantate*, p. 151.

38  Another possible explanation is given in the separate discussion of RV 683 below.

commission but to provide a reservoir of cantatas ready for use on various occasions. If so, one of those occasions would have arrived after no more than two years, when Vivaldi drew on the 1731 stock for no fewer than five of the nine cantatas supplied to Dresden.

The status of the manuscripts transmitting the alto cantatas provokes thought. Remarkably, not one of them (there are only five such cantatas: RV 670, 671, 674, 676, and 677) is a composition manuscript or a fair copy. All appear to be transposed and altered versions of soprano cantatas. This implies that Vivaldi had little occasion to conceive such works in their original form for alto – even for Anna Girò.

Bringing up the rear, RV 682, an 'accompanied' cantata for soprano, is noteworthy in two respects. First, its date of copying is no earlier than 1734, which makes it the 'latest' of the cantatas.[39] Second, it was copied by an unpractised hand encountered nowhere else among Vivaldi's manuscripts. Since the composer himself made a few corrections to dynamic marks, the manuscript must originate from his *atelier*. The copyist was possibly one of Vivaldi's two nephews, Pietro and Daniele Mauro, who were sons of his sister Cecilia Maria. Pietro (1717–after 1780) first tried his hand at being an operatic tenor (nicknamed 'il Vivaldi') and occasional impresario but abandoned the stage after a few years for the more pacific life of a music copyist, in which he achieved greater professional success.[40] Daniele (born 1717) appears to have been a music copyist from the start.

Its conventional text – the return of a spurned lover to his beloved – provides no hint of the place or occasion for which RV 682 was required. During the 1730s Vivaldi travelled a great deal on the Italian mainland to direct performances of his operas, and this cantata could have been intended just as well for Ferrara or Ancona as for Venice.

## Individual Works

### RV 650: *Allor che lo sguardo* (ARA)

The arias of this cantata illustrate the two main approaches to forming the ritornello and accompaniment of a cantata aria. In the first, the ritornello material is strongly instrumental in character and independent of the vocal melody; motives extracted from it become the accompaniment in the vocal periods. Sometimes there are hints, at least initially, of ground bass treatment, but the ritornello soon dissolves into its fragments: where others use 'themes', Vivaldi prefers 'motives' or even mere 'figures'.

In the second aria, the ritornello opens with a pre-echo of the first vocal phrase or phrases before moving to a cadence. During the vocal periods the accompani-

---

[39] This date, derived from Everett's findings, is given in the Critical Notes of Francesco Degrada's edition, but no reason is provided. The manuscript employs varieties of B5 and B47 paper.

[40] In 1760 the diarist Pietro Gradenigo identified him as the best music copyist in Venice (Venice, Museo Civico Correr, Ms. Gradenigo 67, vol. 6, f. 91v).

ment changes to neutral, functional material that sustains the momentum and provides the necessary harmonic underpinning without drawing attention to itself. This option is preferred in swiftly moving arias that have no time to develop material independently in the bass part.

The first aria uses the mediant minor as a substitute for the dominant in the middle of the 'A' section. In fact, the dominant is completely ignored throughout the movement. This particular substitution is very common indeed in Vivaldi's music, recalling a similar 'deviation' in a few of Domenico Scarlatti's keyboard sonatas. Strangely enough, the tonal structure of the 'B' section is not always adjusted to take account of the earlier change, although this happens in the present case.

Many of the phrases in the second aria are duplicated – that is, presented twice in succession. This is a *galant* mannerism that began to gain currency in the late 1720s. It is most familiar today from Scarlatti's sonatas, which cultivate it in an extreme form, but is commonly encountered in Italian music of the 1730s. An almost Scarlattian addiction to it is seen in the first movement of Vivaldi's very late (1740) concerto 'con molti istromenti' RV 558. In RV 650 the repetitions are less blatant, partly because the phrase-structure is less quadratic, but the shape of things to come is clearly visible.

RV 651: *Amor, hai vinto, hai vinto: ecco il mio seno* (RARA)

The first aria of this cantata is truly magnificent. With its use of the *passus duriusculus*, extravagantly wide leaps and aggressively dotted rhythms, it recalls the tragic grandeur of the sonatas RV 6 (for violin) and RV 53 (for oboe), both likewise in C minor. The agitation represents the tossing of a ship, and the chromaticism is a response to the opening phrase of text, 'Passo di pena in pena' ('I go from one torment to another'), which, in bar 22, is further illustrated by a melodic augmented second. This interval is shown in Example 5.2, which opens three bars earlier at a point where a descending sequence in the bass, characterized by Malagueña Fifths (in bar $20_1$, reproducing bar $3_2$ of the opening ritornello), is complemented by a freshly devised vocal phrase that, instead of attenuating the effect of parallel fifths, actually intensifies it. Rarely does Vivaldi sound more Hispanic! In the B section, where the poet speaks of thunder and lightning, a new mode of accompaniment takes over, in the shape of oscillating demisemiquavers recalling the rumble of distant thunder depicted by obbligato cello in the slow movement of the 'Winter' Concerto, RV 297.[41]

The second aria, in the highly contrasted key of A minor, is perhaps less memorable but maintains the high level of invention and craftsmanship.

---

[41] This part is missing from some modern editions, and consequently from some modern performances – but only because some extant examples of the Le Cène edition (1725) lack this part, which was engraved on a separate page.

Ex. 5.2 Vivaldi, *Amor, hai vinto, hai vinto: ecco il mio seno*, RV 651: 'Passo di pena in pena', bars 19–22

## RV 655: *Era la notte quando i suoi splendori* (RARA)

This, in contrast, is one of the weakest of Vivaldi's cantatas. It is starved of tonal contrast, commuting back and forth between E minor, G major, and B minor. The opening recitative sets the tone by closing in the key of its start: E minor. If one were to look for merit in this cantata, one might find a little comfort in the neat way in which the descending quaver phrase spanning a fifth that opens the first aria in the continuo is later brought back underneath the voice. But the second aria, a never-ending stream of clichés, is irredeemable.

## RV 656: *Fonti del pianto* (ARA)

The opening line of this cantata was originally 'Fonti di pianto', which is how it also appears in the Dresden source. The Turin manuscript carries the instruction to the copyist 'Un Tuono basso' ('A tone lower'). This cannot refer to the copy in Dresden, which is at the same pitch. Possibly, therefore, the alteration from *di* to *del* was made by Vivaldi immediately before the no longer extant transposed version was copied.

'Pianto' ('lamentation') is the keyword of the opening aria. Vivaldi chooses to illustrate it not only with the traditional Neapolitan Sixth but also with the device known in modern musicological parlance as 'minorization' – a momentary move across to the parallel minor key. Although it was Neapolitan composers above all who popularized minorization, Vivaldi was an early exponent. As so often in Domenico Scarlatti, the quickfire alternation of major and minor keys sharing a tonic is sometimes the most striking feature of his movements.[42] The closing bars

---

[42] Transmodal modulation, which includes minorization, is discussed with reference to Vivaldi in Michael Talbot, 'Modal Shifts', 30–33.

Ex. 5.3  Vivaldi, *Fonti del pianto*, RV 656: bars 37–48

of the second vocal period, reproduced in Example 5.3, show this kind of modulation in action. Characteristically for Vivaldi, the reversion to the major occurs with a bump, at the last possible moment (bar 48).

The repeated-quaver accompaniment in the bass of this example is a form of *Trommelbaß* extremely common from the 1720s onwards in both slow and quick tempos. It tended to replace the fussier ways of elaborating a single harmony (with chord-inversions, passing notes, auxiliary notes, etc.) inherited from the Corellian tradition.

The second aria, following a pattern often observable in Vivaldi's cantatas, has a weaker 'personality'. It is perhaps a little too garrulous for its own good, but develops its rather simple material attractively enough.

Both arias have their 'A' sections hinged on the mediant minor, as remarked earlier for RV 650.

### RV 657: *Geme l'onda che parte dal fonte* (ARA)

Whereas Vivaldi's best continuo cantatas from the Mantuan period tend to be the ones containing popular elements, those from the later period place a premium on virtuosity and drama. RV 657 is second to none in those qualities.

Ex. 5.4 Vivaldi, *Geme l'onda che parte dal fonte*, RV 657: bars 7–21

Its opening aria is breathtakingly rich in illustrative detail. The first vocal period, shown as Example 5.4, depicts in turn the whirling of water (oscillation between adjacent notes) as it issues from a fountain (a downward cascade), the wilting of a flower in the evening (sluggish crotchets in the bass), the depth of valleys and the height of mountains (abrupt leaps between registers), and finally the lament (a slow chromatic progression in a 'scissors' movement culminating in an augmented sixth) of a nightingale (piping birdcalls). Here, the old 'mono-motivic' approach lies dead and buried. In the second vocal period the same motives appear in the same order, attractively varied. The 'B' section mixes them with new material illustrating a broken heart (with a 'beating' motive in the bass).

Ex. 5.4  Vivaldi, *Geme l'onda che parte dal fonte*, RV 657: *cont.*

It contains the longest melisma of the aria, which runs without pause for seventy-two triplet semiquavers and a quaver (bars 55–8). But this is not empty display: it is Vivaldi in total control and deploying the full force of his imagination. The second aria, 'Deh non partir sì presto', is scarcely less vivid, using a cascading staccato figure in the bass (representing the pouring out of liquid refreshment – the *ristoro* of which the text speaks?) to provide musical interest and thematic unity. Add to this a thoughtfully contrived central recitative (ending with the unusual final cadence shown as Example 3.2), and we have an exceptional work – which also requires an exceptional singer.

### RV 660: *La farfalletta s'aggira al lume* (ARA)

The butterfly (*farfalletta*) is a very familiar image in the cantata repertory. It stands for the male lover who flits hither and thither, attracted by the 'lights' (eyes) of beautiful nymphs. In the opening aria the idea of flight is suggested by soaring figures in the vocal part, while the bass contributes an independent, rigorously developed motivic idea. The second vocal period of this movement includes a very clear and attractive reprise of the opening theme. In the second aria the dominant musical figure, shared by both parts, is a descending demisemiquaver scale representing the 'black veil' of Night.

This is a fine, representative cantata. However, its key, A major, is very individual. Overall, Vivaldi's cantatas show a very strong bias towards the 'flat' keys. Part of the reason for this preference may be the preponderance of the darker passions. Even the cantatas with violins adhere to this bias, which is not shared by his instrumental music, where D major and E major appear with great frequency.

### RV 662: *Par che tardo oltre il costume* (ARA)

This is the companion piece to RV 660, and it possesses the same admirable qualities of spaciousness, exuberance, and attention to pictorial detail. In the first aria, the effect of acceleration produced by starting the vocal part with a pair of minims (for *Par che*), graduating to crotchets (*tardo*), and ending the phrase with two semiquavers followed by a 'snatched' minim (*oltre il costume*) suggests the release of a coiled spring. This is a Neapolitan feature that Vivaldi employs in some bravura arias of his later operas (e.g., 'Sorge l'irato nembo' in *Farnace* and 'Tra inospiti rupi' in *La fida ninfa*). The asymmetry that the device naturally imparts fits his penchant for non-quadratic phrase structure especially well.

Like many of the late cantatas, RV 662 opens with a movement in moderate tempo (the marking in the Turin source is 'Larghetto', altered to 'Andante' in the Dresden manuscript). The florid style of the Neapolitans, abounding in triplet semiquavers or demisemiquavers, had the general effect of slowing down the pulse at all tempo levels. Without its shortest notes, this aria would have worked well enough at ordinary 'Allegro' speed. In an important but little-known study of tempo in Vivaldi's concerto allegro movements, Karl Heller showed how the fairly uniform concept of 'Allegro' as it existed around 1710 (the time of *L'estro armonico*) later fractured into slower ('Allegro non molto') and faster ('Allegro molto') varieties.[43] The slowing down that resulted from the move to shorter note values sometimes took a tempo out of the 'Allegro' category altogether. Hence the popularity of such marks as 'Larghetto' and 'Andante' in Vivaldi's later arias, and his evident difficulty (expressed through alterations to the tempo indication) in finding terms appropriate to the situation.

The bass part is so active and expressive in both arias that this cantata, like RV 657, can be performed successfully with cello alone. There is no evidence that this ever happened at the time, and one cannot infer Vivaldi's intentions merely from scrutinizing the notes on the page. What one can claim, however, is that the use of cello alone was sanctioned by the performance practice of the period and that – at an empirical level – such a solution would 'work' very effectively in the present case.

## RV 663: *Scherza di fronda in fronda* (ARA)

The curious origins of this cantata's first aria were discussed earlier. It must be acknowledged frankly that neither the original material of the first aria nor its arrangement can elicit much admiration. The never-ending parade of quavers in the bass – reducing to uniformity what had been pleasantly varied in the operatic aria – is wearisome, even crude. How to render a functional bass attractive is shown by the second aria, 'Vorrebbe amar il cuor'. Its ritornellos refer to the main theme of the vocal part, but the 'athematic' accompaniment to the vocal sections employs five main rhythmic modules: three crotchets, six quavers, minim plus crotchet, crotchet plus minim, and dotted minim. The secret of Vivaldi's success is to form these modules into unpredictable patterns that sometimes cut across the

---

[43] Karl Heller, 'Tendenzen der Tempo-Differenzierung im Orchesterallegro Vivaldis', in Eitelfriedrich Thom (ed.), *Die Blasinstrumente und ihre Verwendung sowie zu Fragen des Tempos in der ersten Hälfte des 18. Jahrhunderts: Konferenzbericht der 4. Wissenschaftlichen Arbeitstagung Blankenburg/Harz, 26.–27. Juni 1976*, Magdeburg /Leipzig: Rat des Bezirks/ Zentralhaus für Kulturarbeit, 1977, pp. 79–84.

vocal phrases. As soon as the listener risks finding a pattern tedious, another comes to replace it.

### RV 664: *Se ben vivono senz'alma* (ARA)

This cantata, likewise, is not among Vivaldi's best. Its very title violates Italian prosody, since his setting of the first line makes an *ottonario* out of what should, for conformity with the rest of the stanza, be a *settenario* ('Se ben vivon senz'alma'). Some of the melismas in the first aria are object lessons in the kind of *fioritura* that Marcello (and Berlioz) deplored. Vivaldi subjects the first syllable of *moverli* in bars 23–6 to an elaborate melisma in short notes that one would take to express physical movement. But the 'moving' in question is only figurative: the poet is seeking to move the wood, meadow, and stream to pity. Vivaldi's over-literal interpretation is thus quite inappropriate, even ludicrous.

Things do not improve in the second aria, whose jejune accompaniment, mostly in 'hopping' octaves, fails to bring life to a dull vocal line.

### RV 666: *Sì, sì, luci adorate* (RARA)

This is an efficient but singularly soulless cantata. Both arias suffer somewhat from an excess of repetition. In the first aria, the unrelieved dactyls (quaver plus two semiquavers) in the accompaniment eventually produce monotony, while the culprit in the second aria is the phrase-structure, which, by its division into predominantly one-bar segments, robs the music of fluidity.

### RV 667: *Sorge vermiglia in ciel la bella Aurora* (RARA)

In its original version, this cantata has the widest vocal compass ($g$–$b''$) of any continuo cantata by Vivaldi. The author of the poetic text must have been familiar with the destined singer's prodigious range, since keywords expressing spatial extremes (literal or figurative) occur in three of the four movements. The first recitative has *ciel*, *dolente*, *l'ombre*, *sol*, and *muore*; the first aria, *lungi* and *muore*; the second aria, *atterra*, *ciel*, and *terra*. Vivaldi accepts with gusto the invitation to luxuriate in pictorialism. Example 5.5 gives complete the opening recitative, which moves very eloquently between contrasted registers and tonalities.

In the first aria, 'Nasce il sole, ed io sospiro', one hears echoes of 'Passo di pena in pena' from RV 651 (coincidentally or not, the phrase 'di pena in pena' occurs in the opening recitative). The use of the *passus duriusculus* in conjunction with a 'self-accompanied' line (bar 5) is noteworthy; so, too, are Malagueña Fifths in association with extravagant, zigzagging leaps (bars 11–14). Perhaps the two cantatas are close in date.

The second aria, 'Ardi, svena, impiaga, atterra', is a typical 'fury' aria of the kind familiar from Vagaus's 'Armatae face et anguibus' in *Juditha triumphans* or Cato's 'Dovea svenarti allora' in *Catone in Utica*. Unusually, however, it is not the protagonist's own fury that this aria expresses, but that of his beloved heaped on his head, which will never be strong enough to break his fidelity to her. The

Ex. 5.5 Vivaldi, *Sorge vermiglia in ciel la bella Aurora*, RV 667: opening (Turin version)

Ex. 5.6  Vivaldi, *T'intendo, sì, mio cor*, bars 5–7

histrionic quality of this splendidly full-blooded aria is enhanced by a few aptly inserted phrases where the voice moves in octaves with the bass.

### RV 668: *T'intendo, sì, mio cor* (ARA)

This lone setting of a Metastasio text may not be Vivaldi's most accomplished cantata, but it is not without charm. Strikingly, the first vocal period of the first aria opens with a chord that is neither the tonic nor the dominant: the subdominant. The phrase in question, shown as Example 5.6, is almost identical in outline to the one that opens the 'Peccator videbit et irascetur' movement of Vivaldi's *Beatus vir*, RV 597/795. Beginning a section or movement in an 'off-tonic' manner, as here, is a typically Vivaldian quirk. Unexpectedly, this phrase reappears in a triple-metre paraphrase in the second aria, three bars after the start of the first vocal period. Such inter-aria relationships are rare in Vivaldi's cantatas – far less common, for instance, than those between the outer movements of his concertos – and the recurrence looks accidental rather than deliberate.

The existence of settings of versions of the same text by at least three other composers (Leo, Porpora, Pescetti) contemporary with Vivaldi provides an opportunity for stylistic comparison. Degrada has already done this in respect of the setting by Leo.[44] Such comparisons are, of course, dangerous, since if the basic specifications (tempo, metre, mode, vocal compass, etc.) of the movements in question differ too much, the basis for a useful comparison shrinks: one is no longer comparing like with like. The Leo setting is perhaps too different in this respect to offer good material for comparison. Porpora's setting is more suitable – especially in its second aria, 'Placido zeffiretto', which, like Vivaldi's aria, is in 3/8 metre and even shares one significant thematic particle (I–II–I in the rhythm dotted quaver, semiquaver, quaver).

The 'B' section of both arias is quoted up to the first main cadence as Example 5.7. At first sight, Vivaldi's setting appears unsophisticated in comparison with Porpora's. Its bass is content to stride along in quavers without engaging thematically with the voice, and all the phrases except the last are three bars in length. However, this rather brazen approach reaps dividends: the melody, which has a clear thematic relationship to the 'A' section, possesses great robustness and shapeliness. Nor is the bass line devoid of artistry: its rhythmic permutations (similar to those described earlier for RV 663) and its repeated use – also in

---

[44] Degrada, 'In margine all'edizione critica delle cantate di Antonio Vivaldi', pp. 360–70.

Ex. 5.7  Comparison of settings of the second aria of *T'intendo, sì, mio cor* by Vivaldi and Porpora

Ex. 5.7  Comparison of settings of the second aria of *T'intendo, sì, mio cor: cont.*

inversion – of a broken triad in close position lend it both personality and consistency. Most important, Vivaldi shows his understanding of the usefulness of 'irregular' (here, three-bar) musical units. Because the listener is programmed to expect binary designs – these are built into the rhythms of the body and of daily life – the imposition of ternary designs creates ambiguity in the sense that the opening bar of one unit is initially 'heard' as the closing bar of its predecessor. This interplay between the 'actual' (ternary) and 'background' (binary) phrase structures binds the music together and increases its fluidity.

Porpora starts promisingly enough. Like Vivaldi, he finds that *settenario* lines fit naturally into three bars of 3/8 metre. The bass response in bar 70 and its overlap with the next three-bar vocal phrase are nicely contrived. Things start to go wrong, however, when Porpora next imitates the voice. His failure to make the soprano re-enter in bar 78 slackens the tension at the wrong point (in mid-period) by suddenly introducing quadratic phrase structure. The change of the bass design in bars 79–81, where one would have expected simple sequential repetition, may have been conceived by Porpora as a subtlety but comes across only as a needless inconsistency. From this point onwards, the passage degenerates into inconsequential note-spinning. The erudite *cadenza sfuggita* in bar 92, where the bass takes over with ritornello material, comes too late to rescue the situation.

Running out of steam early is a classic characteristic of the weaker composer – and sometimes also of good composers in their weaker moments, Vivaldi not excepted. On other occasions, Porpora can do far better than this, but he never seeks to go beyond a well-mannered blandness. He was massively popular and influential in Venice after he settled in the city – the first of many eminent Neapolitan musicians of the generation following Vivaldi to do so. The theatrical agent Owen Swiney, in his letters to the Duke of Richmond reporting on his search for singers in Venice, described the success of Porpora's first Venetian opera, *Siface* ('The Musick is excellent; and commended by every body of a True Taste') but noted the chagrin of the local musicians ('The Masters of Musick,

Their Protectors & adherents [. . .] are sworn Enemies to it; or, rather, to the composer of it, who is look'd upon, by 'em, as a Foreigner, or an interloper').[45] Supported by the Grimani family, proprietors of the S. Giovanni Grisostomo theatre, and enjoying a high profile throughout the whole year by virtue of his tenure of the post of *Maestro di coro* at the Ospedale degli Incurabili, Porpora went from strength to strength. Incredibly, it was he, rather than a native composer, who was chosen to write the gala opera *Imeneo in Atene* that celebrated the return of Cardinal Pietro Ottoboni from a long exile in the autumn of 1726.

To end up by joining what one cannot beat is a universal human tendency, and it is certain that Venetian composers studied Porpora's music carefully, appropriating those elements that seemed to contribute to its public success. In Vivaldi's case, there was little of a strictly compositional nature to learn from his Neapolitan rival. However, the *galant* inflections of the vocal lines, the *cantabile* writing for violins, the simple but sturdy accompanimental patterns, perhaps even the provision of formal stopping points for a vocal cadenza: all these may have left a mark on him. In musical history one is so accustomed to examine the influence of older composers on younger ones that it is easy to forget that, in a world where fashions change quickly, the reverse may equally take place. Even in the domain where he had led the field, the concerto, Vivaldi was not ashamed to pick up a few ideas from Tartini in later life.[46]

### RV 669: *Tra l'erbe i zeffiri* (ARA)

The first aria of this unassuming cantata shows a remarkably single-minded application of the modular principle of construction. The germinal motive for the whole movement, vocal part as well as bass, is a short figure announced in the first bar:

This little idea seems laughably plain: a pattern of even, repeated notes with a little 'flick of the tail' that propels it into the next bar. However, Vivaldi knows that the simplest motives are the most malleable, therefore capable of being the most pervasive. This figure is used in one form or another (also in inversion) in the great majority of bars in the bass. Wherever its termination will not fit, he simplifies the figure to six repeated semiquavers. In the vocal line, the figure is used for long melismas on the *mor-* of *mormorio*, revealing (six bars into the first vocal period) that it is not wholly abstract in intention but aims to depict the murmuring of a brook. Many of Vivaldi's aria ritornellos give the impression of being afterthoughts, created only after the essentials of the vocal line have become fixed in the composer's mind. There is no shame in this: exactly the same could be said of many piano introductions to Schubert songs. Here, however, the voice fastens on to the motive as if it were an *objet trouvé* that just happened to

---

45 Letter of 28 December 1725, transcribed in Gibson, *The Royal Academy of Music*, pp. 361–2.

46 Such as the use of the orchestral violins, playing in two parts, to accompany the principal violin. Earlier, Vivaldi had preferred to use violins and viola, or unison upper strings.

suit the purpose. This probably illusory impression arises from the fact that the motive is introduced not at the head of the first vocal period but mid-way through it.

Art conceals art once again in the second aria, 'Nel mar la navicella', whose ritornello is a sinuous unbroken series of quavers. Vivaldi's obvious intention here is to represent a ship ploughing slowly and evenly through calm waters. In a different metre and rhythm, this movement might be a barcarole. Here, however, one senses the regular movement of a galley's oars. The vocal line has just enough variety to preserve the aria from monotony.

### RV 670: *Alla caccia dell'alme e de' cori* (ARA)

A comparison between Vivaldi's and Porpora's setting of this text reveals differences similar to those found earlier in RV 668. Vivaldi is boldly direct, careful to maintain momentum and always focused on the next cadence. Porpora tends to drift and lose himself in flaccid passage-work. It is interesting how much more economical Vivaldi is than Porpora in his choice of keywords to highlight through melismatic treatment. In the first aria he limits himself to *va* ('goes'); in the second, to *volo* ('flight'). In each case, the choice is both poetically and musically apt: the dynamism of the huntress Clori, on the prowl to ensnare male lovers, receives emphasis, and pre-cadential tension is generated in just the right place. (*Va* and *volo* are the final words of their respective semistrophes, but Vivaldi takes the melismas back into the body of the period by repeating the close of the text non-melismatically in a concluding phrase.) By comparison, Porpora is indiscriminate in his melismatic emphasis of keywords, none of which coincides with Vivaldi's two. He has *barbara* ('barbarous'), *amanti* ('lovers'), *alme* ('souls'), *beltà* ('beauty'), and *stende* ('extends') in the first aria, *spiegar* ('unfurls') and *solo* ('alone') in the second. The result is that, although the melismas display clearly enough Porpora's mastery of *bel canto*, they confuse rather than clarify the poetic expression and musical structure.

Vivaldi's word-setting is on occasion not supple enough to fit the words comfortably. The *ottonario* opening the second aria, 'Preso sei, mio cor piagato') is strait-jacketed into four statements of the rhythmic module quaver + crotchet in 3/8 metre, each quaver broken into two semiquavers placed on the first beat of the bar. This brutal iambic formula destroys the natural links between syllables and words, chopping the line up into the four segments *Preso*; *sei, mio*; *cor pia-*; and *-gato*. Sung insensitively, these four bars can easily sound grotesque. This is one of the many instances where Vivaldi's drive for motivic regularity overrides the legitimate demands of word-setting.

### RV 671: *Care selve, amici prati* (ARA)

This one of Vivaldi's weaker cantatas. The first aria lacks unity: its ritornello material has no obvious connection, apart from the use of triplet semiquavers, with the vocal material, and the whole consists of empty routines. The second aria is marginally better. Rather oddly, the sinuous figure that obviously represents the flowing brook is applied indiscriminately, and therefore confusingly, to more than one keyword – a fault similar to the one to which Porpora fell victim in his setting of *Alla caccia*. It appears in association with *placido* ('peaceful'), *ombroso* ('shady') and *accorderò* ('I will tune'), as well as with its proper object, *l'onda* ('the wave').

## RV 679: *Che giova il sospirar, povero core* (RARA)

This is a superb composition. If Faustina was, as suggested above, the intended performer, she will have been well satisfied. Both recitatives are simple, as are all the recitatives in the Meiningen volume. In the first aria, which expresses bitterness at Irene's rejection of the lover's advances, Vivaldi achieves a marvellous 'mixed' *affetto*, where tenderness and anger mingle. Example 5.8 shows the end of the 'A' section. The tenderness is expressed at the start by the limpid diatonicism and the 'stroking' figures in the violins. Towards the end of the ritornello, however, the mood darkens as Vivaldi first shifts abruptly from F major to F minor and then modulates successively to G and A minor, as if to depict mounting anger, before falling back meekly into F major. The well-contrasted second aria, 'Cupido, tu vedi', is bittersweet in a different way. Its mode is minor, but it has a raciness that belies the presence of such words as *pena* ('pain') and *affanno* ('horror') in the text. In fact, Vivaldi anticipates already in the 'A' section the inner contentment that he asks Cupid in the 'B' section to restore.

Bar 29 of the example contains the only instance in Vivaldi's cantatas where a fermata appears over the notes of the dominant chord preceding a cadence as an invitation to the singer to insert a cadenza. With this addition, the last barrier separating the cantata aria from the operatic aria is crossed. Such cadenzas were short (their accommodation within a single breath was recommended by contemporary theorists) and non-thematic: the idea that, in addition to demonstrating technical skill, the performer should refer back to material heard in the course of the movement had yet to take root.

In the second aria the first violin doubles the voice throughout. This is very normal for arias of the 1720s and later. Vivaldi very rarely asks the violins to provide a counter-melody to the vocal line, although independent accompanimental phrases, as illustrated in Example 5.8, are common. The main preoccupation, it seems, is that the vocal line should be heard clearly. In this aria the accompaniment during the vocal periods is *senza basso* throughout.

## RV 681: *Perché son molli* (ARA)

Equally impressive in its own way is this early cantata. Its poetic theme is unusual. The singer describes in the first aria how his tears are bringing unhappiness to Arcadia. The recitative describes his resolve to leave the fields and forests and seek a solitary cave in which to continue his lamentations without troubling others. In the second aria he presents his vision of an Arcadia restored to happiness – in his absence. Could this be an allusion to some real event?

The tone of the first aria is predominantly pastoral in the blissful vein that one knows so well from Vivaldi (for example, in the chamber concerto aptly titled *La*

Ex. 5.8  Vivaldi, *Che giova il sospirar, povero core*, RV 679: bars 26–34

Ex. 5.8 Vivaldi, *Che giova il sospirar, povero core*, RV 679: *cont.*

*pastorella*, RV 95). Here and there, however, little disruptive touches – syncopation in the vocal line, Neapolitan Sixths, chromatic inflections – are used to express disquiet.

The recitative, whose opening is illustrated as Example 5.9, is a catalogue of special effects that seem tailor-made to establish Vivaldi's credentials as a proficient composer of vocal music.[47] The movement opens with ordinary 'accompanied' recitative, then switches, in bar 5, to 'obbligato' recitative. The phrases punctuating the lines or hemistiches of the text employ, at first, repeated notes in various rhythmicizations, then broken chords *all'unisono*. To mark the climax of the rising harmonic sequence, there is one bar of 'measured' recitative (bar 15), followed by a descending *tirata* to depict the desolate wails of the forest beasts.

The ninth added (as the fourth note in the soprano part) to the leading-note seventh in bar 2 is a Vivaldian trademark. If nothing else had survived from this cantata, that bar would have sufficed to confirm his authorship.

In contrast, the second aria conjures up an image of nymphs and swains dancing on the Arcadian equivalent of a village green. Its off-tonic opening (with subdominant harmony) and 'sawing' rhythms propel it on its merry course. The scoring in the vocal periods is once again *senza basso*.

### RV 682: *Vengo a voi, luci adorate* (ARA)

This very late cantata has a slightly tedious first movement filled with rather obvious *galant* effects (inverted dotting, slides, triplet semiquavers, etc.) and a perfunctory central recitative. It springs to life, however, in the second aria, which is exceptional among Vivaldi's cantatas in featuring a main theme employed elsewhere in his music. The works sharing it are the violin concerto RV 213 (third movement) and a newly discovered flute concerto in G major.[48] The theme is based on a *jeu d'esprit*: a second violin part consisting merely of a gently syncopated monotone at the top of the texture. In harmonic terms, this is an 'inverted pedal' that, like all pedal-notes, has the privilege of grating against the other notes without apology. Vivaldi maintains the pedal throughout the movement, although he has to alter its pitch from time to time in step with changes of key. The greatest dissonance occurs during the tailpiece to the second vocal period, which unexpectedly moves to the parallel minor key, where it remains until the final cadential phrase. As Example 5.10 illustrates, the clash of the dominant minor ninth ($a^{b\prime\prime}$) against the pedal note ($g\prime\prime$) is a very apt way of expressing the 'tormento' that is the subject of the voice's melisma.

### RV 683: *Amor, hai vinto, hai vinto: ecco il seno* (RARA)

This is the queen of Vivaldi's cantatas: the cantata to which one would bring a sceptic full of received ideas about our composer's 'flight from counterpoint', 'lack of feeling for the voice', 'over-use of sequence', 'disregard for the text', and

---

[47]  In the example, the lowest notes of the upper stave are those of the reconstructed viola part.
[48]  On this flute concerto, see Michael Talbot, 'Miscellany', *Studi vivaldiani*, iv (2004), p. 120.

Ex. 5.9 Vivaldi, *Perché son molli*, RV 681: 'Dunque, già ch'il mio duolo', opening

Ex. 5.9  Vivaldi, *Perché son molli*, RV 681: *cont.*

Ex. 5.10 Vivaldi, *Vengo a voi, luci adorate*, RV 682: 'Sempre penare', bars 32–41

Ex. 5.10  Vivaldi, *Vengo a voi, luci adorate*, RV 682: *cont.*

the other strictures that, while they may on occasion find justification, fall far short of a complete and fair picture.

Its opening simple recitative, which begins brightly and unassumingly, soon takes on darker hues; a deceptive cadence (*cadenza sfuggita*) in bar 11 is especially fine. Generally speaking, Vivaldi avoids 'learned' – as opposed to vivid – effects in his cantatas, but when he strikes, he chooses his moments well.

The first aria, marked 'Larghetto Andante', is the only instance in Vivaldi's cantatas of fugal treatment. The first and second entries (the subject and its answer) occur in the ritornello. The third and fourth entries of the exposition arrive in the first vocal period. Middle entries are heard during the second vocal period, which includes a striking passage (bars 34–7) in which the head of the subject is treated in stretto imitation. The 'B' section is given over to contrasting material dominated by a rumble in the continuo part signifying thunder (as in the equivalent section of RV 651) but preserves a motivic connection with the 'A' section by continuing to use a figure employed there as a second countersubject (this figure, consisting of four semiquavers, begins on a low note and then leaps to a twice-repeated higher note). The subject and the main countersubject, shown in Example 5.11, initially perform a typically Vivaldian 'scissors' motion: the subject, progressing slowly by step (to express the word *passo*) but including a prominent augmented second (for *pena*), moves in contrary motion with the quicker, more conventionally shaped countersubject. This is exactly the formula – right down to the prominent augmented second – used at the start of Vivaldi's *Sinfonia al Santo Sepolcro*, RV 169. When the two subjects come together in parallel thirds just after the start of the second bar, the effect is wonderfully poignant. The second countersubject (both violins, bars 4–5) – really just a little tag – contributes greatly to the effect by its gentle abrasion, as a pedal-note, against the C natural of the subject.

There is much to admire in this movement besides the fugal devices. The passage-work is fresh and sparkling, and there is a good admixture of simple homophonic effects that gain in power from their alternation with contrapuntal

Ex. 5.11 Vivaldi, *Amor, hai vinto, hai vinto: ecco il mio seno*, RV 683: 'Passo di pena in pena', opening

passages. In the vocal periods, the alto is doubled by the first violin an octave higher. This is the conventional way of doubling an alto part instrumentally and lends the music an attractive sheen.

Vivaldi provided two independent settings of the second recitative. The first to appear in the autograph score is a simple recitative. The second is orchestrally accompanied; this is the version appearing in the separate part for alto (with bass), which, employing different paper from the rest of the parts and the score, may have been substituted for an earlier part that included the simple recitative. There is no hint, however, that the accompanied recitative was composed at a later date than its companion movements.

Rather oddly, the tonal design of these two recitatives is quite different. The simple setting begins in C major and ends with a half-close in E minor; the accompanied setting starts with a dominant seventh in A minor and closes on the dominant of D minor. Both settings conform to Vivaldi's principle, described in Chapter 2, of avoiding a 'zero' progression between adjoining recitatives and arias, but it is hard to discern an underlying reason for the difference. The setting with strings mixes 'accompanied' and 'obbligato' recitative in the manner described for RV 679, but with greater spaciousness and material of more individual character. Tempo contrasts between 'Presto' and 'Adagio' sections are prescribed.

The second aria, 'Se a me rivolge il ciglio', makes no attempt to scale the emotional heights of its predecessor. In the narrative of the poem, the first aria expresses the descent into desperation; the second aria, the stirrings of hope. Light and bubbly though it is, there is nothing facile about the second aria. Vivaldi's writing for the strings is particularly appealing: the constant crossing of the two violin parts, which allows each to operate over a wider range than is normal in Italian music of the time (compare, for example, Albinoni and Torelli), creates fascinating textural patterns, often entailing incidental dissonance, that stand alone in the literature of the late Baroque.


## RV 684: *Cessate, omai cessate* (RARA)

This cantata opens in *maestoso* fashion with a stately accompanied recitative headed by six bars for strings alone that form a kind of prelude. This mini-sinfonia bears a strong resemblance to the introductory ritornello to Vivaldi's *Beatus vir* in C major, RV 597, with its *saccadé* ('alla francese') rhythms and short *tirate*. The point of this preface is revealed when the alto opens with the word *Cessate* ('Cease'). For something to stop, it must obviously already have started.

The original first aria (the one belonging to the incomplete variant known as RV 684a) was conventional and, to judge from its opening, uninspired. Its replacement reveals the experimental streak in Vivaldi's handling of the string orchestra. The accompaniment to the 'A' section is in three strands. The highest strand, for united violins, is to be played *pizzicato* – except for one instrument, presumably the principal violin, which is directed to play with the bow. The middle strand, for violas, is played *pizzicato*. The lowest strand has the cellos playing *arco*, the double basses *pizzicato*. The closest parallel is found in Vivaldi's aria 'Sento in seno ch'in pioggia di lagrime' (*Giustino*, II.1), where, amid a sea of *pizzicato*, one first violin, one second violin, and one double bass retain their bows. During the tailpiece to the second vocal period in the cantata, all the strings use their bows, but the initial scoring returns for the final ritornello. The vocal line is finely chiselled and full of rhythmic artifice. One so often finds in Vivaldi that rhythmic variety in one part (or group of parts) is compensated for by uniformity in the other parts. This is what occurs here. The regularity and evenness of the string accompaniment act as a foil to the ever-changing rhythmic patterns in the alto part.

For the 'B' section, Vivaldi switches to 3/8 metre and changes the tempo from 'Larghetto' to the slightly faster 'Andante molto'. At a surface level, this section is quite different, although a search for significant musical shapes reveals that the descending third is prominent in both sections. In his earlier vocal music, Vivaldi is less fond than many of his contemporaries of pointing up a contrast between the text of the two semistrophes of an aria stanza by creating a comparable musical contrast. His natural inclination is towards monomotivic treatment, as practised in his instrumental music. After c.1720 he shows greater readiness to introduce contrast of this kind. It was, of course, especially favoured by the Neapolitan composers who were simultaneously his competitors and models. What is remarkable, perhaps, is that this is the only cantata aria by him to differentiate the two sections by metre and tempo.

In the 'B' section, where the viola provides a *bassetto*, the acoustic pitch of the alto frequently dips beneath the bass part, creating six-four chords. However, the 'heard' pitch stays above and no harmonic solecism is apparent. This is a peculiarity of instrumentally accompanied song that is observable just as clearly in a Schubert song if, for example, it is sung by a tenor instead of a soprano. A single, accompanied voice always sounds like an upper part, regardless of its true pitch.

Another recitative with strings follows, mingling 'accompanied', 'measured', and 'obbligato' styles freely. The second aria is a superb *aria d'azione* of the kind Anna Girò liked to sing. Particularly admirable is the way Vivaldi stitches together the motives making up the vocal part. In Example 5.12, the alto part of the entire 'A' section, the first vocal period comprises five segments, identified in the example by letters from A to E. There are the usual subtleties of phrase structure (segment A has a three-bar antecedent followed by a four-bar consequent) and textual illustration (segment C felicitously represents *alta* not only as 'loud' but also as 'high'). The second vocal section, ending in bar 74, repeats the sequence of events but replaces segment B by a new one, F, and omits segment D. Segment A, somewhat modified, replaces the tonic key by the dominant; segment C is unaltered in pitch and key; segment E is transposed from dominant to tonic. The tailpiece is unusually elaborate. It begins in bar 75 with a return of the earlier omitted segment D (now set to the text of A). This is followed by new versions of C and B. Segment D then returns (its words borrowed this time from C), and segment E, in a double statement (the second of which is elaborated), brings up the rear. Every thematic element has the opportunity to undergo development and variation – and in the 'B' section segments B and E, preserving the continuity, appear alongside new material. It is difficult to know what to admire more in this aria: the systematic approach taken to its construction, or the little deviations from regularity that create surprise. The two aspects, at any rate, are in perfect balance.

### RV 796: *Usignoletto bello* (ARA)

Unpretentious yet stylish, this continuo cantata has a lot in common with the lighter cantatas of the Mantuan period, to which, as was explained earlier, it is probably very close in date. The main reason why the G major anonymous version is likely to be earlier than the E flat major version is given by Francesco Degrada in the Critical Notes to his edition: it is that certain accidentals notated correctly as sharps in the first version appear incorrectly as sharps (where they should be naturals) in the second. Scribe 4 presumably transposed his copy at sight and failed to make the necessary adjustment. Of course, both versions could

Ex. 5.12  Vivaldi, *Cessate, omai cessate*, RV 684: 'Nell'orrido albergo', bars 22–102, vocal line

Ex. 5.13 Vivaldi, *Usignoletto bello*, RV 796: 'Come te cantando anch'io', opening

be transpositions of a primitive version in a third key: unless an autograph source turns up, there is no way of knowing for sure.

Among the most attractive features of this cantata are the ritornellos of its arias, which reassemble elements of both the vocal melody and its bass. If one examines the first seven bars of the second aria, 'Come te cantando anch'io' (the whole passage is shown as Example 5.13), one notes first of all a short phrase of decidedly 'bass-like' character. The purpose of this phrase might be found puzzling – until one recognizes it as a suitable accompaniment to the opening vocal phrase, which one is presumably expected to anticipate in the continuo realization. The next phrase is a paraphrase, one octave lower, of the second vocal phrase. Bars 3–6 develop sequentially in a syncopated rhythm the motive occurring as notes 2–5 of the vocal part and take it to a cadence. This is yet another demonstration of the 'logical yet unpredictable' nature of Vivaldi's inspiration. It is ironic that he should have earned from many modern commentators the reputation of always seeking easy solutions, whereas the reality is that he is sometimes almost perverse in his avoidance of them!

# CHAPTER SIX

# The Dresden Cantatas

## *Vivaldi and Dresden*

After the Ospedale della Pietà in Venice, the institution with which Vivaldi enjoyed the longest professional relationship was the court of Dresden, seat of the Saxon electors, who, during the same period (1712–40), were also kings of Poland. The seeds for this association were sown by the accession, in 1694, of Friedrich August I (1670–1733), known as 'Augustus the Strong'.[1] In 1696 the Polish throne became vacant. This monarchy was elective, and in a disputed contest Friedrich August emerged as the winner, being crowned as Augustus II at Cracow on 15 September 1697. A condition of becoming king of Poland was that he should embrace Catholicism. Saxony was staunchly Lutheran, and the elector initially made his conversion a merely personal matter. The electress, Christiane Eberhardine, and most of the court remained true to Protestantism.

In 1704 a Russian–Swedish alliance ousted Friedrich August as king of Poland in favour of his rival, Stanisław Leszczyński (father of the princess whose marriage to Louis XV Vivaldi was later to celebrate in RV 687). The elector did not, however, lose hope of regaining his throne. He refused to return to Lutheranism, and in 1708 enraged his court and subjects by transforming Dresden's former opera house into a Catholic court chapel (*katholische Hofkirche*). His patience was rewarded, for in 1709 the Russians and Swedes fell out, so that in the following year Friedrich August was able to reclaim the Polish throne.

To make it more likely that the Polish crown would remain in the hands of his dynasty (the Wettins), Friedrich August had to ensure that his similarly named son, born in 1698, also became a Catholic. This entailed removing him for a number of years from the influence of Christiane Eberhardine and the court. The solution was to send him on a prolonged, ostensibly educational, tour of Europe. The prince travelled *incognito* – that is, with an assumed rank lower than his real

---

[1] Good sources of information on the electors of Saxony and their cultivation of music in the early eighteenth century are Fürstenau, *Zur Geschichte der Musik und des Theaters am Hofe zu Dresden*, vol. 2, and Wolfgang Horn, *Die Dresdner Hofkirchenmusik 1720–1745: Studien zu ihren Voraussetzungen und ihrem Repertoire*, Kassel, etc.: Bärenreiter, 1987. A useful account in English is contained in Janice B. Stockigt, *Jan Dismas Zelenka: A Bohemian Musician at the Court of Dresden*, Oxford: Oxford University Press, 2000.

one – in order to avoid problems of protocol, and his retinue, which included Catholic priests, was kept very small. The tour started with his journey to Frankfurt in late 1711 for the coronation of Charles VI as German emperor. For reasons both religious and cultural, Italy was the prince's main destination. He made three separate sojourns in Venice. The first ran from 5 February to 17 March 1712; the second, from 21 May to the end of November 1713; the third and longest, from 13 February 1716 to 20 July 1717.[2] Between the first and second visits the prince was officially received into the Catholic Church (at Bologna, on 27 November 1712). The news was kept secret from the court until the prince's return to Dresden in 1717.

Some time in February 1712 the young Friedrich August visited the Pietà. In the Pietà's *vacchette* (account-books recording daily transactions) there is an entry for 29 February noting the expenses relating to this visit. Under the same date, there is a separate entry for 35 *lire* and 10 *soldi* paid to Vivaldi for 'un libro di suonate' ('a book of sonatas'). This payment cannot relate to compositions supplied by Vivaldi directly to the Pietà, for these were always copied free of charge by the *figlie di coro* themselves. The payment must refer instead to instrumental compositions presented by the Pietà to Friedrich August as a gift. 'Suonate' might even be used here in a generic sense to refer to concertos as well as, or even instead of, sonatas, in which case *L'estro armonico* (of which the publisher Estienne Roger doubtless sent Vivaldi complimentary examples) might provide the answer. The SLUB possesses an example of Vivaldi's Op. 2 violin sonatas in the edition engraved in 1712 by Roger, to which the entry could equally well refer.[3] If so, the sonatas must have been very handsomely bound to have cost so much. Otherwise, the compositions were probably a set resembling the 'Manchester' violin sonatas of c.1726 presented in manuscript to Cardinal Ottoboni.[4]

There are no reports of a visit to the Pietà by the prince during his second Venetian sojourn. He is likely, however, to have attended services with music there without fanfare. Regarding the third visit, we learn of his attendance at an oratorio presented by the *figlie di coro* on 5 March 1716.[5] The identity of this oratorio and its composer is uncertain; it could perhaps have been Vivaldi's *Juditha triumphans*, which may, however, have been performed later in the same year.

By the time of his third visit, the prince was in late teenage, and it was thought fit to enlarge his retinue by sending a select group of musicians to join him in

---

2    Some minor discrepancies in the dates exist in the primary literature. The diary of Antonio Benigna (Venice, Biblioteca Nazionale Marciana, It. VII-1620 (7846), f. 8r) claims that the third visit began on 9 February 1716 and ended on 24 July 1717. The dates for the same visit given above are taken from Venice, Archivio di Stato, Cerimoniali, Reg. 4, ff. 26r and 27v.

3    On the date of this publication, see Rudolf Rasch, 'La famosa mano di Monsieur Roger: Antonio Vivaldi and his Dutch Publishers', *Informazioni e studi vivaldiani*, xvii (1996), 89–135, at 114–15.

4    Since mentioning the volume, which was first brought to my attention by Micky White, in my 'Miscellany' column in *Informazioni e studi vivaldiani*, xx (1999), 135–9, at 138, I have come round to the view that this was most probably the published Op. 2 (which is preserved in Dresden) rather than a manuscript volume (of which no trace survives there).

5    Venice, Archivio di Stato, Inquisitori di Stato, Avvisi, Busta 706, 7 March 1716 (Francesco Alvisi), f. 2v.

Venice. Foremost among them was Johann Georg Pisendel (1687–1755), a promising violinist who had briefly studied under Giuseppe Torelli in Ansbach and was a keen partisan of the Italian style in preference to the French style that the players of the *Hofkapelle* at that time favoured. Pisendel became a pupil and intimate of Vivaldi. In the SLUB there exists, in fact, a manuscript of a concerto movement in A minor by Pisendel containing corrections in Vivaldi's hand.[6] While in Italy, Pisendel made it his business to amass as much instrumental music by local composers as possible. He succeeded both in persuading composers to donate or sell compositions to him and in gaining access to their scores, which he then copied on small-format manuscript paper (German scholars call these copies his *Reisepartituren*, or 'travelling scores'), suitable for bringing or posting back to Dresden.[7] Today the SLUB possesses manuscripts of fifteen sonatas, twelve independent sinfonias, and ninety-one concertos by Vivaldi.[8] Most of these are of works collected by Pisendel in 1716–17 in Venice, although several are preserved only in the form of scores or parts prepared subsequently in Dresden by assistants of Pisendel (who included the young Quantz) or by copyists working for the *Hofkapelle*.

At least two other musicians came from Dresden as members of the prince's chamber ensemble (*Kammermusik*). One was the oboist Johann Christian Richter (1689–1744), for whom Vivaldi must have written the oboe sonata RV 53 and perhaps also RV 28 and RV 34, if it is true that these have been misidentified as violin sonatas. Another was the keyboard player Christian Petzold (1677–1733). The double-bassist Jan Dismas Zelenka (1679–1745) may have joined the group at some stage, although much of the time he appears to have been in Vienna, studying composition with Johann Joseph Fux.

There is considerable evidence that Vivaldi composed music for the prince's *Kammermusik* or its individual members during their stay. Especially noteworthy are some early chamber concertos – works written for a small group of players without orchestra.[9] This experience prepared the way for the Vivaldi 'cult' that grew up subsequently in Dresden.

Only a few months after his arrival in Venice, Friedrich August, acting on behalf of his father, engaged Heinichen as a 'second' *Kapellmeister* (the existing *Kapellmeister* being Johann Christoph Schmidt, who thenceforth would take a back seat). This appointment confirmed the new orientation, towards Italian music, that the *Hofkapelle* was destined to take. More significant still was the recruitment of Antonio Lotti, then serving as first organist of S. Marco, to lead a troupe of Italian singers who were to revive opera at the court. Lotti and the other

---

6   Shelfmark: Mus. 2421-0-14.
7   Albinoni and Vivaldi both inscribed autograph manuscripts of compositions to Pisendel. Other composers with whom Pisendel had personal contact were Benedetto Marcello, Antonio Montanari, and Giuseppe Valentini (the last two during his visit to Rome in 1717).
8   These figures are based on Landmann's catalogue, discounting variants of the same work, lost compositions and spurious items.
9   See Michael Talbot, 'Vivaldi's *Quadro*? The Case of RV Anh. 66 Reconsidered', in Enrico Careri and Markus Engelhardt (eds), *Italienische Instrumentalmusik des 18. Jahrhunderts: Alte und neue Protagonisten* ('Analecta musicologica', xxxii), Laaber: Laaber-Verlag, 2002, pp. 9–32, at pp. 28–30.

members of the company belonging to the *Cappella ducale* received leave of absence at the elector's request and arrived in Dresden in September 1717. They were to remain there for more than two years, making a major contribution to the celebrations surrounding the wedding of the prince to Habsburg princess Maria Josepha in 1719. In 1720, when their most important task had been completed, the Italian company was dismissed: their inflated salaries had aroused jealousy among the regular members of the *Hofkapelle*, and their arrogant behaviour had caused dissension.

It appears that after the return of Pisendel and his companions Vivaldi was solicited independently for compositions by the Saxon court. Two concertos in particular – RV 576 and 577 (coincidentally, both in G minor) – bear inscriptions connecting them not with individual members of the orchestra but with the court itself. The first is headed, in the partly autograph manuscript today in Turin, 'p[er] S[ua] A[ltezza] R[eale] di Sas[soni]a'; the second, 'p[er] l'Orchestra di Dresda'. RV 576 has a very unusual scoring that includes five 'treble' wind instruments: a principal oboe (partnering a principal violin), two other oboes, and two recorders. It may have been performed as *Tafelmusik* during a *Türkischer Fest* held (appropriately) at the Turkish Palace on 1 September 1719, as part of the wedding celebrations.[10]

In 1725 the court engaged a fresh set of Italian singers for use both in opera and in the *concertante* church music that Heinichen and others were now providing. Concurrently, however, it pursued a longer-range strategy aimed at providing the *Hofkapelle* with a cheaper, more compliant and more permanent vocal group. In 1724 Count Ämilius Villio, the Saxon ambassador to Venice, was instructed to select three young female and four young male singers for training in preparation for their eventual engagement in Dresden.[11] Lotti assisted the ambassador in his choice. The boys, all castratos, were trained first in Bologna and later in Venice. They comprised the sopranos Venturio Rocchetti and Giovanni Bindi, and the altos Domenico Annibali and Casimiro Pignotti. Bindi, whose compass was unusually high, reaching at least *d'''*, received lessons from Porpora. All the castratos were trained at the conclusion of their studies by the famous alto Antonio Campioli.

The female singers remained throughout in Venice. The soprano Maria Santina Cattanea was trained by Pietro Scarpari, *Maestro di canto* at the Pietà and at other *ospedali*. Like the male singers, she was accommodated in the ambassador's house. In contrast, the sisters Rosa and Anna Negri in September 1724 became boarders (*figlie a spese*) at the Pietà, for which privilege the court paid the Pietà 300 ducats per annum.[12] As usual, each boarder was entrusted to a *figlia*

---

10 See Irmgard Becker-Glauch, *Die Bedeutung der Musik für die Dresdener Hoffeste bis in die Zeit Augusts des Starken*, Kassel and Basel: Bärenreiter, 1951, p. 105. In Becker-Glauch's description of the instruments, based on a contemporary ink drawing by Carl Heinrich Jakob Fehling, a principal violinist and principal oboist (featured in the score) stand in the doorway adjoining the banqueting room.

11 The main source of information on the singers and their training is Fürstenau, *Zur Geschichte der Musik und des Theaters am Hofe zu Dresden*, 2, pp. 159–60 and 166.

12 Venice, Archivio di Stato, Ospedali e luoghi pii diversi, Busta 658, Parti, and ibid., Reg. 1005, Quaderno cassa, f. 551.

*privilegiata*, an older member of the *coro* (usually a *maestra*, aged at least 40). Rosa, her name augmented to 'Maria Rosa', was assigned initially to *Maestra* Maddalena 'dal Soprano' (1676/77–1728), Anna (as 'Anna Bolognese') to Meneghina 'dalla Viola' (1688/89–1761).

During their training in Venice all these singers, especially the Negri sisters, must have become acquainted with Vivaldi. When, fully trained, they arrived in Dresden in the spring of 1730, they formed yet another 'bridge' between the composer and the Saxon capital.

Meanwhile, the death of *Konzertmeister* Volumier in 1728 allowed Pisendel to step into his shoes and intensify the cultivation of Vivaldi's instrumental music. It is from this period – the late 1720s – that the regular copyists of the *Hofkapelle* appear to have devoted their attention to his works, many of which, under Pisendel's guidance, were 'customized' for the orchestra, receiving extra wind parts and sometimes even compositional modifications.

So far, however, Vivaldi's vocal music had been all but ignored by the *Hofkapelle*. It may well be that his *Magnificat* (RV 610 or one of its variants), which is listed in inventories of the sacred repertory of the *Hofkapelle*, had already arrived – and the case of the two cantatas RV 663 and RV 796, which do not belong to the main Dresden group, has already been discussed in Chapter 5. Then there are miscellaneous pre-1733 operatic arias: sixteen arias from *Arsilda, regina di Ponto* (autumn 1716) – presumably a souvenir of Friedrich August's last visit; one aria from *Orlando finto pazzo* (autumn 1714); and three unplaceable arias.[13] All are notated in two-stave score and perhaps originated as singers' parts (which were always notated together with the bass part). Otherwise, Vivaldi was represented only by his instrumental music.

The catalyst for change was the death of Augustus the Strong on 1 February 1733. His son's accession as Friedrich August II gave hope for new appointments to, and promotions within, the *Hofkapelle*. The successor to Heinichen, who had died in 1729, was already chosen. This was Johann Adolf Hasse, who is described as 'Primo maestro di cap[p]ella' to the king of Poland and elector of Saxony already in the libretto of his opera *Dalisa*, which opened in Venice (with Anna Girò in the cast) in May 1730. The expression 'Primo', however, betrays the fact that the Saxon-Polish court, divided, as it was, between two sites (Dresden and Warsaw), needed more than a single *Kapellmeister* to attend to its musical needs. Already during Heinichen's régime (leaving aside the marginalized Schmidt), there had been room for Lotti to provide operas, and for Ristori and Zelenka to provide sacred music. There was, in theory, almost unlimited scope for composers from outside Dresden to be recognized as 'purveyors of music' to the court under a suitable title.

Bach's reaction to the succession of Friedrich August II is well known. He composed a 'short' Mass (a *Kyrie* in B minor and a *Gloria* in D major that are the starting point of the future *Mass in B minor*, BWV 232), which he sent to the court in 1733. This canny gift eventually, in 1736, earned him the title of *Hofcompositeur*. Zelenka, deeply disappointed at not succeeding Heinichen,

---

[13]   Mus. 1-F-30, pp. 37-70; Mus. 1-F-30, pp. 195–201; Mus. 2389-J-1, pp. 1–7.

whose *de facto* replacement he had become during the latter's declining years, tried a new strategy to attract the incoming elector's attention: he composed a series of eight 'demonstration' arias (ZWV 176) designed to prove his suitability for operatic composition, a task not previously entrusted to him. (Sadly, these arias by a normally excellent composer show exactly why such a commission would have been hazardous: they are overlong and insensitive in their word-setting.)

Vivaldi appears to have attempted something more ambitious than Zelenka: a portfolio of music for solo voice (soprano and alto) embracing several genres. There are four components in this portfolio:

1. Twenty-four arias and a terzet in full score taken from five recent operatic productions (*La fede tradita e vendicata*, 1726; *L'Atenaide*, 1729; *Farnace*, 1731; *Semiramide*, 1732; *La fida ninfa*, 1732).[14]
2. Nine chamber cantatas (including one, RV 678, with obbligato flute).[15]
3. Two motets (RV 627 and 632) for soprano and strings.[16]
4. A setting for soprano, flute, and strings of the psalm *Laudate pueri Dominum* (RV 601).[17]

The coherence as a group of the thirty-seven items listed above – the Dresden compilation – is established by various factors. First, there is the evidence of paper and rastrography.[18] Second, all the pieces originate from the composer's domestic *atelier*, the assistants being Scribes 4, 14, and 16. Third, there are notable similarities of musical style and working methods.

Significantly, the eight continuo cantatas belonging to the group in Mus. 1-J-7 (but not RV 796 and RV 663, which precede them in the volume) are numbered from 1 to 8 in Zelenka's handwriting. This implies that they reached Dresden together.[19] Zelenka's custody of the court's vocal music (with Heinichen dead, Hasse itinerant and Ristori resident in Warsaw, he was the senior composer in Dresden, however inadequately recognized) was probably inimical to Vivaldi's cause. Unlike Pisendel, he had no ties of friendship binding him to the Venetian, whom he may well have considered an undeserving interloper. None of the manuscripts making up the Dresden compilation shows any sign of having seen active use in performance.

The vocal specifications of the items are highly variable. One composition – the *Laudate pueri Dominum* – appears to be tailored to Bindi's ultra-high compass. It is noticeable, however, that three cantatas also belonging to the 1731 compilation (RV 657, 662, and 667) have had the upper end of their compass

---

14 SLUB, Mus. 2389-J-1, pp. 8–169.
15 Mus. 1-J-7, pp. 72–113.
16 Mus. 2389-E-1 (RV 632) and Mus. 2389-E-2 (RV 627).
17 Mus. 2389-E-3.
18 As discussed in the Critical Notes of the works published in *NEC*. See also note 22.
19 Similarly, RV 627 and 632 are included as consecutive items (14 and 15) in Zelenka's inventory of the sacred music in his custody (*Inventarium rerum musicalium variorum authorium ecclesiae serventium quas possidet Joannes Dismas Zelenka*), reproduced in facsimile in Wolfgang Horn, Thomas Kohlhase, Ortrun Landmann, and Wolfgang Reich, *Zelenka-Dokumentation: Quellen und Materialien*, 2 vols, Wiesbaden: Breitkopf & Härtel, 1989, 2, pp. 169–218, at p. 215.

taken down a note or two. Clearly, Vivaldi was aiming for diversity, perhaps following the 'scatter-gun' principle (according to which a range of different products is more likely to find favour, even if only in part, than a collection of uniform products). The absence of any mention of specific singers in the group of manuscripts suggests that the Dresden compilation was despatched to Saxony without a prior commission and without suggestions regarding performance, even though Vivaldi must have had a good idea of who was available.

Vivaldi's connection with the court was renewed in 1740 when the new electoral prince, Friedrich Christian, visited Venice. At the Pietà, on 21 March, the prince was treated to a serenata, *Il coro delle Muse*, on a text by Carlo Goldoni set to old music by the Pietà's inactive *Maestro di coro*, Gennaro D'Alessandro. At four strategic points in this composition a sinfonia and three concertos with 'novelty' scoring purchased especially from Vivaldi were inserted. The prince liked what he heard, especially Vivaldi's concerto with 'echo' violin, RV 552.[20]

Strange to relate, Vivaldi's relationship with the Saxon court persisted even beyond the grave. In the 1750s the Venetian copying shop of Iseppo Baldan supplied huge quantities of ostensibly up-to-date Italian sacred vocal music to the *Hofkapelle*, which was seeking to renew its repertory. Most of the works were by Baldassarre Galuppi, who had by then become the *doyen* of Venetian composers. Perhaps encountering a shortage of genuine Galuppi compositions, Baldan slipped in a couple of Vivaldi works from the composer's final cycle of psalms for the Pietà (1739), which he may have acquired via the composer's nephew Daniele Mauro, one of his employees. Only in recent years have these two works falsely attributed to Galuppi, the *Beatus vir* RV 795 and the *Nisi Dominus* RV 803, been restored to their true composer.[21]

## The Cantatas of the Dresden Compilation

Table 6.1 lists the nine cantatas forming the group. As the first column shows, all five continuo cantatas for soprano are copies, three with significant revisions, based on the manuscripts of existing works preserved in Turin. RV 657 is a special case. Its paper-type, B48, links it to the 1731 compilation, and the hand is that of a professional Venetian copyist, Scribe 14, who is known to have prepared manuscripts of music by several composers of the time, including Cervetto, Giacomelli, Hasse, Martinelli (Vivaldi's successor at the Pietà as *Maestro de' concerti*), and Porta.[22] Everett's view that it was prepared soon after the other

---

[20] Dresden, Staatsarchiv, Geh. Kabinett. Loc. 355, *Journal der Reise des Kurprinzen Friedrich Christian von Rom nach Wien*, f. 263. The four works by Vivaldi were taken back to Dresden in a souvenir volume, today shelfmarked Mus. 2389-O-4.

[21] The story is recounted in detail in Michael Talbot, 'Recovering Vivaldi's Lost Psalm', *Eighteenth-Century Music*, i (2004), 61–77.

[22] Paul Everett, 'Vivaldi's Italian Copyists', *Informazioni e studi vivaldiani*, xi (1990), 27–86, at 56–7. I must acknowledge here my indebtedness to extracts from an unpublished essay, 'The Manuscripts of Vivaldi's Cantatas', prepared by Paul Everett in 1995. In particular, Everett's essay distinguishes for the first time what I describe in this book as the '1731 compilation' and the 'Dresden compilation'. It also suggests for the first time that the Dresden manuscript of RV 657 was not intended originally for inclusion in the group.

Table 6.1 The cantatas of the 'Dresden compilation' of c.1733 contained in SLUB, Mus. 1-J-7, pp. 4–12

| RV | Pages | Paper | Rastrography | Hand | Manuscript type | Voice | Compass | Accompaniment | No. |
|---|---|---|---|---|---|---|---|---|---|
| 655(2) | 72–9 | B9 | 10/183.2(2) | Scribe 16, then autograph | supervised copy | Soprano | $d'-g''$ | continuo | 2 |
| 656(2) | 80–87 | B9 | 10/183.2(2) | Scribe 4 | supervised copy | Soprano | $f-a''$ | continuo | 3 |
| 657(2) | 64–71 | B48 | 10.186.9(1) | Scribe 14 + autograph | copy with autograph modifications | Soprano | $c'-b''$ | continuo | 1 |
| 662(2) | 96–101 | B5 | 10/190.6(4) | autograph | composition copy | Soprano | $c'-b^{b''}$ | continuo | 5 |
| 667(2) | 88–95 | B5 | 10/190.6(4) | autograph | composition copy | Soprano | $b-a''$ | continuo | 4 |
| 674 | 114–20 | B9 | 10/183.2(2) | autograph, then unknown scribe | composition copy | Alto | $b^b-e^{b''}$ | continuo | 6 |
| 676 | 121–8 | B9 | 10/183.2(2) | Scribe 16, then autograph | supervised copy | Alto | $a-e''$ | continuo | 7 |
| 677 | 129–36 | B9 | 10/183.2(2) | Scribe 16, then autograph | supervised copy | Alto | $b-e''$ | continuo | 8 |
| 678 | 102–13 | B5 | 10/190.6(4) | Scribe 4, then autograph | supervised copy | Soprano | $d'-a''$ | flute + continuo | – |

(Turin) manuscript for a purpose unconnected with Dresden fits the evidence well: only the later autograph alterations to it, resulting in the lowering of its compass at the top end, relate directly to the Dresden compilation. And the inclusion in the Turin score, as afterthoughts, of the modifications subsequently introduced to the Dresden score (a unique occurrence) provides added proof of the lateness of the conversion.

Vivaldi's use of assistants – the practised Scribe 4 and the inexperienced Scribe 16 – seems to have been motivated by a need to work very quickly. The general principle adopted was that when the music was taken without alteration from an exemplar, the work was entrusted to a copyist. When compositional alterations were anticipated, Vivaldi copied the score himself. Thus RV 662 and RV 667, which both required a compression of the vocal compass, are entirely in his hand. The same is true of the alto cantata RV 674 up to bar 18 of the second aria, at which point Vivaldi entrusted the copying of the notes to an unidentified assistant. In seven instances (RV 655, 656, 667, 674, 676, 677, and 678) the composer reserved for himself the writing of the underlaid text and other verbal instructions. This follows a pattern familiar from his sacred vocal music and dramatic music, which was also one widely practised in copying shops, where a senior copyist often took sole charge of titles and words. There is probably more than one reason why Vivaldi chose to add the verbal text himself. First, it provided a convenient opportunity to check the accuracy of the notes as he went through the score. Second, he was undoubtedly proud of the fluency and clarity of his handwriting, which, at its most calligraphic (as in the title-page of the 'Manchester' sonatas), is aesthetically very pleasing and expressive of his artistic personality. Third, and perhaps most important, the presence of his handwriting on a manuscript provided 'brand identity': irrefutable evidence of his authorship and his personal involvement in the preparation of a manuscript.

Of the five continuo cantatas for soprano, two (RV 655 and 656) are essentially unchanged from their earlier state. The other three (RV 657, 662, and 667), however, have had their vocal line amended so that it stays within the range $b–b''$. In RV 662 this is coupled with some light cutting; in RV 657, with rhythmic simplification. In every case, the bass remains exactly the same; in fact, Vivaldi shows remarkable skill in making the alterations without needing to change it. The nature of the revisions can be illustrated by comparing three bars near the end of the 'B' section in the original Turin version of RV 657 with their Dresden counterpart (Example 6.1).

RV 674, 676, and 677 – all large-scale continuo cantatas for alto preserved nowhere else – seem to form a coherent subgroup. The literary quality of their texts is higher than average and pays especial attention to the recitative stanzas, none of which is shorter than ten lines. The structure is RARA in each case. All the texts have vivid, dramatic qualities crying out for musical illustration. The collective compass of the three cantatas, $a–e''$, would have suited the voice of Anna Girò excellently, and one wonders whether she was their original singer.

The discussion of individual works that follows is limited to the four cantatas of the Dresden compilation unique to that source.

Ex. 6.1  Vivaldi, *Geme l'onda che parte dal fonte*, RV 657: 'Deh non partir sì presto', bars 49–51

## Individual Works

### RV 674: *Perfidissimo cor! Iniquo fato!* (RARA)

The boldness and eloquence of this cantata's opening recitative have already been illustrated in Example 2.1. The first aria, 'Nel torbido mio petto', has one of Vivaldi's 'obsessive' basses. It remains in semiquavers practically throughout, and the second, third, and fourth semiquavers – a kind of triple upbeat – are nearly everywhere set to the same note.[23] The result is a clear impression of ostinato treatment, even though only short fragments recur in unaltered shape. Predictably, the monolithic rhythm of the bass is offset by a splendid plasticity of rhythm in the vocal part. Here, the keyword is *sdegno* ('scorn'), on which Vivaldi lavishes a wealth of rolling melismas.

The second recitative is notable for its elegant tonal design. Starting in B flat major, Vivaldi moves sharpwards along the circle of fifths from C minor to F sharp minor (with ellipsis occurring between C minor and D minor, and between E minor and F sharp minor); he then moves back from F sharp minor to D, where he effects an instant shift from major to minor, and ends the movement in G minor, close to his starting point.

The second aria, 'Più amar non spero, no', is the epitome of Vivaldi's habit of basing a movement on the smallest imaginable musical particle. Here, this is a rising semitone starting on the weak second or fourth quaver of a 2/4 bar and concluding on the first or second beat. The bass and the voice take turns in treating this motive intensively. A glorious moment arrives at the end of the second period (to which there is no separate tailpiece), where a close paraphrase of the ritornello theme supplies the bass to a vocal line that at various points reinforces the former's upward semitonal thrust with parallel movement. This passage is shown as Example 6.2. The 'B' section of this aria has a splendidly rhetorical conclusion: a threefold statement of the single word *svanì* ('vanished') set to the semitonal motive and separated by rests.

---

[23]  An extract from the bass is quoted as Example 3.5.

Ex. 6.2  Vivaldi, *Perfidissimo cor! Iniquo fato!*, RV 674: 'Più amar non spero', bars 38–50

### RV 676: *Pianti, sospiri e dimandar mercede* (RARA)

This cantata begins strikingly with a dominant seventh chord, the seventh being placed in the vocal part. Similarly dissonant opening chords are commonplace in internal recitatives, but this is the only such example from an opening recitative of a Vivaldi cantata. It heralds the intensely dramatic nature of the work to follow.

The 'A' section of the first aria, 'Lusinga è del nocchier', is dominated by a vigorous but not violent bass line that makes copious use of dotted rhythms. When the voice enters, it soon becomes clear that this rhythm is an illustration of the phrase *venticel legger* ('light breeze'). Very soon, the voice applies the same rhythm to a melisma on the 'l'on-' of *l'onde* (the waves), making it clear that the motion of the winds is transferred to the waters.

If the 'A' section relates how a steersman (*nocchier*) is persuaded to set sail because of the apparently favourable weather (a metaphor for a lover's hopes at the start of a new romantic attachment), the 'B' section tells us that, scarcely out of port, he is assailed by strong, dangerous winds. The new situation calls for a different, more vigorous, style of accompaniment, which in Vivaldi's hands becomes a figure in demisemiquavers resembling an Alberti Bass. Cleverly, Vivaldi does not introduce it immediately, beginning the 'B' section as if (as happens so often in his cantata arias) it were a kind of development section for the

Ex. 6.3 Vivaldi, *Pianti, sospiri e dimandar mercede*, RV 676: 'Lusinga è del nocchier', bars 24–9

earlier material. When the demisemiquavers begin, the surprise is total. Example 6.3 shows the end of the 'A' section and the start of the 'B' section.[24]

In the second aria, 'Cor ingrato, dispietato', Vivaldi subtly expresses the lover's indignation at the rebuffs to his advances by employing a 'stamping' motive in even quavers. What is remarkable and admirable in Vivaldi's technique of word-painting is his willingness to go beyond simple pictorialism relating to surface details in order to capture background moods. The most celebrated instance of this in his music is perhaps the depiction of Judith's racing heartbeat in

---

[24]  In the example, the 'dotted' groups (dotted semiquaver plus demisemiquaver) are notated in the source as even semiquavers; the alteration is made by analogy with earlier passages.

her aria 'Veni, veni me sequere fide' from *Juditha triumphans*, which, unusually, offers an 'interpretation' on the composer's part of a situation not described in the text.[25] In the present aria, the 'stamping' motive is all the more effective for referring obliquely, rather than directly, to the content of the poem.

### RV 677: *Qual per ignoto calle* (RARA)

This cantata is set to the most interesting poem of any among Vivaldi's cantatas. The text is based on a simple simile, in which the lover is likened to a pilgrim travelling at night along an unfamiliar path. He is beset by fears, both rational and irrational, and prays for the advent of daylight: the reciprocation of his love.

A brief arioso in the first recitative (bars 10–12) introduces us to a 'lightning' motive (a rapid scale) in the vocal part and a 'thunder' motive (a broken chord moving first up and then down) in the bass. These two motives are remembered and requoted in the arias that follow. The 'thunder' motive pervades the bass part, and makes periodic appearances in the vocal part, of the first aria, 'Quel passagier son io'. Arguably, the recurrence is here musically rather than textually motivated, for the placid 'Andante' tempo makes the rising and falling of the motive more graceful than threatening. In the second, faster aria, 'Qual dopo lampi e turbini', the significance of the motives is most definitely textual as well as musical: the *lampi* ('flashes of lightning') are represented, as before, by scales, though now both falling and rising, while the *turbini* ('squalls') become rapid semiquaver oscillations between two notes.

There is an interesting oddity in the text of this aria. Its two semistrophes each consist of six lines: five *settenari sdruccioli* plus one *settenario tronco*. The only rhyme present is the 'key' rhyme linking the two final lines. However, this otherwise perfect symmetry is contradicted by the imagery of the text. The first four lines of the first semistrophe deal with the horrors of the night; the joys of daytime emerge in the fifth line and continue without interruption into the second semistrophe. A composer setting the text has, therefore, to recognize the dual nature of the first semistrophe and respect the bridge that its last two lines form to the second semistrophe.

| | |
|---|---|
| Qual dopo lampi e turbini | Just as, after lightning and squalls, |
| appar l'Aurora fulgida | the bright dawn appears, |
| a dissipar le tenebre | banishing the gloom |
| d'oscura notte orribile | of a dark and dreadful night, |
| e il pellegrino timido | and returning to cheer |
| ritorna a consolar; | the timid pilgrim; |
| | |
| così men fiero e rigido, | so, too, if the adorable eyes of my |
| se volgi a me l'amabile | beloved turn once more to me |
| ciglio, ridente e placido, | and become less hostile and unyielding, |
| pieno d'amor, di giubilo, | happy, calm, full of love and rejoicing, |
| scordato di mie lacrime, | forgetting all my tears, |
| benedirò il penar. | I will bless my former suffering. |

---

[25]  See the discussion of this aria in Talbot, *The Sacred Vocal Music of Antonio Vivaldi*, pp. 430–31.

Ex. 6.4 Vivaldi, *Qual per ignoto calle*, RV 677: 'Qual dopo lampi e turbini', bars 10–18

Vivaldi's solution is exemplary. When the fifth line is reached, the 'lightning' and 'squall' figures disappear, being replaced by a simple bass motive (quaver rest, quaver, crotchet) that expresses the hesitancy of *timido*. This motive carries over into the 'B' section. Example 6.4 shows the point of transition during the first vocal section. It is interesting that this aria, like the one preceding it, has no detached tailpiece following the second vocal period. This 'modern' feature has the effect of broadening the sweep of both movements.

'Qual dopo lampi e turbini' shows Vivaldi at the height of his powers: alert to the nuances of the text and displaying genius (no weaker word is fitting) in the invention and controlled development of memorable motives.

Since another setting of the same text exists, a comparison is in order. The sole source for the second, anonymous setting is a volume in the British Library containing twenty-four items: twenty-one cantatas (two with instruments), a duet, an aria, and an incomplete movement.[26] The cantatas comprise six by Hasse, three by A. Scarlatti, two each by Arrigoni, G. Bononcini, and Mancini, and single examples by Bigaglia, D'Astorga, Lotti, and Porpora. Of the two unattributed cantatas, one is by Gasparini. This leaves unclaimed the cantata *Qual per ignoto calle*, which occupies ff. 63–70. Like ten other items in the collection, it is written

[26] London, British Library, Add. Ms. 4,213.

in a hand, probably Neapolitan, identified by Josephine Wright as that of 'Scribe A'.[27]

In the volume, cantatas by a named composer are invariably placed consecutively. Since *Qual per ignoto calle* is preceded and followed by cantatas attributed to Carlo Arrigoni, both similarly for alto and copied out by 'Scribe A', his possible authorship is the first we need to examine.[28] Arrigoni (1697–1744) was a Florentine lutenist, tenor, and composer. From 1731 to 1736 he worked in London, where, in 1732, he published a set of ten *Cantate da camera*. John Walter Hill's article on him in the *New Grove* (2001) is uncomplimentary, describing him as a composer of 'modest ability' and perceiving a lack of 'directional flow' in his music.

The two Arrigoni cantatas in the same volume and the ten published ones provide useful comparators. The anonymous cantata certainly possesses notational features linking it to his practice. Both of its recitatives end with an effective 2/4 bar: that is, a bar in which, after the conclusion of the music on the second beat, no minim rest is appended in order to 'complete' the 4/4 bar. This rather unusual manner of notation is encountered often in Arrigoni's cantatas. Some of the appoggiaturas, which include several rising from below, are fully written out: this is a feature that Arrigoni shares with Hasse. The cut time (2/2) of the second aria of *Qual per ignoto calle* is encountered many times in Arrigoni's cantatas. It is a typically Neapolitan feature originating from church music but successfully transferred to secular music in a *galant* vein (Vivaldi employs cut time very rarely indeed, and then mostly in borrowed movements).

Stylistic features linking the anonymous cantata to Arrigoni include beginning the second vocal section exactly as the first, making extensive use of the *Trommelbaß* and fitting three syllables to a group of four semiquavers in the pattern 1 + 2 + 1.

The evidence is not quite strong enough for the cantata to be assigned with certainty to Arrigoni, but it certainly favours his authorship. With this proviso, the remaining discussion will assume that he was indeed the composer.

It is obvious from a first glance that Arrigoni's aesthetic, like that of Leo in *T'intendo, sì, mio cor*, is poles apart from Vivaldi's. The emphasis is on vocal display, not expression of the passions. Consequently, word-painting and mood-painting are optional extras – not part of the essence of the work. The major-key brightness of the two arias is not a response to the character of the text but simply the 'default' choice of the period among up-and-coming composers. As Sir John Hawkins lamented in his preface to the second edition (1788) of William Boyce's *Cathedral Music*, 'the sweet modulation of the keys with the minor third' had almost become a thing of the past. Vivaldi was born too early to lose interest altogether in minor keys (although the incidence of minor-key works decreases somewhat in his later music), but Arrigoni, almost a whole generation younger, exemplifies perfectly the new taste.

---

27  Wright, 'The Secular Cantatas of Francesco Mancini', pp. 85–9.
28  Perhaps significantly, the succeeding cantata, *Ti sento, Amor, ti sento* (ff. 71–6), has a vocal compass (*g–d''*) identical with that of the anonymous *Qual per ignoto calle*.

Ex. 6.5 Carlo Arigoni (?), *Qual per ignoto calle*: 'Qual dopo lampi e folgori', opening

Example 6.5 shows the opening of Arrigoni's second aria, which has no initial ritornello. The theme resembles the *soggetto* of a fugue in the strict style, but its contrapuntal promise evaporates soon enough. For *lampi* and *folgori* (replacing the *turbini* of Vivaldi's text) we have the tamest, most fleeting word-painting. The chosen way of representing *timido* – starting with repeated notes and graduating to semitones, thence to tones and wider intervals – is fine as a compositional conceit: the only problem is that the result is so ineffectual in musical terms. Arrigoni drifts: he seems to be unable to take hold of a strong idea and run with it. In contrast, Vivaldi rarely drifts: he may choose to play with a single chord interminably, milking it for its sonority, but he always keeps sight of his next goal.

RV 678: *All'ombra di sospetto* (RARA)

This cantata with a single obbligato instrument is the lone successor to RV 680. Its choice of partnering instrument, the transverse flute, makes it perhaps the most endearing of Vivaldi's cantatas. Around 1730 the flute was just entering the most glorious period of its entire history. Its soft tone, capacity for dynamic shading, and agility made it the perfect vehicle for civilized, *galant* music-making, while its portability and kindness to the player's posture and facial expression made it the ideal instrument for a gentleman. Frederick the Great's choice was not accidental. Vivaldi was the earliest major composer in Italy to write obbligato parts for the flute – some appear in his chamber concertos of the mid-1710s – and his Op. 10 (Amsterdam, 1729) was the first-ever published collection to consist entirely of concertos for flute and strings.[29]

Vivaldi will have known that the Saxon *Hofkapelle* boasted three excellent flautists, all of them also active as composers: Pierre Gabriel Buffardin, Johann Joachim Quantz, and Johann Martin Blochwitz. It is idle, in our present state of knowledge, to speculate on which particular flautist, if any, he had in mind for the cantata's baptism. Although Quantz knew Vivaldi's music well and had copied some of it out for Pisendel, Vivaldi may not have known him personally – even Quantz's autobiography does not claim that the two men came into direct contact. As the senior flautist, Buffardin probably had priority in any performance at court. (But, as observed earlier, there is no sign that RV 678 ever entered the active repertory of the *Hofkapelle*.)

*All'ombra di sospetto* is all about arias. Its two recitatives are merely efficient, and the first is exceedingly short: four lines of poetry occupying five bars.

From its opening note, the first aria, 'Avvezzo non è il core', is a hymn of praise to the *galant* style. It oozes slides, appoggiaturas, Lombardic rhythms, trills, and fussy ornaments. The superabundance of these features is there for a special purpose – to illustrate the words *finti vezzi* ('false charms') and, later on, *lusinghiero* ('flattering') – although one suspects Vivaldi of revelling in them for their own sake. The ornate style of writing for the flute resembles very strongly that of Pietro Locatelli in his Op. 2 sonatas (1732). The point is not that Vivaldi imitated Locatelli, or the reverse, but that both composers appreciated around the same time the way in which a flute could embody the *galant* aesthetic more successfully than a violin, their own instrument, ever could. The way in which Vivaldi gradually draws the partners, voice and flute, into co-operation is as methodical as in RV 680. The first vocal period (bars 7–11) is entrusted to the soprano alone. The second begins with the voice alone (bars 13–14); in bar 15 the flute joins in, discreetly accompanying; in bar 17 the two enter into an imitative sequence; in bar 20 they move into parallel sixths, in the manner of a love duet, to prepare for the cadence in bar 24. The third vocal period is constructed similarly. Its five-stage plan is: voice alone – imitation – ritornello for flute – voice alone – parallel motion. Example 6.6 shows the first eight bars of the second vocal period.

---

[29] On Vivaldi's cultivation of the flute and recorder, see Federico Maria Sardelli, *La musica per flauto di Antonio Vivaldi*, Florence: Olschki, 2000.

Ex. 6.6 Vivaldi, *All'ombra di sospetto*, RV 678: 'Avvezzo non è il core', bars 13–20

Ex. 6.6  Vivaldi, *All'ombra di sospetto*, RV 678: *cont.*

The brisk second aria, 'Mentiti contenti', is a touch disappointing. Being in the same key as the first, it goes over much of the same ground, and its phrase structure and rhythm are perhaps a little too four-square. However, the fluent interaction between the upper parts and the methodical development of the ideas are as good as before. The strong presence of triplet semiquavers (all but absent from the first aria) injects an attractive new element.

## Postscript: The Spurious Works

The work-list of every major composer of cantatas from Vivaldi's period has its due quota of spurious compositions. Among the main musical genres, cantatas were especially liable to anonymous or misattributed transmission. As Chapter 1 showed, cantatas circulated by Vivaldi's time almost entirely in manuscript; the publications that in the case of the sonata and concerto provided, up to a point, a deterrent to wilful misattribution and a means of correcting accidental error were thin on the ground (not that publication was in itself proof of authenticity). Moreover, cantatas circulated singly rather than in groups. They tended to be collected not in volumes dedicated to music by a single composer but in ones holding a variety of works associated with a single singer or patron – or even merely whatever individual pieces a music-lover searching for cantatas was able to obtain. Among such volumes one may distinguish between albums, into which the works are copied consecutively, and binder's collections, in which the separate fascicles containing each work are ordered by the collector and then bound. Missing and erroneous attributions are equally common in the two types.

Discussions of authorship concerning early eighteenth-century music in manuscript probably understate the rôle of deliberate falsification by professional copyists. The case of RV 795 and 803 – sacred works by Vivaldi marketed under the name of Galuppi – may be more typical than we realize. Buyers, especially foreigners who were not professional musicians, were not in a strong position to challenge attributions made by copyists. This was especially true of the cantata genre, where there was an exceptionally high degree of conformity, among poets and composers, to established norms, and therefore less opportunity to use a simple rule of thumb (for example, a preference for a given movement-plan) for the determination of authorship. Asked by a customer to supply a given number of cantatas by a specified composer, copying shops probably acted honestly when their stocks permitted, but when they ran short, they must often have substituted the desired name surreptitiously. In any case, among ordinary music-lovers authorship was less of a 'big issue' in the eighteenth century than it has become since the nineteenth century. Pieces were either liked or disliked, irrespective of whose name stood at the head of the score. So copyists could rest assured that, unless their customer was a professional musician or a connoisseur (and probably not even then), their guilty secret would remain safe.[30]

Other misattributions were more innocent, arising from an attempt to provide an author for an anonymous work existing alongside attributed works, the name of whose composer could be appropriated. In attributing the anonymous setting of *Qual per ignoto calle* to Arrigoni initially on the basis of the two cantatas surrounding it, I acted in exactly the same way as countless collectors and librarians have done before me. But whereas I sought to strengthen the attribution by considering evidence of other kinds, bibliographical and stylistic, most people in the same position have not. The *Anhang* of the Ryom catalogue is so large precisely because the anonymous sacred works in Vivaldi's collection were once widely believed to be his – simply by virtue of being contained in the same volumes as ones genuinely composed by him.

Before examining each of the four continuo cantatas that I believe to be misattributed in their original sources to Vivaldi, it will be useful to consider what they would look like if genuine. The sources all date from around 1710, and therefore cannot be expected to transmit works of the same level of maturity as the Mantuan group or the slightly earlier RV 681 and (possibly) RV 796.

One would expect a Vivaldi cantata of c.1710 – roughly contemporary with the Op. 2 violin sonatas – to be compact in its dimensions and very moderate in its use of *fioritura*. There would be a higher incidence of contrapuntal interaction between the voice and the bass than in his later cantatas. The underlaid text would be organized rather informally, with much repetition of phrases and some jumbling (as in the early sacred vocal works). The 'A' section would always contain two vocal periods, although the ritornello connecting them would probably be brief. Dance-like rhythms (siciliana, giga, gavotta, etc.) would be favoured. The harmony would use Neapolitan Sixths and diminished sevenths abundantly.

The first cantata, *Prendea con man di latte*, RV 753, was already in 1985 the subject of an article by Colin Timms that questions its authenticity.[31] Its sole source is a volume in the Bodleian Library, Oxford, which contains an assortment of cantatas and duets ascribed to sixteen composers active either side of 1700.[32] The hand that attributed RV 753 to Vivaldi (its heading is 'Cantata d'Antonio Vivaldi') penned the ascriptions of fifteen further cantatas, whose authors are

30 I discuss the rise of concern with authorship in the nineteenth century in 'The Work-Concept and Composer-Centredness', in Michael Talbot (ed.), *The Musical Work: Reality or Invention?*, Liverpool: Liverpool University Press, 2000, pp. 168–86.
31 Timms, ' "Prendea con man di latte": a Vivaldi Spuriosity?'.
32 Oxford, Bodleian Library, Mus. Sch. D. 223; the cantata appears on pp. 80–86.

named as Ariosti (twice), Benati, Bononcini (three times), Caldara (twice), Ceruta, Mancia, Mancini, A. Scarlatti (twice), Steffani, and Stradella. The covers of the volume bear the name of its earliest known owner, Isabella Aubert, and a date, 1711. The title written inside confirms Isabella's ownership but gives the volume the date of 1714. Timms suggests that the discrepancy arose when an old binding was used for newly acquired music.[33] Isabella Aubert was possibly related to John Aubert, a French musician in the service of Ann of Denmark in London. A later owner was the organist and composer Raphael Courteville (c.1690–1772).

A date of composition before 1711 would accord very easily with the fact that the text of RV 753 was also set by Francesco Bartolomeo Conti, who – perhaps not coincidentally – visited London on at least two occasions during the first decade of the eighteenth century. (Conti's birth date, 1682, is quite late, but we know that he was already writing cantatas by 1706.)[34]

As an argument against Vivaldi's authorship, Timms mentions the tonal poverty of the cantata. The two recitatives both start and finish in the same key (C minor and G minor, respectively). Both arias are in C minor, and the first, by creating a 'zero' progression after the preceding recitative, violates Vivaldi's normal tonal principles. Internal modulation is minimal in all movements.

Other counter-indications highlighted by Timms are the extreme concision of all the movements and the short-windedness of the phrases. Indeed, there are no melismatic phrases extending further than three notes in the whole of the work. At a more technical level, one could raise the fact that the 'A' sections of both arias consist only of a single vocal period, a sure sign of early date. The first aria employs a *Devise* – very fashionable around 1700 but not employed in any known Vivaldi cantata. The harmony is bland throughout and includes some extended passages in parallel motion (such as bars 46–8 in the second aria) that seem at odds with Vivaldi's habit of making the bass relatively independent in contrapuntal and melodic respects.

Not a whiff of Vivaldi's idiolect emerges from this insipid cantata. Because of the numerous uncharacteristic features in it, one is probably safe to exclude it from the canon of his works.

The three cantatas RV 672, 673, and 675, all for alto and continuo, are no longer regarded as authentic works by the community of Vivaldi scholars, although – irritatingly – they are still occasionally performed from modern editions under his name.[35] They are preserved in the same hand in the same anthology: Ms. 772 of the Conservatorio Statale di Musica 'Luigi Cherubini', Florence.[36] All three copies identify the composer simply as 'Vivaldi'. The other composers represented (at least by name) include Albinoni, Aldrovandini,

---

[33] Timms, ' "Prendea con man di latte" ', p. 65.

[34] Hermine Weigel Williams, *Francesco Bartolomeo Conti: His Life and Music*, Aldershot: Ashgate, 1999, pp. 104–5.

[35] See Chapter 1, pp. 22–3.

[36] The anthology comprises two volumes. The three cantatas are nos. 11 (RV 675), 13 (RV 673), and 14 (RV 672) in the second volume.

Ex. 6.7 *Filli, di gioia vuoi farmi morir*, RV 672: opening

Benati, Bononcini, Pistocchi, Sabadini, and Tosi. Once again, the date of compilation appears to be close to 1710.

Common stylistic traits suggest that the composer of the three cantatas, whatever his true identity, is the same person. All employ for the arias a rigidly quadratic phrase structure, which is occasionally disguised by overlapping, so that a new phrase begins in the final bar of its predecessor. The opening of RV 672, *Filli, di gioia vuoi farmi morir*, shown as Example 6.7, illustrates the point. Melisma is used in the three cantatas almost as sparingly as in RV 753. Harmonic asperities are not shunned. RV 673, *Ingrata Lidia, ha vinto il tuo rigore*, opens with a 7-4-2 chord (bolder than anything Vivaldi ever attempted at the start of a work), while RV 672 even takes a leaf out of Vivaldi's book by adding a ninth to the diminished seventh opening its second recitative.

A concordance not mentioned, to my knowledge, in previous literature may hold the vital clue to the authorship of RV 673 and, by extension, of all three cantatas. Giovanni Bononcini's setting of the same text was mentioned earlier.[37] But there is also a version of RV 673, transposed to A flat major for soprano, in Berlin.[38] This manuscript is attributed to Giuseppe Boniventi.

---

[37] See Chapter 3, p. 71.
[38] Berlin, Staatsbibliothek 'Preußischer Kulturbesitz', Mus. ms. 30266, pp. 47–56. The bass of the Berlin version is a little more elaborate in places than that of the Florence version, suggesting

Boniventi remains a shadowy figure. He was born, probably in Venice, in 1670 or slightly later, and came to the public's attention as a composer of operas in 1690. In 1712 he became *Kapellmeister* to Margrave Karl III Wilhelm of Baden-Durlach, although he returned permanently to Italy in 1717. Vivaldi collaborated with him, as we saw, on *Filippo, re di Macedonia* in 1721. His last known opera, *Bertarido, re dei Longobardi*, dates from 1727, at which point he fades into total obscurity.

Only one other cantata by Boniventi is known: the continuo cantata for alto *Infelice Dorinda*.[39] The present state of knowledge does not allow one to assert that *Ingrata Lidia* conforms to his style, but the old-fashioned features present in all three cantatas make him a far more likely candidate than Vivaldi.

The aria in F minor with which RV 672 opens, illustrated in Example 6.7, ends its 'B' section with a cadence in the supertonic, G minor. This is an act of boldness (or crudity?) foreign to Vivaldi. The 'A' section of the same aria consists of only one vocal period; that of the second aria has a first vocal period marked for repeat. Neither feature occurs in Vivaldi's continuo cantatas.

In RV 673, the strongly deviant features in relation to Vivaldi's style all occur in the second aria. They are (a) the single vocal period in the 'A' section; (b) the appearance of a *Devise*; and (c) the commencement by the alto of the 'B' section over the final note of the ritornello ending the 'A' section (Vivaldi prefers to keep the 'A' and 'B' sections discrete).

RV 675, *Piango, gemo, sospiro e peno*, employs a strict *basso ostinato* in its first aria. The 'A' section is formed from four statements of the four-bar theme (in the familiar *lamento* design), framed by single ritornello statements of the same theme; the 'B' section contains another four statements, transposed to the dominant. This formula is exactly the same (except for the number of repetitions) as that used by Albinoni in 'Pianger lungi dal nume che s'ama', the final aria of *Lontananza crudel* (Op. 4 no. 5). It suggests the late seventeenth century rather than the period (not much before 1705) of Vivaldi's first attempts at composition. Example 6.8 shows the first two, not very imaginative, vocal phrases over this bass.

There is an ironic twist to the story of this aria. In 1966 Bernhard Paumgartner proposed it as the model for J. S. Bach's great chorus 'Weinen, Klagen, Sorgen, Zagen' (from the homonymous cantata, BWV 12), of which the 'Crucifixus' of the *B minor Mass* is an elaborated contrafactum. His theory stemmed from similarities in the openings of their texts (*Piango/Weinen, gemo/Klagen, sospiro/Sorgen, (e) peno/Zagen*) and in their common employment, in 3/2 metre, of a

---

partial recomposition either at the time of the transposition or independently. Which version is the earlier is impossible to judge on the basis of the two manuscripts alone. What appears to be a later copy of the Berlin version is preserved in Brussels, Bibliothèque du Conservatoire, 15.153.

[39] Venice, Biblioteca Querini-Stampalia, Miscellanea Ms. 1128, ff. 40–3. The parallelism between the openings 'Ingrata Lidia' and 'Infelice Dorinda' makes one wonder whether the two cantatas belonged to the same cycle. Johann Sigismund Kusser's commonplace book in Yale University, Beinecke Rare Books and Manuscript Library, Osborn Music MS. 16, lists (p. 184) a further continuo cantata attributed to Boniventi, *Ferma pur l'incauto voto* (with thanks to Rashid-Sascha Pegah for informing me).

Ex. 6.8  *Piango, gemo sospiro e peno*, RV 675: bars 9–16

*passus duriusculus* articulated in crotchets over four bars as an ostinato theme.[40] The problem with the claim is that not only Bach himself but also his librettist, Salomo Franck, would have had to be familiar with this very obscure piece in order to unite the textual parallelism with the musical one. Since both the segmented treatment of the tetrameter (an *ottonario* in Italian terms) and the use of the *passus duriusculus* for a 'chaconne' bass were commonplace, it is hardly necessary to look beyond coincidence. Recent Bach scholarship tends to reject the theory.[41]

The rest of RV 675 remains similarly remote from Vivaldi's musical language. Its second aria reintroduces the *passus duriusculus*, this time continued freely. In its melodic line a few *notes échappées*, uncharacteristic of early Vivaldi, appear before cadences.

40  Bernhard Paumgartner, 'Zum "Crucifixus" der H-moll-Messe J. S. Bachs', *Österreichische Musikzeitschrift*, xxi (1966), 500–3.
41  John Butt (*Bach Mass in B Minor*, Cambridge: Cambridge University Press, 1991, p. 54) states: 'It is perhaps foolish to look for a single model'.

# CHAPTER SEVEN

# Vivaldi's Cantatas in Perspective

## *The Cantata within Vivaldi's Oeuvre*

The cantata stands a little apart from the other domains that Vivaldi cultivated. One symptom of this is the rarity with which the material of his cantatas – and, above all, of his continuo cantatas – recurs in his works belonging to other genres. Whereas a slow movement of a violin sonata may pop up as that of a concerto, or the theme of a concerto ritornello reappear in an operatic aria, such specific links involving themes in the fullest sense (as opposed to motives and figures) are hardly ever encountered between his cantatas and his other music. Since Vivaldi was in general such an inveterate self-borrower, we need to consider why.

Part of the reason lies in simple statistics. The great majority of Vivaldi's cantatas are for voice and continuo. Vivaldi began to compose them in quantity (during the Mantua years) at a point when continuo arias were beginning to disappear entirely from his (and other composer's) operas. The opportunity for exchange in bulk between cantata arias and operatic arias was therefore lost. In any case, Vivaldi had developed a sensitivity for the text–music relationship that prevented him from making such exchanges too freely. Most cantata aria texts differ from most operatic aria texts in style and content. The elegiac, pastorally tinged tone of a typical cantata aria corresponds to that of only a very small subtype of operatic aria. It is significant that in those instances where there has been exchange of material between the cantata and another domain, the cantata text is either borrowed from that domain (as in the first aria of RV 663) or the domain is instrumental (as in the second aria of RV 682).

Close thematic affinities between Vivaldi's continuo cantatas and 'solo' sonatas are minimal. There are of course remoter affinities based on common phrase structure or harmonic progression, but one would have expected these in any case. The composer seems to have respected to an extraordinary degree Mattheson's injunction to keep vocal and instrumental styles separate. Two Vivaldi sonatas, RV 2 for violin and RV 53 for oboe, show the influence of the cantata in an unexpected way: by prefacing the opening slow movement with a continuo ritornello – something very unusual for that genre. A handful of concertos do likewise in their central slow movement.

The world of Vivaldi's cantatas is therefore surprisingly self-contained. But it is far from narrow. Within it, one discovers by turns cantatas that are simple or complex; easy or difficult; concise or expansive; cool or impassioned; insipid or inspired. The vast difference in quality between a masterpiece such as RV 677 and a pot-boiler such as RV 664 has several possible causes. One is certainly the rush to meet deadlines. Some of the cantatas surviving in composition manuscripts already betray their ephemerality through a chaotic appearance, the result of haste, while others, more neatly presented, suggest greater calmness and reflection in the act of composition. The degree of stimulation Vivaldi received from the text would also have varied. It was not necessarily the best poetry, in conventional literary terms, that inspired him, but the most picturesque – containing the vital keywords capable of firing his musical imagination. Finally, the qualities, not only vocal but also dramatic, of the singer must have played an important part. It is no accident that the most difficult among the cantatas contain a disproportionately high number of the most successful. In a nutshell: to elicit the best from Vivaldi, one needed a relaxed schedule, a vivid text, and a superlative singer.

It is a little meaningless to say that the best of Vivaldi's cantatas are the equal of his best sonatas and concertos, since the canons by which one has to judge are so different. A sonata is 'pure' music, while a cantata is 'applied' music. It is not enough for a cantata to be melodious, attractively harmonized, and well constructed: it also has to express something lying beyond the sphere of music. A better comparison can be made with Vivaldi's motets. Here, too, one notes the uneven quality and the similar reasons that cause it. Excellent though some of the motets and *introduzioni* are, even the best of them – *In furore iustissimae irae*, RV 626, and *Nulla in mundo pax sincera,* RV 630, are two examples – fail to achieve the psychological penetration of a cantata such as *Qual per ignoto calle*. If the motets are more frequently heard in modern performance than the cantatas, this is because of the general modern bias towards orchestral textures and the 'aura' that any sacred work enjoys (in Vivaldi's case amplified by the prestige of his choral works, to which they are ancillary).

How do Vivaldi's best cantatas rank alongside those of his major contemporaries? In most instances, one can find some quality or other in which he plainly comes off second-best. He has neither the grand sweep nor the human warmth of Handel. He lacks the contrapuntal finesse of Stradella and Scarlatti. He does not have the zest for quirky experimentation of Gasparini or Marcello. The smoothness of Bononcini and Hasse eludes him. He does not begin to approach the tunefulness of Albinoni. What he does possess in greater measure than most of them, however, is a superb command of musical imagery, a tight control of musical flow, and a real gift for the intensive treatment of musical material – the incipient *thematische Arbeit* accurately perceived by Wörner. His fondness for thematic economy is, of course, double-edged: when the material is strong, the piece springs to life; when it is weak, its repetition only drags the music down.

The mention of Albinoni brings one back to the polar opposition of the two great Venetians – so often misleadingly 'twinned' – on which Schmitz insisted. The quotation, as Example 7.1, of the opening of an early cantata by Albinoni will demonstrate a style of melody that Vivaldi could easily have imitated but chose not to cultivate.[1] It is unproductive to break down such a melody into constituent

---

1   *Allor che il mondo in letargo profondo* (Ostiglia, Biblioteca Greggiati Mss. Musiche B 260, pp. 35–42). This cantata, which is preserved anonymously within a group of cantatas ascribed to

Ex. 7.1 [Albinoni], *Allor che il mondo in letargo profondo*: 'Vaghe stelle, deh venite', opening

Albinoni (or ascribable to him on the basis of concordances), is surely by him as well, since it bears clear marks of his idiolect.

motives: one appreciates it, rather, as an unbroken, sinuous line, of which one takes the full measure only when it is completed. The melody flows effortlessly from one peak to another, and the three peaks in the example are organized in a logical and satisfying progression. The note $e''$ flat arrives already in bar 3; $f''$ in bar 9; and $a''$, just before the end, in bar 12. This is the method of composition described in Chapter 2 as 'top down'. In contrast, as any example taken from a Vivaldi aria will show, our composer flaunts, rather than conceals, his building blocks.

Loss as well as gain is inherent in the modular approach. In the whole of Vivaldi's cantatas there is no melody suitable for humming in the bath. For him, melody is the end-product of notes in motion, not a *Gestalt* in the process of realization. On the credit side, Vivaldi's liberation from conventional approaches to melodic formation allows him greater latitude in the expression of the text. By the late Baroque, most composers were rationing word-painting in vocal parts quite severely so as not to interfere too much with the natural melodic flow. The unusually high density of word-painting in Vivaldi's cantatas could be viewed almost as a throwback to the principles of Monteverdi's *seconda pratica*: 'Prima le parole, poi la musica'. In Vivaldi's case, however, one should perhaps speak of the primacy not of the word itself, but of the image underlying the word. It is revealing that the sonnets attached to *Le quattro stagioni* when the concertos were eventually published, in 1725, as Op. 8 nos. 1–4 were not the actual germ of the programme but an afterthought based on the musical depictions.

It is understandable that Vivaldi's cantatas elicited little appreciation in their time. Today, with our composer-centred approach, we can value them for the qualities they have in common with his music in general and especially for their original features. In contrast, the early eighteenth century was, if anything, genre-centred. Each educated listener had an ideal concept of what a genre was like (these ideals are enshrined in the minute descriptions of each genre penned by Mattheson, Scheibe, and Quantz), and compositions were valued for their success in conforming to that concept. The evident success of anonymous compositions in reaching performance and achieving wider circulation through copying and even (though rarely) publication proves the point that the ability to associate a piece securely with a composer, although growing in importance during the eighteenth century, had not yet become the *sine qua non* that it is today. Their very 'average' qualities, coupled with their huge number, account for the exemplary status in their day of Giovanni Bononcini's cantatas. It was precisely their 'deviant' qualities that barred the way to a wider appreciation of Vivaldi's cantatas and limited their circulation. Had we not had the good fortune to recover a large part of his musical archive (something that has happened to few composers of his time), they might well have remained almost as marginal to our concerns as they were for Schmitz almost a century ago.

To a great extent, the fortunes of Vivaldi's cantatas are bound up with those of the late Baroque cantata in general. In other words, where the performance of cantatas flourishes, those of Vivaldi will flourish too.

## Approaches to Performance

We have already broached, in Chapter 1, the problem of finding a suitable performance context for cantatas in modern conditions. In an ideal world, one might
think of recreating the eighteenth-century *conversazione* – not so very different
from the nineteenth-century soirée – and have cantatas performed in the atmosphere of something like a Schubertiad among friends. This is unlikely to happen
on a significant scale for a number of reasons, all obvious. The intimacy of the
surroundings would reduce the likelihood of raising sufficient ticket income to
offset the cost of paying professional musicians to participate. More fundamentally, such a gathering would fall between two stools: it would be too planned to
achieve credibility as an informal event, too spontaneous to be successful as a
formal event. The clock cannot, alas, be put back.

However, there is much that can be done, and is being done, to make the traditional concert format friendlier to Baroque cantatas. Items can be introduced
orally by the performers. Explanations can be provided of historical or mythological characters. The texts can be printed in programmes with parallel translations
into the vernacular. Singers can 'dramatize' their performance and become a little
less statuesque than their counterparts in Lieder. Most obviously, variety can be
sought in the accompaniment in order to characterize individual compositions
more strongly and delight the ear.

Thirty years ago, cantatas were almost uniformly performed with an accompaniment of harpsichord and cello. The harpsichordist read from a carefully
prepared realization that not infrequently was far too elaborate for its own good –
slowing down the pace and drawing too much attention to itself. The voicing of
chords was often unfortunate, leaving too large a gap between the bass and the
fistful of notes in the right hand.[2] In part, the fussiness of harpsichord realizations
was the consequence of a lack of ornamentation by the singer. Someone had to
keep the movement going, and this became the keyboard player's task by default.

Since those days, the introduction of plucked instruments (lute, theorbo, and
guitar), of genuine improvisation (or performance in a manner suggestive of real
improvisation) and of styles of keyboard accompaniment consonant with descriptions of the time (short attacks, full participation of the left hand in chords, the
addition of acciaccaturas, etc.) have worked wonders. There is still, however, a
reluctance to pare down the accompaniment to the minimum. Performance with
harpsichord or spinet alone is not rare, but the use of cello alone has not yet taken
root. Doubtless, it will do so before long, since it is already becoming established
as a valid mode of performing chamber sonatas for one instrument and bass.[3]

The last frontier to cross is that of self-accompanied performance by a singer-

---

2    This defect probably arose both from a subconscious desire to avoid leger lines underneath the
     treble stave and from a more deliberate decision to keep the left hand free for the bass line alone
     (thus separating the composer's contribution in the clearest possible manner from the editor's),
     although I suspect that an unthinking transference of typical piano textures was also to blame.
3    David Watkins's accompaniments to Corelli violin sonatas, which use multiple-stopping to
     produce intermittent chords, are a case in point.

harpsichordist, which we know was extremely common at the time, especially among amateur musicians. In truth, it is the very unfamiliarity of the idea, within the tradition of classical concert music, that acts as the greatest barrier. There must already be countless specialist singers who rehearse in private, as Farinelli and Faustina once did, to their own keyboard accompaniment. Of course, not every Vivaldi cantata – perhaps only a minority of his cantatas – is suited to such treatment. Both the vocal line and the accompaniment need to be simple enough for performers to be able to divide their attention. An example of a cantata that fits this description perfectly is *Usignoletto bello*, RV 796. Example 7.2 illustrates – as much as any musical notation can convey what is supposed to be an improvised element – the type of realization that can be handled easily by a singer seated at the keyboard. The texture is free-voiced, lying comfortably under the fingers. The activity is greatest when the voice is silent, since the performer's concentration is then undivided. At all times, the bass line remains paramount. When the voice sings, the realization reduces its independent rhythmic activity almost to zero, replicating the rhythm of either the bass or the voice.

In a way, it is rather fortunate that we are so ignorant about the circumstances of the first performances of Vivaldi's cantatas. In recent years, great attention has been paid to what the Baroque composer 'intended' as the performing forces for a given composition, and this intention has been equated – quite illegitimately, in my opinion – with the forces used for the first performance. So if we discover that when a vocal work by Bach was given its first outing without *ripieni* (the extra singers who made up a supporting choir) or a *concerto a cinque* by Albinoni was introduced to the world with precisely five players plus continuo, we are invited to think that this was precisely the ensemble 'for which the composer wrote'. But Baroque composers were not so blinkered as to put all their eggs in the basket of the first performance. They hoped for later performances, many of which would be given under changed conditions, including differences in the size and make-up of the performing ensemble. A great amount of elasticity is built into the composition from the start. If we are talking about authenticity in relationship to eighteenth-century music, the first thing to remember is that pragmatism was the most 'authentic' quality of all during that period. Instead of looking for single 'right' ways to perform Baroque music, we should be seeking to maximize the number of admissible ways. Naturally, there need to be limits; but these limits must be credible within the world in which eighteenth-century music actually operated, not ones imperiously imposed today in a spirit of musicological one-upmanship. What would we think of a musicologist of the twenty-second century who agonized over whether Hindemith conceived his *Ludus tonalis* for a Steinway or a Bechstein? Nowhere is it more desirable to tolerate experimentation at the margins of the possible than in the Baroque cantata, given the relatively unfavourable modern environment.

The one-instrument-per-part debate is highly germane to Vivaldi's cantatas with string accompaniment. Richard Maunder's recent book on the Baroque concerto is a radical reassessment that – in my view, too dogmatically – states the case for regarding 'single' strings as the norm.[4] My recommendation would be to

---

[4]  Richard Maunder, *The Scoring of Baroque Concertos*, Woodbridge: Boydell Press, 2004.

Ex. 7.2  Vivaldi, *Usignoletto bello*, RV 796: opening with realized continuo

U - si - gno - let - to  bel - lo     che  su  quel  ra - mo - scel - lo,

Ex. 7.2  Vivaldi, *Usignoletto bello*, RV 796: *cont.*

adopt an entirely pragmatic position on the issue. As Quantz makes clear in his *Versuch*, what is important is not the absolute size of the ensemble (little account was taken in the eighteenth century of the difference in tone-colour between a single instrument and a group of like instruments playing in unison) but the relative size of its components.[5] If the balance is right and the volume of sound fills the auditorium without swamping it, the mode of performance will be satisfactory.

The question of vocal ornamentation also poses a challenge. In Vivaldi's day it was mandatory to ornament reprised 'A' sections in *da capo* arias heavily, and lighter ornamentation was permissible in the other sections as well. Forty years ago it was not uncommon for the more enlightened editions of Baroque cantatas to propose ornamentation to the performer, much as an editorial continuo realization was set before the accompanist. This one-size-fits-all approach had its all-too-evident weaknesses, although one must give it credit for having introduced singers to the concept of 'improvised' embellishment and for having provided concrete specimens. Such editorial assistance is naturally double-edged: in the short term, it provides ready solutions and has a heuristic value; in the long term, however, it can create a kind of dependence that causes a singer to delay getting to grips with ornamental practice. Direct involvement by the singer is very necessary, since eighteenth-century performers were expected to forge a personal style

5  Quantz, *Versuch einer Anweisung*, p. 185.

of embellishment that foregrounded their strengths and 'trademark' special effects, while disguising their weaknesses. Such ornamentation needs to become second nature to the singer in order to give the effect of genuine improvisation rather than simply 'written-out' embellishment à la Bach. It is easy enough to view samples of embellishment by leading eighteenth-century singers.[6] The problem is that such examples need to be imitated, if at all, only at a very generic level, since what suits one voice will not suit another. I know of no evidence that vocal embellishment was more restrained in cantatas than in operas, but common sense suggests that it was so, in keeping with the more intimate and refined world of the chamber cantata.

However, one should always keep the issue of extempore ornamentation in proportion. It is not a catastrophe if a singer chooses to forego it through inexperience, insecurity, or personal taste, although, as remarked earlier, the result may be to transfer the responsibility for creating variety to the accompanist(s).

Vivaldi's tempo directions should be taken as broadly indicative rather than narrowly prescriptive. Some interesting details emerge from Table 7.1, which gives the tempo markings for all the arias in Vivaldi's thirty-seven authenticated cantatas (omitting the unfinished RV 684a). Where two tempo markings are separated in the same column by an oblique, the second is a later substitution by the composer. Tempi in square brackets are ones supplied by Degrada in *NEC* in the absence of original markings.

Although the RARA and ARA plans were likened in Chapter 2 to the SFSF and FSF plans in sonatas, recitative should not be equated with 'slow movement', or aria with 'fast movement'. The pace of a recitative is entirely dependent on the mood and the choice of note-values, while arias are almost as likely to be slow (marked 'Grave', 'Largo', and their variants) as fast ('Allegro', 'Andante', and their variants). In three instances (RV 659, 661, and 799) both arias are slow; in eleven instances they are both fast. In almost two thirds of the cantatas the first aria is slow, the second fast. Moreover, even when both are classed as 'generically' slow or fast, the faster tempo – Allegro as compared with Andante, or Larghetto as compared with Adagio – is usually placed second. This progression from slower to faster correlates with the general tendency of cantata texts to end more brightly than they begin. This is true for all chamber cantatas of Vivaldi's period.

There are some interesting differences between cantatas of the pre-Neapolitan period ('pre-1725' in the table) and those of the post-Neapolitan ('post-1725') period. An attenuated 'Allegro' ('Allegro (ma) non molto', 'Allegro ma poco') appears in six post-1725 arias but in only one pre-1725 aria. Similarly, an attenuated 'Largo' ('Larghetto') appears as the original marking of seven post-1725 arias but only two pre-1725 ones. It would almost be appropriate to regard 'Larghetto' as a slow 'Andante' rather than a fast 'Largo', as Vivaldi's vacillation between the two terms in RV 662 and 683 seems to imply. There is a clear connection between the slowing down of the beat as a result of the move to shorter

---

6    For example, Robert Donington (*The Interpretation of Early Music*, revised version, London: Faber and Faber, 1974, p. 175) quotes from a manuscript in Vienna a passage showing Farinelli's extravagant ornamentation of an aria by Giacomelli.

Table 7.1 Tempo markings in the arias of Vivaldi's cantatas

| RV | Period | Aria 1 | Aria 2 |
|---|---|---|---|
| 649 | pre-1725 | Largo | Allegro |
| 650 | post-1725 | Larghetto | Allegro |
| 651 | post-1725 | Largo | Andante |
| 652 | pre-1725 | Andante/Andante molto | Allegro |
| 653 | pre-1725 | Andante | Allegro |
| 654 | pre-1725 | Largo/Larghetto | Allegro non molto |
| 655 | post-1725 | Largo/Larghetto | Allegro ma non molto |
| 656 | post-1725 | Andante | Allegro |
| 657 | post-1725 | Andante | Allegro |
| 658 | pre-1725 | Adagio/Largo | Allegro |
| 659 | pre-1725 | Adagio | Larghetto |
| 660 | post-1725 | Andante molto | Largo |
| 661 | pre-1725 | Largo | Largo |
| 662 | post-1725 | Andante/Larghetto | Allegro |
| 663 | pre-1725 | Andante | Allegro |
| 664 | post-1725 | Allegro | Allegro |
| 665 | pre-1725 | Largo | Allegro |
| 666 | post-1725 | Largo | Allegro |
| 667 | post-1725 | Largo | Allegro |
| 668 | post-1725 | [Andante] | Allegro non molto |
| 669 | post-1725 | Andante | Allegro |
| 670 | post-1725 | Allegro | Allegro |
| 671 | post-1725 | Allegro non molto | Allegro ma poco |
| 674 | post-1725 | Larghetto | Allegro non molto |
| 676 | post-1725 | Larghetto | Allegro molto |
| 677 | post-1725 | Andante | Allegro |
| 678 | post-1725 | Larghetto | Allegro |
| 679 | post-1725 | Largo | [Allegro] |
| 680 | pre-1725 | Largo | Allegro |
| 681 | pre-1725 | Largo | Allegro |
| 682 | post-1725 | Larghetto | Allegro |
| 683 | post-1725 | Larghetto/Larghetto Andante | Allegro |
| 684 | post-1725 | Larghetto | Allegro |
| 685 | pre-1725 | Allegro | [Andante] |
| 686 | pre-1725 | Allegro | Allegro |
| 796 | pre-1725 | Andante | Larghetto/Largo |
| 799 | pre-1725 | Andante | Grave |

note-values in the Neapolitan style and Vivaldi's option for 'intermediate' tempo markings. His wavering between 'Largo' and 'Larghetto' suggests to me an uncertainty over the significance of the two terms for the performer during a period of transition rather than a change of mind over the actual tempo, as Degrada has proposed.[7]

Dynamic marks are all but non-existent in the continuo cantatas and very sparse in the 'accompanied' ones. This was an area where performers were expected to work things out for themselves. Most dynamic contrasts are sharp, but since Vivaldi's instrumental music shows that he sometimes employed multi-stage dynamic change (e.g., from *forte* to *piano* and then to *più piano*) and even, perhaps, *crescendo* and *diminuendo* (whose existence in Italian music of the 1730s is attested by Charles de Brosses), performers should not hesitate to vary the dynamic level in subtle ways. Most important is to ensure that the voice at all times emerges clearly from the texture. One thing to remember is that *forte* (in the sense of a full-bodied, if not always literally loud, sound) is the 'default' dynamic at the start of a movement unless expressly contradicted.

Rhythmic assimilation, vertical and horizontal, is a matter that has to exercise the minds of performers of a good many Vivaldi cantatas. Fortunately, *NEC* is very alert to the question, which receives ample discussion in the Critical Notes and Critical Commentary of the volumes affected. The reconciliation of triplet and duplet division of the beat-note is rarely the issue. More common is the contrast between dotted and even two-note groups. Quite often, Vivaldi begins by notating dotted rhythms. When he feels that they are firmly established, he substitutes even rhythms, expecting performers to continue in the same manner. The horizontal assimilation that results is simple and mostly uncontroversial.

Where divergent rhythms occur simultaneously in different parts, however, the solution is not always so clear-cut. Take, for example, the first vocal period of the first aria of *Tremori al braccio e lagrime sul ciglio*, RV 799, shown as Example 7.3. Here, the soprano, after bar 5, never dots a three-note group occupying a beat, whereas the continuo always does. At the start of bar 6 the two rhythmic styles come into conflict. Degrada's edition recommends assimilating the soprano's rhythm to that of the bass, as a result of which the parallel octaves between the notes A and G become more palpable. But perhaps there is a better case for allowing the two parts to follow their separate paths. This kind of rhythmic heterophony is well known from Lieder. It is a strange fact that whenever a voice combines with an instrument, each preserves its separate aural space. This allows rhythmic discrepancies to occur that would be intolerable between two instruments or between two voices. In the example the small difference of rhythm even succeeds in mitigating the effect of the parallel octaves.

And so to a few final remarks. There is every prospect that Vivaldi's chamber cantatas will maintain the steady progress that they have made in recent years towards full recognition by performers and audiences. My additional hope is that they will spearhead a growth of interest by musicians, musicologists, and music-lovers in the Baroque cantata in general. As a composer of cantatas,

---

[7]    In the Critical Commentary for RV 655 he writes: 'It is a common practice of Vivaldi to opt for a livelier tempo when revising a work from an earlier period.'

Ex. 7.3 Vivaldi, *Tremori al braccio e lagrime sul ciglio*, RV 799: 'Quello che senti, o bella', bars 5–8

Vivaldi has an advantage not shared by any other major composer of his time except Handel: his works in several other genres have an unassailable place in the modern performing repertory. These form a permanent bridgehead from which the curious can strike out at any time to explore further. There is never going to be a problem with defending his status as a composer or gaining access to his cantatas. Luckily, too, his cantatas are just the right number for easy assimilation: not so few as to be discountable; not so many as to be forbidding. They are the perfect vehicle for familiarizing modern audiences with the basic features of their once flourishing genre.

Will they remain at thirty-seven? The spate of Vivaldi discoveries in recent years suggests, by the law of averages, that their number will grow. There are, after all, so many possible routes to discovery. The music from private, unpublicized collections that turns up at auction never fails to surprise. As the case of RV 799 proved as recently as 1999, there are still several major libraries whose collections of older musical manuscripts are not yet adequately catalogued.[8] This generally means, also, that the authorship of individual items has not been thoroughly researched. Somewhere, one feels, there are manuscripts of cantatas in the hand of either Vivaldi or his father that do not name the composer and have therefore been listed as anonymous or even ascribed arbitrarily to another composer. Equally, there are likely to be cantatas that even in their own day were transferred, by error or design, from Vivaldi to another composer and need merely an attentive eye to reveal their secret. Or perhaps an old catalogue entry will mention the title of an unknown Vivaldi cantata, which could be enough to lead scholars immediately to the right source. But even if not another note of a Vivaldi cantata is discovered in the future, we already have more than enough to keep us busy for a very long time.

---

[8]   These include the libraries of the Gesellschaft der Musikfreunde in Vienna and the Paris Conservatoire, both extremely rich in cantatas.

# Glossary

*accademia*    The name given, variously, to a teaching institution, a learned society, a music club, and a private concert or recitation of poetry.

acciaccatura    A non-harmonic note added to sharpen the 'bite' of a chord and quickly released after being struck. Gasparini discusses the device at length.

accompagnato    A recitative accompanied by one or more instruments in addition to continuo.

accompanied cantata    A cantata with an accompanying instrument or instruments in addition to a continuo bass.

*affetto*    The prevalent mood of a movement or section.

*ambitus*    The group of closely related keys that have modern key signatures differing by no more than one accidental from each other. The term originates from Heinichen.

arioso    An episode or section in aria style but set to recitative verse.

*bassetto*    A bass part played an octave above the normal bass register by treble or middle-register instruments such as the violin and viola.

*basso ostinato*    *See* ground bass.

bizzarria    The cult, in Italian music, of the strange or perverse for its own sake.

*bricolage*    The improvised and informal assembly of the units, often taken from diverse sources or invented on the spot, making up a whole. (A *bricoleur*, in French, is a handyman.)

*cadenza sfuggita*    A 'deceptive' cadence falling outside conventional categories (such as the ordinary 'interrupted' cadence, V–VI).

*cadenza tronca*    A 'foreshortened' cadence in which the voice closes its phrase over the penultimate note of the accompaniment.

*cantata doppia*    A term ('double' cantata) used by Ireneo Affò for cantatas with the structure RARA.

*cantata morale*    A cantata with an edifying or didactic textual content.

*cantata semplice*    A term ('single' cantata) used by Ireneo Affò for cantatas with the structure RA.

*canto fermo*    An old Italian term for plainsong.

*canto figurato*    An old Italian term for 'figural' (i.e., composed) music.

cavata    An extended contrapuntal section for voice and accompaniment set to a short passage of recitative verse, usually the closing words of a stanza.

chalumeau    A single-reed wind instrument invented just before 1700 and made in several sizes. Its close relative, which eventually supplanted it, was the clarinet.

church aria    A type of aria following the plan of the 'A' section of a *da capo*

|                              |                                                                                                                                                                                           |
| ---------------------------- | ----------------------------------------------------------------------------------------------------------------------------------------------------------------------------------------- |
|                              | aria but lacking a 'B' section. This is the standard form used in church music for settings of verses of psalms, etc.: hence the term.                                                     |
| composition copy             | A copy, normally by the original composer, that at the same time adapts its exemplar.                                                                                                      |
| composition manuscript       | A score representing a composer's first draft of a piece. Most such scores contain evidence of alteration.                                                                                 |
| *concertato*                 | As applied to church music, describes a vocal work with sections for solo voice(s) as well as choir.                                                                                       |
| continuo cantata             | A cantata in which the voice is accompanied only by an instrumental bass part.                                                                                                             |
| *coro*                       | Used in a specialized sense for the body of singers and instrumentalists performing, and receiving musical tuition, at one of the Venetian *ospedali* (q.v.).                              |
| *da capo* aria               | An aria in ABA form, the 'da capo' being the return to the beginning at the end of the 'B' section.                                                                                        |
| *Devise*                     | A 'motto' opening for the voice. This motto is usually identical with the start of the first vocal period, which begins after an instrumental interlude. The term originates from Riemann. |
| diaeresis (*dieresi*)        | The separate pronunciation of adjacent vowels within the same word.                                                                                                                        |
| dialoepha (*dialefe*)        | The separate pronunciation of adjacent vowels belonging to different words.                                                                                                                |
| 'dramatic' voice             | The 'voice' in which the poet assumes the identity of the protagonist, speaking in the first person.                                                                                       |
| *endecasillabi*              | Hendecasyllables, lines with eleven syllables.                                                                                                                                             |
| 'epic' voice                 | The 'voice' in which the poet narrates events.                                                                                                                                             |
| extended binary form         | A type of binary form, common in seventeenth-century arias, that follows the plan ABB or ABB'.                                                                                             |
| fermata                      | A sign (in the shape of an inverted bowl with a central dot) that today signifies a pause. Used in Vivaldi's day also to mark a point for an improvised cadenza.                           |
| *figlie di coro*             | A member (always female) of the *coro* (q.v.) in one of the Venetian *ospedali* (q.v.).                                                                                                    |
| *fioritura*                  | Florid embellishment (referring to a melody).                                                                                                                                              |
| galant                       | Describes the musical style that dominated Italian music from the mid-1720s until well into the second half of the eighteenth century. Its characteristics include treble–bass polarity, symmetrical phrase structure, and elaborate melodic decoration. |
| ground bass                  | A form of continuous variation especially popular in the late seventeenth century. The repeated bass figure is usually identical in melody and rhythm on all its statements, except that some composers permit it to modulate and/or appear in different keys. |
| harmonic ellipsis            | The process whereby a chord usually present as a 'bridge' between two other chords is omitted.                                                                                             |
| harmonic rhythm              | The rate of chord change.                                                                                                                                                                  |
| homometric                   | Describes the use of the same musical metre for all the movements of a work.                                                                                                               |
| homotonality                 | The preservation of the same tonal centre throughout the movements of a work.                                                                                                             |

| | |
|---|---|
| hypermetric | Describes a line of verse that has a surplus of syllables in relation to the chosen metre. |
| iambic prime | Joachim Braun's term for the 'stutter' effect produced when an accented note is immediately preceded by the same note in an unaccented position. |
| inverted pedal | A pedal-note in a middle or high part. |
| keyword | Used in the present study to denote an emblematic word to which a composer lends special emphasis in his musical setting. |
| *lamento* bass | A bass falling stepwise (diatonically or chromatically) from tonic to dominant, used as an emblem of lament. |
| *lezione amorosa* | Literally, a 'lesson in love': a cantata in which the singer gives advice on how to conduct oneself wisely in affairs of the heart. |
| Lombardic rhythms | 'Inverted' dotted groups in which the shorter note (or pair of notes) precedes the dotted note. |
| lyric voice | The 'voice' in which the poet utters his or her own thoughts or feelings. |
| Malagueña Fifths | Stepwise descending perfect fifths (the bass proceeding I–VII–VI–V), whose parallelism is emphasized rather than disguised. |
| melisma | A group of notes set to the same syllable. |
| minorization | A modal shift (q.v.) entailing a temporary move from major to minor. |
| modal shift | A movement to the parallel major or minor key. |
| modulation chain | A sequence of modulations in which each 'link' moves in exactly the same way (e.g., to the major key a whole tone higher) as its predecessor. |
| monometric | Describes a unit of verse, such as a stanza, that remains in the same metre throughout. |
| monomotivic | Describes a section or movement based on a single motive. |
| monothematic | Describes music in which one theme is maintained throughout. |
| Neapolitan Second | The flattened supertonic degree. |
| Neapolitan Sixth | A first-inversion chord on the flattened supertonic, used to express poignancy or *bizzarria* (q.v.). |
| *note échappée* | A short 'inessential' note that differs from a passing note in moving by step away from, rather than towards, its destination. Such notes are characteristic of the French style of Vivaldi's day. |
| obbligato | Describes any prominent, non-optional musical part. |
| *ondeggiando* | Undulating (in imitation of *onde*, waves). |
| *ospedali* | The name given in Venice to charitable institutions caring for a specific category, or to specific categories, of needy persons. The mission of the Pietà, the institution with which Vivaldi was associated, was to care for foundlings (children abandoned in infancy by their parents). |
| paratactic | Describes a form of organization where the units are placed side by side but are not interdependent. |
| *passus duriusculus* | A passage descending by chromatic steps, most commonly taking the form of a descent from tonic to dominant, as in a common form of *lamento* bass (q.v.). |
| *petite reprise* | A repeat, often echo-style, of the last phrase of a section. |

| | |
|---|---|
| *piano* | Describes a line of Italian verse in which the penultimate syllable carries the last stress. |
| *poesia per musica* | Poetry written expressly for setting to music. |
| polymetric | Describes a unit of verse, such as a stanza, that employs more than one metre. |
| polymotivic | Describes a section or movement based on two or more motives. |
| polythematic | Describes music in which several themes appear. |
| 'privileged' key relationship | The author's term for a close relationship between two keys (in Vivaldi's case, E minor and C major, and E flat major and G minor, form such pairs) that occurs with a frequency not explainable by their ordinary harmonic or tonal function in relation to each other. |
| quadratic | Describes a phrase structure whose units are symmetrically balanced at all levels. |
| rastrography | the characteristics of the staves ruled on music paper. |
| 'quoting' voice | The 'voice' in which the poet relays in direct speech the words of a person described in the poem. |
| *récitatif accompagné* | Rousseau's term for an accompagnato (q.v.) in which the instruments play continuously and have no independent thematic ideas. |
| *récitatif mesuré* | Rousseau's term for a type of recitative that has to be sung in strict time. |
| *récitatif obligé* | Rousseau's term for an accompagnato (q.v.) in which the instruments alternate or dialogue with the voice. |
| retransition | A connective passage moving smoothly back to the tonic from the last main key visited. |
| rhythmic assimilation | The practice of performing rhythms not exactly as notated in order to bring them into line with ones heard simultaneously in other parts (vertical assimilation) or at another point in the movement (horizontal assimilation). |
| *rima chiave* (key rhyme) | An end-rhyme linking the last lines of the two semistrophes of an aria text. Rarely absent from aria verse. |
| *rime alternate* | Rhymes following the pattern ABAB. |
| *rime baciate* | Rhymes following the pattern AABB. |
| *rime incatenate* | Rhymes following the pattern ABA BCB CDC. |
| *rime intrecciate* | Rhymes following the pattern ABBA. |
| ritornello | A recurrent instrumental idea employed in arias to introduce, conclude, or punctuate the vocal periods. |
| rounding | The process whereby any feature present at the start of a musical structure returns, after an absence, at its end. |
| *sdrucciolo* | Describes a line of Italian verse in which the antepenultimate syllable carries the last stress. The metre of a *sdrucciolo* line corresponds to the number of actual syllables *minus* one. |
| self-accompanied line | A melodic line that, through frequent changes of register, creates the effect of an upper part accompanied by a bass. |
| semistrophe | 'Half' of a stanza of text that is divided into two portions. These portions correspond to the 'A' and 'B' sections of an aria in binary or *da capo* form. |
| serenata | A dramatic cantata for upwards of two voices, usually with orchestral accompaniment. |

| | |
|---|---|
| *settenario* | A metre, or a line of verse, with seven syllables. Similarly, *quaternario*, *quinario*, *senario*, *ottonario*, etc. |
| *Seufzer* | A 'sighing' figure taking the form of a series of appoggiaturas and their downward resolution, often separated by rests. |
| simple recitative | Recitative accompanied only by continuo. Often made synonymous with *recitativo secco*, although it is possible for a recitative to be 'simple' without being 'dry'. |
| solo cantata | A cantata for a single voice. Often used loosely as a synonym for 'continuo cantata' (q.v.). |
| stretto | A form of imitation between two or more parts in which the imitation begins before the theme has concluded. The device is often used for climactic effect. |
| strophic bass | A form of continuous variation popular in the early seventeenth century. The repetitions of the bass figure preserve its melodic outline but are treated freely in respect of rhythm. |
| *Sujetkantate* | Schmitz's term for an extended cantata on a historical or mythological theme. |
| synaeresis (*sineresi*) | The coalescence of two or more adjacent vowels within the same word. |
| synaloepha (*sinalefe*) | The coalescence of two or more adjacent vowels belonging to different words. |
| syntactic | Describes a form of organization where the units are interdependent and hierarchically ordered. |
| *thematische Arbeit* | The intensive use of thematic material, which is allowed, in a variety of forms, to permeate the texture. A hallmark of Viennese Classical music. |
| *tirata* | A rapid, scalewise 'sweep' of notes (*tirade* in French). |
| tonal closure | The state that exists when a musical unit ends in the key in which it began. |
| tonicization | the temporary treatment of any chord as a tonic in its own right. |
| *Trommelbaß* | A bass lively in rhythm but sluggish in melodic movement. The 'drumming' refers to the multiple repetition of a single note. |
| *tronco* | Describes a line of Italian verse in which the final syllable carries a stress. The metre of a *tronco* line corresponds to the number of actual syllables *plus* one. |
| *versi sciolti* | Unrhymed lines, usually of varying length. Refers in particular to the free mixture of *settenari* (q.v.) and *endecasillabi* (q.v.) in recitative stanzas. |
| 'zero' progression | The harmonic progression (or lack of one) that results when a new section or movement opens on the very chord that concluded its predecessor. |

# List of Vivaldi's Cantatas Published in the *New Critical Edition*

'PR' numbers are the catalogue numbers assigned to volumes of the *New Critical Edition* (*Nuova Edizione Critica*) by the publisher, Ricordi. Following their original appearance in individual volumes, all the cantatas except RV 799 have been collected into larger volumes by the same publisher. Karl Heller is the editor of RV 796; the remainder are edited by Francesco Degrada.

| RV | Title | PR no. | year |
|-----|-------|--------|------|
| 649 | *All'ombra d'un bel faggio* | 1260 | 1984 |
| 650 | *Allor che lo sguardo* | 1258 | 1984 |
| 651 | *Amor, hai vinto* | 1287 | 1988 |
| 652 | *Aure, voi più non siete* | 1297 | 1990 |
| 653 | *Del suo natio rigore* | 1329 | 1994 |
| 654 | *Elvira, anima mia* | 1296 | 1989 |
| 655 | *Era la notte quando i suoi splendori* | 1323 | 1993 |
| 656 | *Fonti del pianto* | 1309 | 1991 |
| 657 | *Geme l'onda che parte dal fonte* | 1310 | 1991 |
| 658 | *Il povero mio cor* | 1327 | 1993 |
| 659 | *Indarno cerca la tortorella* | 1330 | 1994 |
| 660 | *La farfalletta s'aggira al lume* | 1257 | 1984 |
| 661 | *Nel partir da te, mio caro* | 1259 | 1984 |
| 662 | *Par che tardo oltre il costume* | 1314 | 1992 |
| 663 | *Scherza di fronda in fronda* | 1332 | 1994 |
| 664 | *Se ben vivono senz'alma* | 1263 | 1985 |
| 665 | *Si levi dal pensier* | 1331 | 1994 |
| 666 | *Sì, sì, luci adorate* | 1325 | 1993 |
| 667 | *Sorge vermiglia in ciel la bella Aurora* | 1313 | 1992 |
| 668 | *T'intendo, sì, mio cor* | 1265 | 1985 |
| 669 | *Tra l'erbe i zeffiri* | 1324 | 1993 |
| 670 | *Alla caccia dell'alme e de' cori* | 1264 | 1985 |
| 671 | *Care selve, amici prati* | 1288 | 1988 |
| 674 | *Perfidissimo cor! Iniquo fato!* | 1315 | 1992 |
| 676 | *Pianti, sospiri e dimandar mercede* | 1316 | 1992 |
| 677 | *Qual per ignoto calle* | 1326 | 1993 |

| RV | Title | PR no. | year |
|---|---|---|---|
| 678 | *All'ombra di sospetto* | 1322 | 1993 |
| 679 | *Che giova il sospirar, povero core* | 1337 | 1995 |
| 680 | *Lungi dal vago volto* | 1298 | 1990 |
| 681 | *Perché son molli* | 1336 | 1995 |
| 682 | *Vengo a voi, luci adorate* | 1317 | 1992 |
| 683 | *Amor, hai vinto* | 1275 | 1987 |
| 684(a) | *Cessate, omai cessate* | 1274 | 1987 |
| 685 | *O mie porpore più belle* | 1289 | 1988 |
| 686 | *Qual in pioggia dorata i dolci rai* | 1299 | 1990 |
| 796 | *Usignoletto bello* | 1338 | 1995 |
| 799 | *Tremori al braccio e lagrime sul ciglio* | 1360 | 2002 |

# Spurious Works

For discussion of the cantatas believed to be misattributed to Vivaldi, refer to pp. 182–7.

The source manuscript for RV 672, RV 673, and RV 675 is Florence, Conservatorio Statale di Musica 'Luigi Cherubini', Ms 772, date c.1710; that for RV 753 is Oxford, Bodleian Library, Mus. Sch. D. 223, pp. 80–6, date c.1711.

| RV | Title | Publication |
|----|-------|-------------|
| 672 | *Filli, di gioia vuoi farmi morir* | Franco Floris (ed.), Padua: Zanibon, 1958 |
| 673 | *Ingrata Lidia, ha vinto il tuo rigore* | Virgilio Mortari (ed.), Milan: Carisch, c.1947 |
| 675 | *Piango, gemo, sospiro e peno* | Franco Floris (ed.), Padua: Zanibon, 1958 |
| 753 | *Prendea con man di latte* | Meneve Dunham (ed.), Madison, WI: A-R Editions, 1979 |

# Bibliography

Affò, Ireneo. *Dizionario precettivo, critico ed istorico della poesia volgare*, Parma: Carmignani, 1777.

Agricola, Johann Friedrich. *Anleitung zur Singkunst*, Berlin: Winter, 1757.

Antoniotto, Giorgio. *L'arte armonica*, 2 vols, London: Johnson, 1760.

Baretti, Joseph [Giuseppe]. *An Account of the Manners and Customs of Italy*, 2 vols, London: Davies, 1769

Becker-Glauch, Irmgard. *Die Bedeutung der Musik für die Dresdener Hoffeste bis in die Zeit Augusts des Starken*, Kassel and Basel: Bärenreiter, 1951.

Bennett, Lawrence. 'A Little-Known Collection of Early-Eighteenth-Century Vocal Music at Schloss Elisabethenburg, Meiningen', *Fontes Artis Musicae*, xlviii (2001), 250–302.

Besutti, Paola. *La corte musicale di Ferdinando Carlo Gonzaga ultimo duca di Mantova. Musici, cantanti e teatro d'opera tra il 1665 e il 1707*, Mantua: Arcari, 1989.

Bianconi, Lorenzo, and Giovanni Morelli (eds). *Antonio Vivaldi. Teatro musicale, cultura e società*, Florence: Olschki, 1982.

Bizzarini, Marco. *Benedetto Marcello. Le cantate profane. I testi poetici*, Venice: Edizioni Fondazione Levi, 2003.

Boyd, Malcolm. 'Form and Style in Scarlatti's Chamber Cantatas', *Music Review*, xxv (1964), 17–26.

Braun, Joachim. 'The Double Meaning of Jewish Elements in Dmitri Shostakovich's Music', *Musical Quarterly*, lxxi (1985), 68–80.

Brosses, Charles de. *Lettres historiques et critiques sur l'Italie*, 3 vols, Paris: Ponthieu, 1799.

Burney, Charles. *A General History of Music from the Earliest Ages to the Present Period*, 4 vols, London: Becket and others, 1776–89.

Burney, Charles. *The Present State of Music in France and Italy*, London: Becket, 1771.

Burrows, David. 'Style in Culture: Vivaldi, Zeno and Ricci', *The Journal of Interdisciplinary History*, iv (1973–74), 1–23.

Burrows, David L. 'The Cantatas of Antonio Cesti', unpublished dissertation, Brandeis University, 1961.

Butt, John. *Bach Mass in B Minor*, Cambridge: Cambridge University Press, 1991.

Careri, Enrico, and Markus Engelhardt (eds). *Italienische Instrumentalmusik des 18. Jahrhunderts: Alte und neue Protagonisten* ('Analecta musicologica', xxxii), Laaber: Laaber-Verlag, 2002.

Cataldi, Luigi. 'Alcuni documenti relativi alla permanenza di Vivaldi a Mantova', *Informazioni e studi vivaldiani*, viii (1987), 13–22.

Cataldi, Luigi. 'Da "Ah, ch'infelice sempre" a "Cessate, omai cessate". Riflessioni sulle varianti della cantata vivaldiana RV 684', *Studi vivaldiani*, i (2001), 137–52.

Cataldi, Luigi. 'I rapporti di Vivaldi con il "Teatro detto il Comico" di Mantova', *Informazioni e studi vivaldiani*, vi (1985), 88–109.

Cataldi, Luigi. 'Il teatro musicale a Mantova (1708–1732): studi sulle fonti documentarie', unpublished dissertation, Parma, 1983–4.

Cataldi, Luigi. 'L'attività operistica di Vivaldi a Mantova', in Antonio Fanna and Giovanni Morelli (eds), *Nuovi studi vivaldiani*, Florence: Olschki, 1958, pp. 131–45.

Cataldi, Luigi. 'La rappresentazione mantovana del "Tito Manlio" di Antonio Vivaldi', *Informazioni e studi vivaldiani*, viii (1987), 52–88.

Chaikin, Kathleen Ann. 'The Solo Soprano Cantatas of Alessandro Stradella (1644–1682)', unpublished doctoral dissertation, Stanford University, 1975.

Colzani, Alberto, and others. *Il teatro musicale italiano nel Sacro Romano Impero nei secoli XVII e XVIII. Atti del VII Convegno internazionale sulla musica italiana nei secoli XVII–XVIII, Loveno di Menaggio (Como), 15–17 luglio 1997*, Como: A.M.I.S., 1999.

Dean, Winton. 'The Performance of Recitative in Late Baroque Opera', *Music & Letters*, lviii (1977), 389–402.

Degrada, Francesco. 'Note filologiche in margine all'edizione critica delle cantate di Antonio Vivaldi', in Antonio Fanna and Giovanni Morelli (eds), *Nuovi studi vivaldiani*, Florence: Olschki, 1988, pp. 355–85.

Degrada, Francesco. 'Vivaldi e Metastasio: note in margine a una lettura dell' Olimpiade', in Francesco Degrada (ed.), *Vivaldi veneziano europeo*, Florence: Olschki, 1980, pp. 155–81.

Degrada, Francesco (ed.). *Vivaldi veneziano europeo*, Florence: Olschki, 1980.

Dell'Antonio, Andrea. *Syntax, Form and Genre in Sonatas and Canzonas, 1621–1635*, Lucca: Libreria Musicale Italiana, 1997.

Dent, Edward J. 'Italian Chamber Cantatas', *The Musical Antiquary*, ii (1910–11), 142–53 and 185–99.

Donington, Robert. *The Interpretation of Early Music*, rev. version, London: Faber and Faber, 1974.

Dunham, Mary Meneve. 'The Secular Cantatas of Antonio Vivaldi in the Foà Collection', unpublished doctoral dissertation, University of Michigan, 1969.

Eisley, Irving R. 'The Secular Cantatas of Mario Savioni (1608–1685)', unpublished doctoral dissertation, University of California at Los Angeles, 1965.

Eitner, Robert. *Biographisch-bibliographisches Quellenlexikon der Musiker und Musikgelehrten der christlichen Zeitrechnung bis zur Mitte des neunzehnten Jahrhunderts*, 10 vols, Leipzig: Breitkopf & Härtel, 1899–1904.

Eller, Rudolf. 'Vier Briefe Antonio Vivaldis', *Informazioni e studi vivaldiani*, x (1989), 5–22.

Everett, Paul. 'Towards a Vivaldi Chronology', in Antonio Fanna and Giovanni Morelli (eds), *Nuovi studi vivaldiani*, Florence: Olschki, 1988, pp. 729–57.

Everett, Paul. 'Vivaldi's Italian Copyists', *Informazioni e studi vivaldiani*, xi (1990), 27–86.

Everett, Paul. 'Vivaldi's Marginal Markings: Clues to Sets of Instrumental Works and Their Chronology', in Gerard Gillen and Harry White (eds), *Irish Musicological Studies. I: Musicology in Ireland*, Dublin: Irish Academic Press, 1990, pp. 248–63.

Fanna, Antonio, and Giovanni Morelli (eds). *Nuovi studi vivaldiani. Edizione e cronologia critica delle opere*, Florence: Olschki, 1988.

Fanna, Antonio, and Michael Talbot (eds.), *Vivaldi. Vero e falso. Problemi di attribuzione*, Florence: Olschki, 1992.

Fanna, Francesco, and Michael Talbot (eds). *Cinquant'anni di produzioni e consumi della musica dell'età di Vivaldi, 1947–1997*, Florence: Olschki, 1998.

Fechner, Manfred. 'Bemerkungen zu einigen Dresdner Vivaldi-Manuskripten: Fragen der Vivaldi-Pflege unter Pisendel, zur Datierung und Schreiber-problematik', in Antonio Fanna and Giovanni Morelli (eds), *Nuovi studi vivaldiani*, Florence: Olschki, 1988, pp. 775–84.

Fenlon, Iain, and Tim Carter (eds). *Con che soavità: Studies in Italian Opera, Song and Dance, 1580–1740*, Oxford: Clarendon Press, 1995.

Folena, Gianfranco. 'La cantata e Vivaldi', in Lorenzo Bianconi and Giovanni Morelli (eds), *Antonio Vivaldi. Teatro musicale, cultura e società*, Florence: Olschki, 1982, pp. 131–90.

Fourés, Olivier, and Michael Talbot, 'A New Vivaldi Cantata in Vienna', *Informazioni e studi vivaldiani*, xxi (2000), 99–108.

Freund, Cecilia Kathryn Van de Kamp. 'A Study of the Duet Cantatas and Solo Cantatas with Obbligato Instrumental Accompaniment of Alessandro Scarlatti', unpublished doctoral dissertation, North-Western University, 1979.

Fürstenau, Moritz. *Zur Geschichte der Musik und des Theaters am Hofe zu Dresden*, 2 vols, Dresden: Kuntze, 1861–2.

Fux, Johann Joseph. *Gradus ad Parnassum oder Anführung zur regelmäßigen musikalischen Composition*, Leipzig: Mizler, 1742.

Gallico, Claudio. 'Vivaldi dagli archivi di Mantova', in Francesco Degrada (ed.), *Vivaldi veneziano europeo*, Florence: Olschki, 1980, pp. 77–88.

Gasparini, Francesco. *L'armonico pratico al cimbalo*, Venice: Bortoli, 1708.

Gentili, Alberto. 'La raccolta di rarità musicali "Mauro Foà" alla Biblioteca Nazionale di Torino', *Accademie e Biblioteche d'Italia*, i (1927–8), 36–50.

Geyer, Helen, and Wolfgang Osthoff (eds). *Musik an den venezianischen Ospedali/Konservatorien vom 17. bis zum frühen 19. Jahrhundert. Symposion vom 4. bis 7. April 2001 Venedig*, Rome: Edizioni di Storia e Letteratura, 2004.

Gialdroni, Teresa M. 'Bibliografia della cantata da camera italiana (1620–1740 ca.)', *Le fonti musicali in Italia. Studi e ricerche*, iv (1990), 31–131.

Giazotto, Remo. *Antonio Vivaldi*, Turin: ERI, 1973.

Gibson, Elizabeth. *The Royal Academy of Music 1719–1728: The Institution and its Directors*, New York and London: Garland, 1989.

Gillen, Gerard, and Harry White (eds), *Irish Musicological Studies, I: Musicology in Ireland*, Dublin: Irish Academic Press, 1990.

Grout, Donald Jay. *A Short History of Opera*, 2nd edn, New York: Columbia University Press, 1965.

Hanley, Edwin. 'Alessandro Scarlatti's Cantate da Camera: A Bibliographical Study', unpublished doctoral dissertation, Yale University, 1963.

Harris, Ellen T. *Handel as Orpheus: Voice and Desire in the Chamber Cantata*, Cambridge (MA) and London: Harvard University Press, 2001.

Heller, Karl. 'Tendenzen der Tempo-Differenzierung im Orchesterallegro Vivaldis', in Eitelfriedrich Thom (ed.), *Die Blasinstrumente und ihre Verwendung sowie zu Fragen des Tempos in der ersten Hälfte des 18. Jahrhunderts*, Magdeburg/Leipzig: Rat des Bezirks/Zentralhaus für Kulturarbeit, 1977, pp. 79–84.

Heller, Karl. 'Zu einigen Incerta im Werkbestand Vivaldis', in Antonio Fanna and Michael Talbot (eds), *Vivaldi. Vero e falso. Problemi di attribuzione*, Florence: Olschki, 1992, pp. 43–57.

Hill, John Walter. 'Vivaldi's Griselda', *Journal of the American Musicological Society*, xxxi (1978), 53–82.

Hiller, Johann Adam. *Lebensbeschreibungen berühmter Musikgelehrten und Tonkünstler neuerer Zeit*, Leipzig: Dykische Buchhandlung, 1784.

Holzer, Robert R. 'Music and Poetry in Seventeenth Century Rome: Settings of the

Canzonetta and Cantata Texts of Francesco Balducci, Domenico Benigni, Francesco Melosio and Antonio Abate', 2 vols, unpublished doctoral dissertation, University of Pennsylvania, 1990.

Horn, Wolfgang. *Die Dresdner Hofkirchenmusik 1720–1745: Studien zu ihren Voraussetzungen und ihrem Repertoire*, Kassel, etc.: Bärenreiter, 1987.

Horn, Wolfgang, Thomas Kohlhase, Ortrun Landmann, and Wolfgang Reich. *Zelenka-Dokumentation: Quellen und Materialien*, 2 vols, Wiesbaden: Breitkopf & Härtel, 1989.

Hutchings, Arthur. *The Baroque Concerto*, London: Faber, 1961.

King, Alec Hyatt. *Catalogue of the Music Library of Charles Burney, sold in London, 8 August 1814*, Amsterdam: Frits Knuf, 1973.

Kirsch, Dieter. 'Das Bamberger Drittel: Zum Repertoire der Würzburger und Bamberger Hofmusik unter Fürstbischof Friedrich Carl von Schönborn (1729–1746)', in Paul Mai (ed.), *Im Dienst der Quellen zur Musik*, Tutzing: Hans Schneider, 2002, pp. 39–55.

Klemenčič, Ivan (ed.). *300 Years Academia Philharmonicorum Labacensium 1701–2001: Proceedings of the International Symposium held in Ljubljana on October 25th and 26th 2001*, Ljubljana: Založba ZRC, 2004.

Klima, Slava, Garry Bowers, and Kerry S. Grant (eds). *Memoirs of Dr Charles Burney, 1726–1769*, Lincoln and London: University of Nebraska Press, 1988.

Knetsch, Carl. *Das Haus Brabant. Genealogie der Herzoge von Brabant und der Landgrafen von Hessen*, Darmstadt: Historisches Verein für das Großherzogtum Hessen, 19[18]–31.

Kolneder, Walter. *Vivaldi: Leben und Werk*, Wiesbaden: Breitkopf & Härtel, 1965.

Kolneder, Walter. *Antonio Vivaldi: His Life and Work*, London: Faber & Faber, 1970.

Landmann, Ortrun. 'Katalog der Dresdener Vivaldi-Handschriften und -Frühdrucke', in Wolfgang Reich (ed.), *Vivaldi-Studien: Referate des 3. Dresdner Vivaldi-Kolloquiums*, Dresden: Sächsische Landesbibliothek, 1981, pp. 101–67.

Luciani, Sebastiano A. (ed.). *La scuola veneziana (secoli xvi–xviii). Note e documenti raccolti in occasione della settimana celebrativa (5–10 settembre 1941)*, Siena: Accademia Musicale Chigiana, 1941.

Mai, Paul (ed.). *Im Dienst der Quellen zur Musik: Festschrift Gertraut Haberkamp zum 65. Geburtstag*, Tutzing: Hans Schneider, 2002.

Marcello, Benedetto. *Il teatro alla moda* [1720], ed. Andrea d'Angeli, Milan: Ricordi, 1956.

Marpurg, Friedrich Wilhelm. *Historisch-kritische Beyträge zur Aufnahme der Musik*, vol. 1, Berlin: Schütz, 1755.

Martinelli, Vincenzo. *Lettere familiari e critiche*, London: Nourse, 1758.

Mattheson, Johann. *Critica musica*, 2 vols, Hamburg: Author and heirs of T. von Wiering, 1722–5.

Mattheson, Johann. *Der vollkommene Capellmeister*, Hamburg: Herold, 1739.

Maunder, Richard. *The Scoring of Baroque Concertos*, Woodbridge: Boydell Press, 2004.

Mayo, John. 'Handel's Italian Cantatas', unpublished doctoral dissertation, University of Toronto, 1977.

Metastasio, Pietro. *Tutte le opere*, ed. Bruno Brunelli, 5 vols, Milan: Mondadori, 1947–54.

Millner, Fredrick L. *The Operas of Johann Adolf Hasse*, Ann Arbor: UMI Research Press, 1979.

Musketa, Konstanze, and others (eds), *Johann Friedrich Fasch und der italienische Stil: Bericht über die Internationale Wissenschaftliche Konferenz am 4. und 5.*

*April 2003 im Rahmen der 8. Internationalen Fasch-Festtage in Zerbst*, Dessau: Anhalt-Edition, 2004.

Nemeitz, Joachim Christoph. *Nachlese besonderer Nachrichten aus Italien*, Leipzig: Gleditsch, 1726.

Newman, William S. *The Sonata in the Baroque Era*, Chapel Hill: University of North Carolina Press, 1959.

Newman, William S. *The Sonata in the Classic Era*, 2nd edn, New York: Norton, 1972.

O'Donnell, Kathryn Jane. 'The Secular Solo Cantatas of Antonio Lotti', unpublished doctoral dissertation, University of Iowa, 1975.

Oesterheld, Herta. 'Autographe, ja oder nein?', in *Wertvolle Objekte und Sammlungen in den Museen des Bezirkes Suhl,* Meiningen: Staatliche Museen Meiningen, 1974, pp. 91–107.

Over, Berthold. 'Antonio Vivaldi und Therese Kunigunde von Bayern', *Studi vivaldiani*, iv (2004), 3–7.

Parisotti, Alessandro (ed.). *Arie antiche*, 3 vols, Milan: Ricordi, 1895–8.

Paumgartner, Bernhard. 'Zum "Crucifixus" der H-moll-Messe J. S. Bachs', *Österreichische Musikzeitschrift*, xxi (1966), 500–3.

Petrobelli, Pierluigi, and Gloria Staffieri (eds). *Studi corelliani IV. Atti del Quarto Congresso Internazionale (Fusignano, 4–7 settembre 1986)*, Florence: Olschki, 1990.

Pincherle, Marc. *Antonio Vivaldi et la musique instrumentale*, 2 vols, Paris: Floury, 1948.

Pincherle, Marc. *Vivaldi*, Paris: Plon, 1955.

Pincherle, Marc. *Vivaldi: Genius of the Baroque*, New York: Norton, 1957.

Pirrotta, Nino, and Agostino Ziino (eds). *Händel e gli Scarlatti a Roma. Atti del convegno internazionale di studi (Roma, 12–14 giugno 1985)*, Florence: Olschki, 1987.

Quadrio, Francesco Saverio. *Della storia e della ragione d'ogni poesia*, 7 vols, Bologna/Milan: Pisarri/Agnelli, 1739–52.

[Quantz, Johann Joachim.] 'Herrn Johann Joachim Quantzens Lebenslauf, von ihm selbst entworfen', in Friedrich Wilhelm Marpurg, *Historisch-kritische Beyträge zur Aufnahme der Musik*, Berlin: Schütz, 1755, 1, pp. 197–250.

Quantz, Johann Joachim. *Versuch einer Anweisung die Flöte traversiere zu spielen*, Berlin: Voss, 1752.

Rasch, Rudolf. 'La famosa mano di Monsieur Roger: Antonio Vivaldi and his Dutch Publishers', *Informazioni e studi vivaldiani*, xvii (1996), 89–135.

Reich, Wolfgang (ed.). *Vivaldi-Studien: Referate des 3. Dresdner Vivaldi-Kolloquiums*, Dresden: Sächsische Landesbibliothek, 1981.

Riemann, Hugo (ed.). *Auserwählte Kammer-Kantaten der Zeit um 1700*, Leipzig: Breitkopf & Härtel, 1911.

Rinaldi, Mario. *Antonio Vivaldi*, Milan: Istituto Alto Cultura, 1943.

Rinaldi, Mario. *Catalogo numerico tematico delle composizioni di A. Vivaldi*, Rome: Cultura Moderna, [1945].

Rose, Gloria. 'The Cantatas of Giacomo Carissimi', unpublished dissertation,Yale University, 1959.

Rousseau, Jean-Jacques. *Dictionnaire de musique*, Paris: Veuve Duchesne, 1768.

[Rudge, Olga.] 'Catalogo delle opere vocali inedite e dei microfilms della B[iblioteca] Chigi Saracini' in Sebastiano A. Luciani (ed.), *La scuola veneziana (secoli xvi–xviii). Note e documenti raccolti in occasione della settimana celebrativa (5–10 settembre 1941)*, Siena: Accademia Musicale Chigiana, 1941, pp. 74–80.

Rühlmann, Julius. 'Antonio Vivaldi und sein Einfluss auf Joh. Seb. Bach.', *Neue Zeitschrift für Musik*, lxiii (1867), 392–7, 401–5, and 413–16.

Ryom, Peter. *Antonio Vivaldi: table de concordances des œuvres*, Copenhagen: Engstrøm & Sødring, 1973.

Ryom, Peter. 'Inventaire de la documentation manuscrite des œuvres de Vivaldi: I. Biblioteca Nazionale di Torino. Première Partie: le fonds Foà', *Vivaldi Informations*, ii (1973), 61–100.

Ryom, Peter. 'Le recensement des cantates d'Antonio Vivaldi', *Dansk Aarbog for Musikforskning*, vi (1968–72), 81–100.

Ryom, Peter. *Les manuscrits de Vivaldi*, Copenhagen: Antonio Vivaldi Archives, 1977.

Ryom, Peter. *Répertoire des œuvres d'Antonio Vivaldi: les compositions instrumentales*, Copenhagen: Engstrøm & Sødring, 1986.

Ryom, Peter. 'RV 749', *Informazioni e studi vivaldiani*, xiv (1993), 5–49.

Ryom, *Verzeichnis der Werke Antonio Vivaldis (RV): Kleine Ausgabe*, Leipzig: Deutscher Verlag für Musik, 1974.

Sardelli, Federico Maria. *La musica per flauto di Antonio Vivaldi*, Florence: Olschki, 2000.

Sartori, Claudio. *I libretti italiani a stampa dalle origini fino al 1800*, 7 vols, Cuneo: Bertola & Locatelli, 1990–94.

Scheibe, Johann Adolph. *Critischer Musikus*, rev. edn, Leipzig: Breitkopf, 1745.

Schering, Arnold. *Geschichte des Instrumentalkonzerts bis auf die Gegenwart*, Leipzig: Breitkopf & Härtel, 1905.

Schmitz, Eugen. *Geschichte der weltlichen Solokantate*, Leipzig: Breitkopf & Härtel, 1914.

Selfridge-Field, Eleanor. *The Works of Benedetto and Alessandro Marcello: A Thematic Catalogue with Commentary on the Composers, Repertory, and Sources*, Oxford: Clarendon Press, 1990.

Sites, Caroline O. 'Benedetto Marcello's Chamber Cantatas', unpublished doctoral dissertation, University of North Carolina, 1959.

Stockigt, Janice B. *Jan Dismas Zelenka: A Bohemian Musician at the Court of Dresden*, Oxford: Oxford University Press, 2000.

Strohm, Reinhard. *Dramma per musica: Italian Opera Seria of the Eighteenth Century*, New Haven and London: Yale University Press, 1997.

Strohm, Reinhard. *Essays on Handel and Italian Opera*, Cambridge: Cambridge University Press, 1985.

Strohm, Reinhard. 'The Neapolitans in Venice', in Iain Fenlon and Tim Carter (eds), *Con che soavità: Studies in Italian Opera, Song and Dance, 1580–1740*, Oxford, Clarendon Press, 1995, pp. 249–74.

Sutcliffe, W. Dean. *The Keyboard Sonatas of Domenico Scarlatti and Eighteenth-Century Musical Style*, Cambridge: Cambridge University Press, 2003.

Talbot, Michael. 'A Venetian Operatic Contract of 1714', in Michael Talbot (ed.), *The Business of Music*, Liverpool: Liverpool University Press, 2002, pp. 10–61.

Talbot, Michael. 'Anna Maria's Partbook', in Helen Geyer and Wolfgang Osthoff (eds), *Musik an den venezianischen Ospedali/Konservatorien vom 17. bis zum frühen 19. Jahrhundert*, Rome: Edizioni di Storia e Letteratura, 2004, pp. 23–79.

Talbot, Michael. *Benedetto Vinaccesi: A Musician in Brescia and Venice in the Age of Corelli*, Oxford: Clarendon Press, 1994.

Talbot, Michael. 'Francesco Conti's Setting of Pietro Pariati's *Pimpinone*', in Alberto

Colzani and others, *Il teatro musicale italiano nel Sacro Romano Impero nei secoli XVII e XVIII*, Como: A.M.I.S., 1999, pp. 149–66.

Talbot, Michael. 'How Recitatives End and Arias Begin in the Solo Cantatas of Antonio Vivaldi', *Journal of the Royal Musical Association*, cxxvi (2001), 170–92.

Talbot, Michael. 'Miscellany', *Informazioni e studi vivaldiani*, xx (1999), 135–9.

Talbot, Michael. 'Miscellany', *Studi vivaldiani*, iv (2004), 119–26.

Talbot, Michael. 'Modal Shifts in the Sonatas of Domenico Scarlatti', *Chigiana*, nuova serie, xx (1985), 25–43.

Talbot, Michael. 'Musical Academies in Eighteenth-Century Venice', *Note d'archivio per la storia musicale*, nuova serie, ii (1984), 21–50.

Talbot, Michael. 'Recovering Vivaldi's Lost Psalm', *Eighteenth-Century Music*, i (2004), 61–77.

Talbot, Michael (ed.). *The Business of Music*, Liverpool: Liverpool University Press, 2002.

Talbot, Michael. *The Finale in Western Instrumental Music*, Oxford: Oxford University Press, 2001.

Talbot, Michael. 'The Function and Character of the Instrumental Ritornello in the Solo Cantatas of Tomaso Albinoni (1671–1751)', *Quaderni della Civica Scuola di Musica* [Milan], xix–xx (1990), 77–90.

Talbot, Michael (ed.). *The Musical Work: Reality or Invention?*, Liverpool: Liverpool University Press, 2000.

Talbot, Michael. *The Sacred Vocal Music of Antonio Vivaldi*, Florence: Olschki, 1995.

Talbot, Michael. 'The Work-Concept and Composer-Centredness', in Michael Talbot (ed.), *The Musical Work: Reality or Invention?*, pp. 168–86.

Talbot, Michael. *Tomaso Albinoni: the Venetian Composer and his World*, Oxford: Clarendon Press, 1990.

Talbot, Michael. *Venetian Music in the Age of Vivaldi*, Aldershot: Ashgate, 1999.

Talbot, Michael. *Vivaldi*, London: Dent, 1978, 2nd edn 1993.

Talbot, Michael. 'Vivaldi's "Academic" Cantatas for Mantua', in Ivan Klemenčič (ed.), *300 Years Academia Philharmonicorum Labacensium 1701–2001*, Ljubljana: Založba ZRC, 2004, pp. 157–70.

Talbot, Michael. 'Vivaldi's *Quadro*? The Case of RV Anh. 66 Reconsidered', in Enrico Careri and Markus Engelhardt (eds), *Italienische Instrumentalmusik des 18. Jahrhunderts: Alte und neue Protagonisten*, Laaber: Laaber-Verlag, 2002, pp. 9–32.

Talbot, Michael. 'Vivaldi's Serenatas: Long Cantatas or Short Operas?', in Lorenzo Bianconi and Giovanni Morelli (eds), *Antonio Vivaldi. Teatro musicale, cultura e società*, Florence: Olschki, 1982, pp. 67–96.

Talbot, Michael. 'Wenzel von Morzin as a Patron of Antonio Vivaldi', in Konstanze Musketa and others (eds), *Johann Friedrich Fasch und der italienische Stil*, Dessau: Anhald-Edition, 2004, pp. 67–76.

Talbot, Michael, and Colin Timms. 'Music and the Poetry of Antonio Ottoboni (1646–1720)', in Nino Pirrotta and Agostino Ziino (eds), *Händel e gli Scarlatti a Roma*, Florence: Olschki, 1987, pp. 367–438.

Tanenbaum Tiedge, Faun, and Michael Talbot, 'The Berkeley Castle Manuscript: Arias and Cantatas by Vivaldi and his Italian Contemporaries', *Studi vivaldiani*, iii (2003), 33–86.

Thom, Eitelfriedrich (ed.). *Die Blasinstrumente und ihre Verwendung sowie zu Fragen des Tempos in der ersten Hälfte des 18. Jahrhunderts: Konferenzbericht der 4. Wissenschaftlichen Arbeitstagung Blankenburg/Harz, 26.–27. Juni 1976*, Magdeburg /Leipzig: Rat des Bezirks/Zentralhaus für Kulturarbeit, 1977.

Timms, Colin. '"Prendea con man di latte": A Vivaldi Spuriosity?', *Informazioni e studi vivaldiani*, vi (1985), 64–73.

Timms, Colin. 'The Cavata at the Time of Vivaldi', in Antonio Fanna and Giovanni Morelli (eds), *Nuovi studi vivaldiani. Edizione e cronologia critica delle opere*, Florence: Olschki, 1988, pp. 451–77.

Timms, Colin. 'The Dramatic in Vivaldi's Cantatas', in Lorenzo Bianconi and Giovanni Morelli (eds), *Antonio Vivaldi. Teatro musicale, cultura e società*, Florence: Olschki, 1982, pp. 97–129.

Timms, Colin. 'The Italian Cantata since 1945: Progress and Prospects', in Francesco Fanna and Michael Talbot (eds), *Cinquant'anni di produzioni e consumi della musica dell'età di Vivaldi, 1947–1997*, Florence: Olschki, 1991, pp. 75–94.

Tosi, Pier Francesco. *Observations on the Florid Song* [translated J. E. Galliard], London: Wilcox, 1742.

Tosi, Pier Francesco. *Opinioni de' cantori antichi e moderni*, Bologna: Lelio della Volpe, 1723.

Travers, Roger-Claude. 'Discographie vivaldienne', *Informazioni e studi vivaldiani* and *Studi vivaldiani*, i (1980) onwards.

[Villeneuve, Josse de.] *Lettre sur le méchanisme de l'opéra italien*, Naples, 1756.

Vio, Gastone. 'Antonio Vivaldi violinista in San Marco?', *Informazioni e studi vivaldiani*, ii (1981), 51–9.

Williams, Hermine Weigel. *Francesco Bartolomeo Conti: His Life and Music*, Aldershot: Ashgate, 1999.

Wörner, Karl H. *Das Zeitalter der thematischen Prozesse in der Geschichte der Musik*, Regensburg: Gustav Bosse Verlag, 1969.

Wright, Edward. *Some Observations made in Travelling through France, Italy [. . .] in the Years 1720, 1721, and 1722*, 2 vols, London: Ward and Wicksteed, 1730.

Wright, Josephine R. B. 'The Secular Cantatas of Francesco Mancini (1672–1736)', unpublished doctoral dissertation, New York University, 1975.

Zanetti, Emilia. 'Giorgio Antoniotto, il suo trattato "L'arte armonica" (London, 1760) e l'Opera V di Corelli', in Pierluigi Petrobelli and Gloria Staffieri (eds), *Studi corelliani IV*, Florence: Olschki, 1990, pp. 381–404.

# Index to Musical Works

Collections by the same composer bearing opus numbers are listed in the order of those numbers, regardless of the alphabetical sequence of their titles. All other collections, and all individual works (with the exception of Vivaldi's concertos and sonatas, which follow the sequence of their RV numbers), are ordered alphabetically first by genre (if needed) and then by title or incipit. For further references to composers, see the General Index.

# General Index

Word by word alphabetization is used for this index. Terms marked with an asterisk have a related entry in the Glossary.